The Relative Inefficiency
of Quotas

The Relative Inefficiency
of Quotas

James E. Anderson

The MIT Press
Cambridge, Massachusetts
London, England

This book was set in Palatino by Asco Trade Typesetting Ltd., Hong Kong, and printed and bound by Halliday Lithograph in the United States of America.

Library of Congress Cataloging-in-Publication Data

Anderson, James E.
  The relative inefficiency of quotas.

  Bibliography: p.
  Includes index.
    1. Import quotas—Mathematical models. 2. Tariff—Mathematical models.
  I. Title.
  HF1713.A528   1988   382'.52   87-29712
  ISBN 0-262-01103-4

To Jill, Eleanor, and Cecily

Contents

List of Tables

Preface

Most nonspecialists believe (or behave as if they believe) that tariffs and quotas are equivalent. International trade specialists know better, but often act as if nothing generally can be said about the relative inefficiency of the two, or as if nonequivalence were a minor and esoteric matter.

This book shows (1) that for practical purposes there is a strong presumption that tariffs are superior and (2) that the nonequivalence is empirically significant, adding in two case studies about 30% to the unavoidable inefficiency of trade intervention. It assembles in one place research done over the last eight years, introduced by an integrative chapter (chapter 1) that provides perspective at a nontechnical level. Undergraduate majors in economics should find chapter 1 accessible, and even specialists will find some novelty. I have used it for supplemental reading in courses in international economics at Boston College.

Chapters 3, 4, 7, 9, and 10 were previously published, as was a version of chapter 1. I am grateful to the publishers for permission to reprint. The work underlying chapter 3 was funded by the National Science Foundation, and the work underlying chapter 6 by the Bureau of International Labor Affairs, U.S. Department of Labor.

Three of the chapters were joint work with Leslie Young (chapters 4, 7, and 9), on two of which (chapters 4 and 9) he is the senior author. The influence of our joint ideas pervades a good deal of the other chapters. I am also grateful to the many referees and seminar participants who over the years have helped shape my thinking.

1   Introduction

Quantitative restrictions on trade (QRs) have been the main means of increasing protection in the world economy in the last 25 years. Textiles, steel, and autos are well-known examples. Taken with the concurrent reduction in tariffs, it is only slightly inaccurate to treat protection among developed countries as primarily by QRs. Any protection is usually inefficient.[1] A major and unappreciated fact is that the QR method of protection is itself a source of further inefficiency.

The reason is intuitively pleasing to an economist. QRs limit the operation of markets more than tariffs, reducing the efficiency of the price system. There are two aspects: the reduction in *arbitrage efficiency* and the reduction in *competitive efficiency*. Under product heterogeneity, the allocation of quota licenses ordinarily does not achieve a market solution (equal rent in all uses). Thus it destroys the *arbitrage efficiency* of the tariff. The second inefficiency is that under imperfect competition the response of the foreign firms is more limited than under a tariff, which reduces the demand elasticity facing domestic firms and enhances their monopoly power. This destroys the *competitive efficiency* of the tariff. The principal message of this book is that these aspects are ubiquitous, especially the first, and that they are quantitatively important.

The efficiency of the price system can trade off against other values, on the other hand, so there are motives for protection that can reverse the ranking under some assumptions. A second message of this book is that their combined structure is rather special. For practical purposes, protection in developed countries would be more cheaply done with tariffs. Even in special cases where a pure quota might dominate a pure tariff, feasible tariff schedules that vary the tax rate with some variable such as import volume or foreign price will generally dominate quotas.

The conventional wisdom is that tariffs and quotas as a practical matter can usually be treated as equivalent, and that where this rule fails, nothing very general can be said to rank the two. The starting place for the usual analysis is a simple model in which tariffs and quantitative restrictions are equivalent. All undergraduate international trade texts start with this case. While pedagogically convenient, in that it shows that the same incidence analysis developed for tariffs can immediately be used for QRs, the equivalence analysis is fundamentally misleading in suggesting the *practical* equivalence of the two. All the texts with which I am familiar follow the equivalence analysis with only slight attention to giving circumstances in which the two are not equivalent. Sometimes a presumption for tariffs is vaguely sketched (a tariff is more flexible). The undergraduate reader is inevitably left with the impression that nonequivalence is a minor and esoteric matter. This book shows that the nonequivalence is ubiquitous, and empirically important. The equivalence model also dominates the evaluation of protection in practice. For example, the equivalence structure is built into the standard template for case studies of the effects of protection done for the U.S. government. Alternative and operational methods are provided below that demonstrate the dangerous downward bias of standard estimates of the cost of QR protection. On the other hand, for the technically trained, there is a vast technical literature on the nonequivalence of tariffs and quotas. The point of these exercises is often to display sufficient conditions for the ranking to go either way. The impression created is that the ranking depends on special features of models, with no general principles available. This book shows that two important themes dominate the analysis, working always in favor of tariffs.

This chapter develops the common structure of essays written by the author alone and with Leslie Young over the last eight years that establish a presumption against quotas. Section 1.1 reviews the equivalence analysis. Section 1.2 considers the pure case of quota inefficiency. It shows that QRs are substantially inferior to tariffs in the presence of product heterogeneity or imperfect competition. The simplest comparison occurs when the motive is to hit a target level of import aggregate quantity or value. Such constraints most naturally arise due to external factors, such as a desire to reduce dependence on external oil. They also arise due to crude responses to domestic factors, such as a desire to protect employment or to raise a given amount of revenue. In an important special case, the crude response is optimal. Section 1.3 goes behind import control to review the most common motives for protection in more general models. In principle, these could qualify the ranking of section 1.2. Instead, save for special cases, quotas are an inefficient means of achieving protectionist targets in models of realistic complexity.

Section 1.4 concludes with some observations on QRs and political economy. The appendix develops the methodology used in the book in terms of a template model, and indicates how the special cases of the various chapters adapt it. The methods used are likely to have other applications in the analysis of policy, so the reader is encouraged to digest it.

1.1 Tariff and Quota Equivalence

In a competitive model with a single homogeneous product, any tariff has an equivalent quota and vice versa. The only difference between the two (absent administrative costs) lies in who receives revenue from the trade control instrument. In the tariff case, it is the government. In the quota case, it is the holders of licenses to sell in the controlled market. If the government holds a competitive auction to sell the licenses, then the two instruments are identical, (again, absent administrative cost differences).

To see these points, consider the market for clothing imports. P^* is the foreign relative price of clothing, and P is the domestic relative price. Consider a specific tariff t (a tax of t dollars per unit of imports) and a quota Q^0 that yields the same amount of imports. In figure 1.1, S is the foreign export supply curve and D is the home import demand curve. A tariff t shifts up the supply curve facing consumers to S', so that S' and S have the same slope at each quantity. The home country will have imports selling at P, the foreign country will receive P^*, and quantity consumed is Q. A quota in the amount $Q^0 = Q$ (i.e., Q^0 worth of import licenses are issued) will

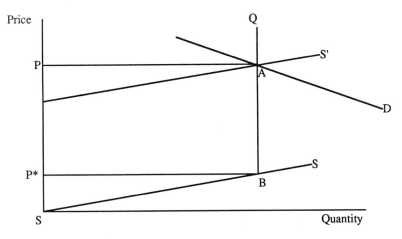

Figure 1.1

make the supply curve facing consumers be the foreign supply curve up to Q and then be vertical beyond it: SBQ. Evidently the price and quantity consequences for importing and exporting countries are identical for the tariff and quota. The revenue associated with either instrument is $PABP^*$, but in the case of the tariff it goes automatically to the government. In the case of the quota, it goes to the holders of the licenses, unless they have paid for the licenses.

One significant complication with QRs is that they are frequently forced on the exporting country. The importer wants to limit trade but requires the exporter to control it. In this case the quota is a voluntary export restraint (VER). The consequences are as in figure 1.1, save that foreign owners of export licenses get the revenue. VERs are especially bad from the viewpoint of domestic national net welfare. In a world welfare analysis, of course, it makes no difference who gets the revenue.

1.2 Tariffs Are Preferred to Quotas: The Pure Case

The simple equivalence model of section 1.1 implies that economists should be indifferent to the choice of an instrument. In fact, in more complex and realistic models there are compelling reasons for believing that tariffs are considerably more efficient instruments for attaining the protectionists' goals. Two important complications are imperfect competition and product heterogeneity. In either case the vague intuition that tariffs are better because more flexible is confirmed. QRs further confine the responsiveness of economic agents in these cases, and this results in reductions in the efficiency of the price system via losses in *arbitrage efficiency* and *competitive efficiency*.

1.2.1 Imperfect Competition

Imperfect competition has long been known to imply tariff dominance (Bhagwati, 1965). Quotas seal off domestic monopolists from the price discipline of the international market, permitting monopolization of the home market segment that cannot be filled from imports. Tariffs, in contrast, leave the potential monopolist as a price taker. The monopolist's well-known profit-maximizing markup formula is $(P - C_Y)/P = YP_Y/P$, where P is the price of the monopolist's output, Y is the quantity of output, C_Y is its marginal cost, and YP_Y/P is the inverse elasticity of demand facing the monopolist. Under a tariff, where the foreign good is a perfect substitute for the home good, the inverse elasticity is zero. Under a quota it is based on the elasticity of the residual, net of imports, demand curve. Output restriction becomes profitable since domestic consumers cannot escape to imports at the margin, and the left-hand side of the equation must rise in response.

Chapter 2 considers the more realistic case where the home and foreign firms are duopolists. Essentially, the Bhagwati insight is shown to carry over to the home duopolist's rational "perceived" demand curve. As compared to tariffs, quotas raise the relevant "perceived" inverse demand elasticities under reasonably general conditions. Equivalence arises if the type of trade instrument has no effect on the nature of competition between firms. If instead, more reasonably, the firms' perceptions of their rivals' reactions are formed rationally,[2] quotas imply less competitive home firm behavior than tariffs that achieve the same quantity or import price. Interestingly, this conclusion holds for either price or quantity-setting duopolists. The quota is then shown to be inferior. This is the *competitive inefficiency* of quotas.

Chapter 2 also considers the case where the home firm is able to see through the government's trade policy to its strategic dependence on the firm's output decision. For example, the government may be using trade policy to hit an employment target. The output game then has a collusive solution, and tariffs are equivalent to quotas. More complex models of this type with asymmetric information are a fruitful area for future research.

A related form of nonequivalence arises when *nations* exercise monopoly power with strategic trade policy, as in the optimal tariff and retaliation literature (Rodriguez, 1974). Again tariffs lead to superior outcomes. Recent game-theoretical literature has been deepening insights in this area, but this chapter will not review it. Save for the singular case of OPEC, such behavior is rare, so it has little to do with the pragmatic analysis of protection.

1.2.2 Heterogeneity

The most basic and ubiquitous reason for nonequivalence is product heterogeneity. In practice, protection is granted for a product class: autos, cheese, oil, etc. An aggregate number of units, e.g., 1.85 million Japanese cars, is authorized. The distribution of the licenses across members of the controlled group (e.g., Toyotas, Subarus, Isuzus, Mitsubishis, Nissans) is left to an administrator. Instead of using the market system to price the licenses, the administrator allocates according to some simple rule, like base year market shares (e.g., if Subaru had 5% of the market in 1979 before the quota system, they receive 5% of the allocation of 1.85 million, or 92,500

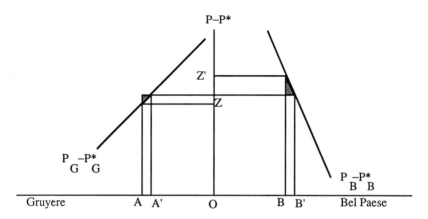

Figure 1.2

units). In general, this system will not imply rent earned on a unit license being the same across products, so long as resale is frustrated (which it usually is) or is inefficient (apparently the case for Hong Kong textile export licenses under the VER system).

Elementary economic theory teaches that exchange is beneficial, and this insight applies to quota licenses too. What would the outcome of a competitive market process for licenses be? Evidently, the rent earned on the use of a license would be the same for all members of a quota constrained group. If not, profitable arbitrage opportunities exist impelling reallocation. Figure 1.2 illustrates this. The aggregate amount of cheese (measured in pounds) across the two categories Gruyere and Bel Paese (G and B), is AB. The allocation of licenses to the two categories depends on a bureaucrat's discretion. In the case shown, $1/2$ of the licenses are given to each. The value of a license to the holder is $P_i - P_i^*$, where i is either G or B. Evidently the allocation leaves a higher premium on B licenses. Transfer of a license from G to B, given the initial allocation, earns additional rent $= (P_B - P_B^*) - (P_G - P_G^*) = ZZ'$. This is also a social benefit under the representative consumer model, since P_i is the marginal social benefit of another unit of imports of category i (measured by consumers' willingness to pay), and P_i^* is the marginal social cost (if a world welfare viewpoint is adopted, or if the country is small; S is horizontal in figure 1.1). A competitive equilibrium in the allocation of licenses will equate the rent, solving for the quantities A' and B' that yield a uniform $P - P^*$ in figure 1.2. The standard gains from trade analysis reveals that the competitive equilibrium yields higher social surplus by the amount of the shaded triangles.

Note that equal rent across uses is equivalent to a specific tax uniform across the product class, save for distribution of the revenue. The shaded triangles are the *arbitrage efficiency* gain due to the tariff. Relative to any allocation, the tariff secures such triangles: this is the arbitrage efficiency property of the tariff. This implies a basic result: given an aggregate constraint on import quantity, a uniform specific tax satisfying the constraint is more efficient than any quota allocation system (save the unique allocation equivalent to the specific tax allocation of imports). Quota inefficiency arises because it prohibits beneficial exchange.

Chapter 3 is an empirical study of the U.S. cheese quota system (from Anderson, 1985); with essentially this structure for 9 categories of imported cheese, I showed that the added inefficiency of the quota allocation amounted to over 15% of the base expenditure on the controlled categories. That is, switching to a specific tax designed to yield the same aggregate cheese imports (announced as a goal by the chief administrator) saved 15% of base expenditure. In an alternative scale, the inefficient quota allocation increased by 30% the unavoidable loss due to the constraint on aggregate imports. Moreover, aggregation bias causes these to be substantial underestimates of the true relative inefficiency. This is a very substantial loss relative to the usual magnitudes found in studies of the cost of protection.

The potential arbitrage efficiency loss of QRs is also ubiquitous, since this is typically the situation of quota-ridden products. No matter how finely the product specification is divided, for manufactured products there are usually remaining elements of heterogeneity. An administrator is then left with the discretion to solve an allocation problem. The prominent industries receiving quota protection are highly heterogeneous (steel, textiles, autos). Even where the product is homogeneous, the allocation issue arises across countries of origin. U.S. sugar import quotas are notoriously inefficiently allocated, for example. VERs are inherently subject to the same allocative inefficiency, since the quota is negotiated with the original market incumbents, with new entrants being sealed off after a small incursion, and initial allocations receiving property right status.

A closely related form of product heterogeneity occurs when the future is not certain. Let a possible outcome of that which is not known (like the annual rainfall next year) be a state of nature. Then in essence, one pound of imported sugar is a different commodity in each state of nature. Let G be a good year for domestic sugar production and B be a bad year.

Note that a fixed quota Q is a given allocation of imports for a fixed time interval (usually a year) that is the same across states of nature (assuming for simplicity that the quota always binds). Is this efficient? Suppose that the constraint on policy is to achieve an average import volume. Since imports are not in principle required to be Q in each state of nature, one can conceive of arbitrage of state-contingent licenses occurring across the product group, subject to the import average constraint.

This can be analyzed as in figure 1.2. Let $Q = OA = OB$. Imports are worth more in the bad year B. Suppose that good and bad years occur with probability 1/2. The permissible average level of imports is then $AB/2$, and any allocation of state-contingent licenses that preserves AB is feasible. Competitive arbitrage equilibrium occurs where rent on use of a license is equal in all states; this is equivalent to a uniform-over-states specific tariff. It is found by sliding the line segment AB along the horizontal axis until the perpendiculars at the end points A and B intersect the inverse demand curves at the same height. The resulting allocation is OA' and OB'. This is the most efficient allocation due to the same gains from exchange argument as above for cheese. A more formal treatment is in chapter 4, based on Young and Anderson (1980).

Such an auction of contingent licenses is infeasible in practice, due to the cost of enumerating a very large number of states and monitoring the volume of exchange in them to impose the average constraint. *Therefore, no quota system can ever achieve in practice the arbitrage efficiency of a tariff.* This is a significant point, since the government is now considering auctions of licenses in future protection cases (e.g., this was in fact the ITC recommendation to President Reagan in the shoe case in 1985). An auction *would* resolve the inefficiency created in the previous type of heterogeneity. It would also provide information on the restrictiveness of the quota, which might reduce the level of protection under the analysis of the political economy model. While desirable, auctions can nevertheless not restore the efficiency of the tariff.

The shifts in the allocation of imports shown in figure 1.2 may of course have negative impact on some deeper government policy goal than aggregate or average imports AB. For example, aggregate or average employment, output, wages, or profits in an import-competing sector may be targeted. In less-developed countries, revenue from trade distortions may be a target. Generally these cases are treated in section 1.3. In the important special case of weak separability, analyzed in chapter 5, the deeper target is affected by the aggregate *value* of imports alone, not by the detailed allocation within-group. Allocations of import value quotas across the heterogeneous types (foreign exchange licenses) can be analyzed as in figure 1.2, dividing the vertical variables by P^* and multiplying the horizontal variables by P^*. The new constraint is in terms of aggregate foreign exchange value of imports, a constant length on the horizontal axis for the transformed variables $P_i^* Q_i$. Under this constraint, a uniform *ad valorem* tariff achieves the competitive equilibrium in arbitrage of foreign exchange licenses. Once again, the appropriate type of tariff has the *arbitrage efficiency* property relative to any quota allocation system. Chapter 4 applies the same analysis where the element of heterogeneity is the state of nature and the constraint is on expected foreign exchange value of imports.

To gain a simple understanding of the argument of chapter 5, suppose for simplicity that an auction of licenses under certainty *did* make a quantity quota equivalent to a specific tariff. The *ad valorem* rate of duty on high priced imports is less than on low priced imports. The substitution effect will lead to *quality upgrading* (Baldwin, 1982; Falvey, 1979). This could imply that in order to meet, for example, an employment constraint, the quota must be tightened, possibly implying that the quantity quota would be inefficient relative to a system that did not induce quality upgrading. Chapter 5 shows that for a protectionist target rate of unemployment (which stands in for a wide variety of domestic economy targets), the optimal trade instrument is a uniform *ad valorem* tariff under production or preference structures weakly separable with respect to the partition between imports and domestic goods. The reason is that under this structure, the choice of goods to demand for input use or consumption proceeds according to a decision tree in which the choice between aggregate expenditure on home and foreign goods is made at the upper level, with allocation among imported goods given the aggregate import expenditure decided at a lower level. Then what matters for the link of imports with domestic goods or factors demand is only the aggregate expenditure on imports. The *arbitrage efficiency* of the uniform *ad valorem* tariff can be secured. Under more general production or preference structures, the circumstances that lead to dominance of the specific tax over the *ad valorem* are shown to be rather special.

Finally, product heterogeneity is significant along the time dimension. Tariffs and quotas generally have different implications for the temporal structure of domestic prices of imports. First, most simply, note that "noneconomic" constraints on the (discounted) sum of the quantity or value of imports over time act like the average constraints in the case of uncertainty and all the same analysis applies. An *ad valorem* tariff leaves the intertemporal import domestic price ratio equal to the foreign; a specific tariff leaves the intertemporal marginal net benefit of imports constant over time. Both are efficient relative to a quota that freezes the value or quantity imported at each point in time, causing intertemporal fluctuations in the license premium.

But more deeply, a quota is a permit to import over an interval of time. Quota licenses (foreign exchange licenses) cannot generally be priced so that they convert into specific (*ad valorem*) tariffs in the presence of uncertainty, since they are effectively *options*. The quota will be restrictive; licenses have positive value, even for years when the limit on imports is not attained. Presumptively, the added distortion of intertemporal relative prices is inefficient if the "noneconomic" constraint is not an absolute annual limit. Chapter 10 sets out a model of option pricing of quota licenses. The use of quota licenses is usually encumbered with restrictions, and the chapter shows that the usual administrative procedures for control of license use are inefficient.

Both the *competitive inefficiency* and the *arbitrage inefficiency* are effectively overcome by the virtues of the invisible hand of the market mechanism. The relative inefficiency of quotas thus rests on the same base as other invisible hand propositions, and is subject to the same qualifications. It could be that quotas outperform tariffs in ameliorating some other distortion, for example. Such claims must be checked on a case-by-case basis. It turns out that typically even when the claim is true, the arbitrage efficiency of the tariff is the dominant consideration.

The next section reviews the principal forms of other distortions, some of which could lead to quota dominance in principle. In practice, tariffs dominate.

1.3 Impure Cases: The Practical Dominance of Tariffs

The principal reasons for protection in developed countries are (1) to raise sectoral-specific employment or wages, or sometimes the associated output or profits, and (2) to limit imports of agricultural price-supported commodities. In less-developed countries, (1) and (2) may be operative, and a host of other second-best claims are made, in which a trade instrument is devoted to fixing a nontrade problem such as a capital market distortion. What lies ultimately behind the protectionist target may be either efficiency or equity motives. Where these might matter to instrument choice, a further consideration is developed.

This section reviews some recent work done on comparing tariffs and quotas under the main forms of motives for protection in the presence of heterogeneity. Employment and agricultural price protection are considered as the most practically relevant cases for developed countries.

There is almost no end to the number of possible second-best cases relevant to less-developed countries, but two interesting ones are revenue constraints and capital market failure. These are reviewed below.

1.3.1 Employment Protection

The most important distortion for explaining protection in industrial countries is in the labor market. Sometimes this is expressed in a concern for employment, sometimes for wages, and sometimes for both. Employment concerns can arise naturally in a representative consumer model in the presence of labor market distortions. Somewhat more awkwardly, distributive justice concerns can explain a desire to protect sectoral employment, wages, or both. Below it is shown that the exact form of the constraint is actually unimportant for the purpose of ranking tariffs versus quotas; a variety of sectoral targets or embedded distortions have the same implications for the ranking of tariffs versus quotas.

In chapter 6, a study of employment protection in the U.S. textile industry (SIC 22), I show that the arbitrage efficiency of tariffs is the dominant consideration, even in a model that does not reduce to achieving the goal by a simple restriction of imports, such as average value or quantity. The optimal (but infeasible) allocation of imports over states is revealing. It requires equality of the marginal net benefit of another unit of imports, $P - P^*$, with the marginal cost to employment, which is proportional to l_Q, the employment displacement effect of another unit of imports. For constant l_Q over states, this implies the optimality of a fixed specific tariff. The closer to linearity the employment function is, the better the tariff will do relative to the quota. Even for nonlinear models the structure that permits quota dominance is very special.

A simulation of a loglinear model of the textile industry (typical of the type of cost-of-protection model used in numerous case studies) reveals that tariffs are 30% less costly (quotas increase by 30% the unavoidable loss due to the constraint) in achieving the same 10% increase in average employment. The aggregation bias due to treating textiles as a homogeneous product implies that this is a substantial underestimate of the true relative inefficiency. Interestingly, tariffs in this study came within a few percent of the optimal (but infeasible) state-contingent tariff or quota system that shifts the protection in each state of nature.

In contrast to this, many union and management lobbyists press for quotas because they argue that their effects are more certain. It is unclear what they mean is more certain: quantity is, but price is less so. Other magnitudes, like employment, may or may not be. In the simulation the difference in the variation in employment under the QR and tariff was trivial. A "noneconomic" constraint on average employment appears consistent with social norms in the United States, but constraints that are risk averse with respect to variation in employment are easily implemented. It is possible with such constraints and the "right" structure that a fixed quota could dominate a fixed tariff.[3] On the other hand, tariff quotas, in which the rate of tariff steps upward with the volume of imports, are feasible and in fact fairly common. Chapter 7, from Anderson and Young (1982), sets out circumstances in which they are optimal. Essentially, high import volume is more damaging. For each range of imports subject to a given tax rate, tariffs dominate quotas due to their arbitrage efficiency. It seems clear that such mixed instruments can almost always dominate a fixed quota.

The design of the textile study seems representative of methods that would be used in most sectors, so I believe the results are representative also. In sensitivity analysis, the ranking of tariffs over quotas was preserved for a wide range of key elasticities, so the results appear to be robust. I conclude that tariffs are significantly more efficient in employment protection.

Output and profit protection motives should lead to the same results, since in this type of model all three move together. Furthermore, it can be shown (see chapter 6) that any fixed distortion that prevents equality of supply price and demand price produces the same qualitative structure of optimal instruments and thus should have the same ranking of tariffs versus quotas. This covers a wide variety of possible qualifications of the invisible hand theorem, including several versions of labor market distortion, regulated prices, fixed markup pricing by producers, fixed excise taxation, etc. For example, if the fixed distortion is g and it affects activity Y, the optimal policy involves $P - P^*$ proportional to gY_Q, where Y_Q is the marginal response of Y to imports.

1.3.2 Agricultural Protection

Agricultural products that are price supported have a variety of restrictions on competitive imports (and occasional export subsidies). In the EEC (European Economic Community) the system of variable levies taxes imports or subsidizes exports to maintain the price target. In the United States, the primary policy instrument is the domestic support purchase program, but import quotas and occasional export subsides arise in order to limit domestic support budgets.[4] What lies behind the support programs are apparently two motives: to raise farm income on average and to reduce its variation. If the former motive dominates (or if the market were reasonably certain, which is counterfactual), the analysis of optimal policy may be entirely subsumed under that of chapter 5, with the arbitrage efficiency of *ad valorem* tariffs presumptively dominant.

The new element is the reduction of variance motive. A deep consideration of the capital market failure that makes this desirable has yet to be done and is beyond the scope of this book. So a "noneconomic" lower limit price is exogenously given. Trade policy alone could be used, leading to variable levies. Or as in the U.S. case, buffer stock policy can also be used.

Chapter 8 considers commercial and buffer policy in the presence of price supports and deficit limits. In the absence of storage cost, it is always welfare improving to add buffering. But the buffer agency is clearly subject to some restriction in its budget. Suppose this takes the form of an average constraint on the net deficit to be covered by a subsidy from general revenue. If the randomness is primarily domestic, the arbitrage efficiency of the tariff is desirable (buy more imports when domestic willingness to pay is high), and the tariff dominates. On the other hand, the arbitrage efficiency of tariffs (buy more imports when external cost is low) turns out to be a disadvantage if the source of randomness is external price shifts. In this case, the quota does a better job of protecting the domestic buffer agency's budget. Greater imports when price is low increase the budget pressure precisely in those states where it is more acute. The optimal policy turns out to be a feasible combination of a specific tariff and an *ad valorem* subsidy on imports, so the appropriate tax system is still superior. The rather bizarre nature of optimal policy is a reminder that price supports are an inefficient method of increasing and stabilizing farmers' incomes. Capital market methods are presumptively preferable, though a satisfactory theoretical treatment is lacking. Empirical work on the ranking of simple tariffs and quotas in practice for agriculture remains to be done.

1.3.3 Revenue Constraints

When trade distortion revenue is important to the government budget (as in many LDCs—less-developed countries), it is *possible* that a fixed quota is superior to a fixed tariff in raising revenue under uncertainty (Young, 1980). Most empirical work is based on demand and supply curves with either (1) additive or (2) multiplicative random terms. For these cases, a fixed specific (1) or fixed ad valorem (2) tariff dominates a fixed quota. Thus quota dominance is unlikely. For more nonlinear types of randomness, the arbitrage efficiency of the tariff can be outweighed by the quota's superior ability to confine trade so that the elasticity of import demand or export supply is closer to its optimal value in each state, given by the inverse elasticity formula. This is advantageous.[5]

For the certainty case, chapter 5 shows that if imports enter preferences or the technology weakly separably and in addition within-group expenditure shares are invariant to aggregate import expenditure, the optimal revenue tariff is uniform *ad valorem*. More generally, the arbitrage efficiency of the tariff creates a presumption in favor of the *ad valorem* tariff, since "nonneutrality" must enter in the right way and strongly to overcome it.

For developed economies, trade revenue is a trivial and disregarded fraction of government receipts, so even aside from the esoteric nature of possible quota dominance under a revenue motive, this seems unlikely to produce a motive for quota preference.

1.3.4 Income Smoothing

Finally, when capital markets are insufficient to ensure adequate risk reduction, there may be reason to intervene in traded goods markets to make trade policy do some of the work of insurance markets at the aggregate level.[6] Aggregate risks such as external price or domestic productivity shocks cannot be diversified, and without complete markets in Arrow's sense (due to transactions cost) individuals bear risk. The social surplus magnitudes of figure 1.2 are now weighted by the marginal utility of income. Chapter 9, from Young and Anderson (1982), is an example of this type of analysis.[7] With no other distortion, the optimal small country policy remains free trade, but a "noneconomic" constraint on average imports introduces trade policy—which then has an income-smoothing component. For domestic shocks, the arbitrage efficiency of tariffs also achieves real income smoothing over states, since the marginal utility of income will be positively correlated with the marginal net benefit of imports $P - P^*$. With external price disturbances, it *can* turn out that QRs dominate tariffs because they do a better job of buffering real income. A rise in the foreign price of imports reduces real income. On arbitrage grounds, it implies purchasing less imports. An increase in permitted imports in the given high price state, on the other hand, would raise income in that state, and hence buffer the real income from the price shock. This type of possibility is most likely when other forms of real income smoothing are few, when the imports controlled account for a large share of expenditure, and when external randomness dominates. For developed economies, at least two and more likely all three of these conditions are not met, but they are relevant for some less-developed countries and other small open economies.

This section has shown that tariffs ordinarily dominate quotas. Even in cases where the opposite is possible, a stepped tariff function, which is feasible, is superior since it can preserve part of the exchange efficiency of the tariff.

What structure could lead to the converse? Evidently, this occurs when the rate of social damage from imports is steeply rising at level Q.[8] It is difficult to think of normal circumstances that imply this property and yet allow positive trade. For example, a zero quota on heroin is no doubt optimal, since even a small amount causes great damage to health. The examples of side effects considered here, such as employment displacement, do not have the same leap in the rate of social damage at a critical value with plausible supply and demand configurations.

The most reasonable exception is in wartime. For example, physical shipping constraints severely limited the import volume capacity of the United Kingdom in 1942, essentially requiring an aggregate fixed quota constraint. Consider applying the analysis of arbitrage efficiency to the problem. Effectively, the marginal transport cost was infinitely responsive to variations in quantity at the limit. Any *arbitrage* efficiencies of reallocation over states would be overwhelmed by the response of transport costs. Also, for reallocation across goods, in the absence of a market for war material, and with the price control system for consumer goods, arbitrage over quota allocations within the aggregate constraint would be likely to impact other "distortions" of large magnitude. It could well be inefficient.[9]

1.4 Political Economy and Quotas: Conclusion

This chapter argues that quotas are an inefficient means of achieving protectionist goals. For a given distortion of trade, national income will be lower; hence an enlighted planner will presume the tariff is better.

Recent developments in political economy models of protection suggest that the preceding discussion of quota inefficiency is incomplete, since it holds the intervention exogenous. Endogenous choice of protection also has interesting implications for the relative inefficiency of quotas. This section will develop a political economy model of relative quota inefficiency and contrast it with a bureaucratic model that attempts to establish the converse.

I assume it is reasonable to characterize the postwar era as one where protection occurs by means of quotas: a quota *regime*. Prior to World War II protection was by means of tariffs: a tariff *regime*. Regime choice is still held to be exogenous to the actions of agents in any particular market for protection. Protection can in fact be either in QR or tariff form. For the United States, it is the outcome of either a "political" or an "administrative" process (see Baldwin, 1987, for a description). Quotas in the form of VERs are generally the outcome of the "political" route along which the president diverts intense lobbying pressure by ordering the Special Trade Representative to negotiate such agreements. The "administrative" route, in which the International Trade Commission hears evidence and makes recommendations to the president upon complaint by interested parties under various legislative mandates, can result in either sort of instrument, at much lower cost to the parties. Protection changes via this route have been trivial in the last 30 years. Thus the United States may fairly be characterized as being in a QR regime in recent times. Prior to the New Deal, protection was obtained through Congress exclusively in the form of tariffs. Thus it was in a tariff regime.

Subsection 1.4.1 develops the political economy model of relative quota inefficiency, and subsection 1.4.2 presents the bureaucrats' alternative.

1.4.1 The Political Economy Model

Relaxing the assumption that the height of the tariff or size of the quota is exogenous, I now shall argue that for a given configuration of political economic forces the market for protection will yield a worse distortion under a quota regime by (a) raising the level of protection achieved and (b) generating greater resource loss in "rent-seeking" behavior for any level of protection achieved.

In political-economy models protection is regarded as a commodity subject to supply and demand analysis like any other (see Baldwin, 1987, for a review). In implausible circumstances, the amount of protection exchanged on political markets would be socially optimal; ordinarily this is a zero level. The main reason this outcome is never observed is the free rider problem in the organization of consumers, who lose from protection. Smaller producer and labor groups have lesser free rider problems and sharper perceptions of their interest in protection. Thus they are able to obtain "excess" protection in the political market.

There are four factors that shift the supply curve to the right under a QR regime relative to a tariff regime. First, quotas have an impact on price that

by its nature is more difficult to establish than tax rates, which are published. In practice, even for a sophisticated investigator, it takes a great deal
of work to find the gap between P^* and P. Frequently it cannot be done at
all with any degree of accuracy. Thus the implied subsidy to domestic
production and employment is hidden more effectively. For the naive
consumer, QRs do not immediately suggest any increase in price, particularly when lobbying campaigns emphasize irrelevant but plausible catch
phrases like "fair" market share and "level playing fields." By lowering
consumer group resistance the pursuit of protection via QRs is made
cheaper for interest groups: the cost curve is lowered.

A second factor is also operative in some circumstances. General government revenue is often less valuable to officials and politicians than a smaller
amount of rent more directly under their control. The lucky recipients of
annual quota licenses can easily be identified and shaken down for campaign contributions and other political favors in return for renewal of their
annual licenses. This is particularly so if resale is forbidden (which simplifies
finding the rent) and if government does not sell them in the first place
(which transfers the rent from the general revenue to the license holders).
Both are nearly universal practice. Even in the case of VERs, where the
recipients are foreign nationals, the identifiability of the beneficiaries is
useful to governments and bureaucrats. The sugar quota is infamous for the
degree to which political/national "security" motives dominate economic
considerations in the allocation of licenses. A trade tax, in contrast, simply
dumps into general government revenue the entire sum $PABP^*$ in figure
1.1. If this is less valuable to key officials and politicians than a smaller sum
that can be recaptured from license holders, a QR regime lowers the supply
curve for protection.

Third, bureaucrats enjoy extra prerogatives under a QR regime. The
quota limit is a number with much less apparent significance than a tax. It
must be interpreted relative to a technical model that relates it to the
employment or other target of protection. Further, the quota must be
allocated to individuals by some process that subdivides the original single
number into hundreds of further numbers. All this requires extra staff and
allows the agency to display competence in producing "scientific" numbers. If resale is prohibited, as in the U.S. cheese import quota system,
further staff members are required to monitor the use of licenses. These
features serve to lower resistance to protection among bureaucrats, which
shifts the supply curve for protection facing the lobbyists to the right.

Fourth, quota licenses that are not auctioned transfer rent to potential
opponents of protection (importers and foreign exporters). They may thus

not oppose the lobbying efforts of proponents, or offer only token resistance. This shifts the supply curve for protection to the right.

Finally, two factors shifts the demand curve for protection to the right under a QR regime relative to a tariff regime. First, the identifiability of beneficiaries may help ease the free rider problem. Pursuit of protection costs money, which must be raised by voluntary subscription. The rent transfer implied by the gift of a quota license may convert an opponent into a proponent who will contribute to the lobbying for protection. There was some suggestion in the press that Toyota and Nissan were in this position in the last stages of the Japanese auto VER debate.

Second, under imperfect competition (see below), the rents earned by protected firms will be higher under a QR regime than with a tariff that permits the same volume of imports. Thus they should be willing to spend more in pursuit of those rents, shifting the demand curve to the right.

The last observation points to the other source of relative inefficiency of a QR regime in the political economy model. Rent-seeking behavior involves the expenditure of real resources on capturing or defending rents. Krueger (1974) has argued that this is greater under a QR regime. Bhagwati and Srinivasan (1983, for example) have disagreed without a detailed consideration. Most analysts have sided with Krueger, also without a detailed consideration. The above arguments imply higher protection under a QR regime, hence higher absolute amounts of waste on rent seeking. But the last two factors imply higher relative rent seeking. This is compounded by factors having to do with heterogeneity. QRs confront bureaucrats with an allocation problem that tariffs solve automatically. Considerable rents accrue due to the allocation problem, and considerable resources are spent to capture or defend such rents.

The political economy model implies that when "constitutional" arrangements establish a QR regime, the level of protection will be higher than if a tariff regime obtained, and that expenditures on rent seeking will be higher. In principle these are testable propositions, but in practice it would be hard to control for all other factors to find episodes of protection where the only difference is in the permitted mode of protection. Casual empiricism supports the conclusion in two ways. First, the experience of LDC trade liberalizations under QRs is usually that the extent of trade increase is a surprise; protection was greater than informed analysts expected. Second, many QRs in developed countries have very high tariff equivalents (where they can be measured). They are not only high with respect to current tariff levels (which is scarcely surprising) but high with respect to historic high tariffs, such as Smoot-Hawley. Their distortionary effect is exacerbated by the generally low tariffs on non-QR imports, so that they have a great effect on relative price.

The political economy model suggests that a simple method of reducing the attractiveness of QRs is routinely to establish government monitoring of foreign and domestic prices of quota-constrained categories. No other category of government subsidy has so little accountability, so this should not be objectionable in principle. The cost of the necessary staff additions at the Bureau of Labor Statistics should be part of the cost-benefit analysis of any QR proposal. Alternatively, government auction of quota licenses would establish a similar information base.

Finally, the choice of regime can be encompassed within the political economy model. Above, this is treated as exogenous, but it is of course ultimately endogenous. Cassing and Hillman (1985) have initiated discussion of this point, asking whether politicians should prefer a tariff or a quota regime. Their answer is that it is ambiguous, an answer also suggested by the discussion above. The outcome for interest groups is also ambiguous. Consumers, of course, should prefer a tariff regime.

The nature of the arguments above suggests a further relative defect of quotas. Milton Friedman connects the efficiency virtues of the market to its virtues in preserving individual freedom. The connection holds in comparing tariffs and QRs: the arbitrage efficiency property of tariffs also protects liberty. In contrast to quotas, tariffs are *anonymous* in their effects; beneficiaries need not be related to officials or judged "worthy" in order to receive benefits. Obnoxious and inevitable features of QRs are their secretiveness (because it is so difficult to monitor them), absence from public review, dispensation by arbitrary officialdom, and most important, creation of personality.

1.4.2 The Bureaucrats' Weak Case for Quotas

For completeness consider three reasons often proposed by bureaucrats in favor of quotas. They appear weak on reflection.

1. One reason given is that quotas are more certain in their impact on the domestic market than tariffs, sometimes expressed as concern about "import surges." Protectionist lobbyists have succeeded in diverting policy analysis from essentials with this classic bit of propaganda, suggesting storm surges falling on an unprotected shore.

In an environment with random shifts in the relevant demand and supply curves, an increase in imports can be caused by either an outcome of the random process or a change in the underlying parameters of supply and demand. If it is the latter, any form of intervention should in general be altered following a resimulation of the model on which the original intervention was based.

If it is the former, a little reflection reveals that more certainty about quantity means less certainty about price. The price of the import is what controls the position of the demand curve for the domestic product. Thus it is not clear that this argument has any merit even considering only the interests of the domestic import-competing firms or workers.

The preoccupation of this view with quantity usually comes from the fundamental error of ignoring substitution effects. Outside the economics profession this error is nearly universal, despite such examples as the recent humiliation of the "limits-to-growth" modelers (e.g., Forrester, 1971).

A more sophisticated error leading to a focus on quantity is based on the mercantilist view of the world as heavily cartelized in all markets. Imperfectly competitive environments lead, however, to quotas being relatively inefficient (see chapter 2).

2. In international political terms, bureaucrats argue that the VER is superior to a tax because (a) it avoids multilateral negotiating over the tariff retaliations automatically produced under GATT and (b) it provides compensation to the foreigners losing markets in the form of quota rents. This argument is not really compelling outside the short run. First, VERs are not much simpler to negotiate than taxes. In fact, such trade arrangements typically end up in increasingly cumbersome multilateral negotiations. Over time the arrangements become more and more complex, as new entrants are subjected to VERs while "fairness" compels continued compensation of the original incumbents. Second, it has always seemed to me somewhat implausible to rationalize a selfish national policy under the guise of its ability to subsidize foreigners. Even if this is accepted, the advantage of VERs over tariffs in compensating the original incumbents becomes a disadvantage as new entrants must be dealt with. If distributive justice is to be served, it is generally the newest entrants who are most worthy of special consideration. In any event, compensation could equally well be served by voluntary export taxes. Another layer of complexity is added by "noneconomic" criteria, as in the recent (1986) debate over inclusion of South Africa in the textile agreement. Thus the "bureaucratic cost" of "orderly marketing arrangements" (OMAs, multilateral VERs) is not in practice lower than for tariff changes under GATT. Indeed, it seems higher in the long run.

3. Government officials claim that the above argument implies that VERs are very flexible, and can thus easily be removed when the need has passed. In practice this claim rings hollow. The textile industry has been protected for almost 30 years and has long since become competitive in the eyes of analysts. The only example of removal extant is that for Japanese autos, and the degree to which trade in autos has actually liberalized is debatable. Furthermore, it seems clear that had Chrysler been joined in its campaign to keep the VERs by GM and Ford, the campaign would have succeeded. The latter wanted an end to the VERs in order to bring in more imports from their Japanese affiliates.

If protection cannot be avoided, it should be done with taxes in normal times. If the rent transfer property of VERs is a significant contributor to international harmony, it should be accomplished by voluntary export taxes (VETs). Foreign governments would secure the revenue, which they could use to dispense trade adjustment assistance or any other worthy cause.

Appendix 1.A: The Reduced Form Primal Methodology

The methods used in succeeding chapters are specializations of a general *reduced form primal* model. This appendix offers a formal treatment of the general case. There are two reasons for doing so. First, the underlying unity of the work will be more clearly revealed, and the reader's passage across chapters eased.

Second, the usefulness of the *reduced form primal* method seems to be under-appreciated in the profession. Dual methods offer added simplicity over primal methods by embedding optimizing behavior and obtaining the dependence on price that is usually the focus of econometrics and partial analysis of the behavior of agents. *Reduced form primal* methods embed *market equilibrium* requirements into dual methods. On the other hand, by inverting to make prices depend on quantities, they appear to be a step backward. Their main general advantage over dual methods for welfare economics is that the derivatives with respect to quantities are *equilibrium* prices, hence have an immediate interpretation in terms of taxation (see Deaton, 1979, for a similar argument). Primal methods also have first derivatives in terms of prices, but these equal equilibrium prices only at an optimum. Thus they are not directly useful in evaluating away from an optimal point. The power of this feature of the *reduced form primal* method is revealed in the numerous applications below to the ranking of second-best instruments.

The models of this book have in common a representative consumer whose interests are advanced by a benevolent government planner, subject to unavoidable distortions. These are usually in the form of "noneconomic" objectives that constrain the planner's actions. Some concern is paid to relating the "noneconomic" to deeper "economic" targets, but they are always exogenous to the planner (thus suppressing political economy for simplicity). Imports are usually infinitely elastically supplied by the world economy for simplicity, in order to suppress the routine "optimal tariff" effect.

Some aspects of general equilibrium linkages are used throughout. The revenue accruing to trade interventions is usually assumed to be distributed back to consumers without altering their decisions at the margin. Profits in domestic import-competing activities are also distributed to consumers without altering decisions at the margin. Prices in domestic import-competing activities are jointly determined with domestic prices of imports; further interaction with the domestic economy is usually suppressed by the assumption that relative prices in the rest of the economy are not altered by a change in output in the import-competing sector.

Subsection 1.A.1 sets out a general canonical model. Subsection 1.A.2 notes its specializations in succeeding chapters.

1.A.1 The General Model

The indirect utility function of the representative consumer is $V(P, H, I)$, where P is the domestic price of imports, H is the domestic price of import competing goods, and I is consumer expenditure. Other prices r are suppressed in the numeraire. When dealing with randomness, $V(P, H, I)$ is for a given realization of the random process (state of nature, indexed by s) and welfare is the mean of V, $E[V(\cdot)]$; i.e., additive separability over states of nature is imposed on preferences. When dealing with a set of imports with no randomness, P is a vector. When domestic and foreign goods are perfect substitutes, P and H are identical.

Expenditure is constrained by income (in the absence of intertemporal shifting via assets). Various aspects of general equilibrium linkage are developed, depending on the purpose of the exercise. In partial production equilibrium, the sources of consumer income are exogenous income I^0, government revenue, G, and profits in the domestic import-competing sector, π: $I = I^0 + G + \pi$. When a general equilibrium of production is developed, $I^0 + \pi$ becomes the revenue function $R(H, r)$. When the other domestic good is developed explicitly, its production is X and consumption is Z. Consumers always take I as exogenous. G will be the rent on quota licenses or the tariff revenue: $G = [P - P^*]Q$, where Q is the quantity imported and $[P - P^*]$ is the margin between P and the foreign price P^*. The home industry profits π are a function of the import-competing good's price H, $\pi(H)$. When randomness is studied, the producer decisions are assumed for simplicity to all occur ex post, after uncertainty is resolved. Then output is π_H by Hotelling's lemma. Finally

$$I = I^0 + [P - P^*]Q + \pi(H), \tag{A.1}$$

or

$$I = R(H, r) + [P - P^*]Q. \tag{A.1'}$$

Market equilibrium constrains prices in terms of quantities. For a given set of binding (for simplicity, with later relaxation where it is useful) import quotas Q^0, the market clearing prices satisfy

$$-V_P/V_I = Q^0 \qquad \text{(using Roy's equality),} \qquad\qquad\qquad \text{(A.2)}$$

$$-V_H/V_I = \pi H \qquad \text{(using Roy's equality and Hotelling's lemma).} \qquad \text{(A.3)}$$

Substituting (A.1) into (A.2)–(A.3) yields a system of equations sufficient to determine P, H in terms of Q^0.

Denote the reduced form price functions based on the implicit solution to (A.1)–(A.3) as $P(Q^0)$, $H(Q^0)$. Substitution back into the indirect utility function yields the *reduced form primal utility function*:

$$v(Q^0) = V(P(Q^0), H(Q^0), [P(Q^0) - P^*]Q^0 + \pi(H(Q^0)) + I^0), \qquad \text{(A.4)}$$

or

$$v(Q^0) = V(P(Q^0), H(Q^0), [P(Q^0) - P^*]Q^0 + G(H(Q^0))). \qquad \text{(A.4')}$$

Due to the envelope properties of efficient production and consumption, and equilibrium as expressed in (A.2)–(A.3), the first derivative of (A.4) or (A.4') is remarkably simple:

$$v_Q = -V_I Q^0 P_Q + V_I Q^0 P_Q + V_I[P - P^*]$$

$$\qquad - V_I DH_Q + V_I YH_Q \qquad\qquad\qquad\qquad\qquad \text{(A.5)}$$

$$\qquad = V_I[P - P^*],$$

where D is the consumption of the domestic good and Y is its production. By market clearance $Y = D$; hence the second equality follows. (A.5) is the marginal net benefit of an additional unit of imports. With no constraints the optimum is attained where $v_Q = 0$, which implies free trade.

LEMMA   Under risk aversion, $V_{II} \leqslant 0$, v is concave in Q.

Proof of Lemma   The lemma holds if the second derivative matrix is negative semidefinite. Let $\Phi = (P, H)$ and $\Psi = (Q, D - Y)$, the excess demands. The prices are implicit functions of Q through

$$Q = Q(P, H, G(H) + [P - P^*]Q),$$

$$0 = D(P, H, G(H) + [P - P^*]Q) - R_H(H).$$

To obtain the second derivative matrix of $v(\cdot)$, I first obtain the price derivatives Φ_Q. Using the Slutsky decomposition and the envelope theorem, market clearance requires

(i) $\Phi_Q = [\partial \Psi^{\text{comp}}/\partial \Phi]^{-1}\{K - \Psi_I(P - P^*)'\}$,

so that Φ_Q equals

$$\Phi_Q^{\text{comp}}\{K - \Psi_I(P - P^*)'\}.$$

Differentiating (A.5),

(ii) $v_{QQ} = V_I P_Q + [P - P^*][(\partial V_I/\partial \Phi)' + V_{II}\Psi']\Phi_Q + V_{II}[P - P^*][P - P^*]'.$

P_Q is the matrix formed by deleting the last row of Φ_Q: $P_Q = I^{\Psi'}\Phi_Q$. Now use the Slutsky decomposition for the marginal utility of income:

(iii) $\partial V_I / \partial \Phi = V_{II}(-\Psi) + V_{I\Phi}^{comp} = V_{II}(-\Psi) - V_I \Psi_I$.

Substituting (iii) into (ii),

(iv) $v_{QQ} = V_I I^{\Psi'} \Phi_Q + V_{II}[P - P^*][P - P^*]' + V_I[P - P^*](-\Psi_I')\Phi_Q$.

Collecting terms and using (i),

(v) $v_{QQ} = V_I\{I^{\Psi'} - [P - P^*]\Psi_I'\}\Phi_Q^{comp}\{I^{\Psi} - \Psi_I(P - P^*)'\}$
$\qquad\qquad + V_{II}[P - P^*][P - P^*]'$.

Under the hypothesis of risk aversion $V_{II} \leqslant 0$ so the second term is negative semidefinite. The matrices to the right and left of Φ_Q^{comp} are transposes and Φ_Q^{comp} is negative semidefinite; hence the first term is negative semidefinite.   QED

The canonical problem facing the planner is to maximize (A.4) (or its expectation) over the heterogeneous elements of Q^0 (or Q^0 for each state of nature). The constraint is assumed to be a concave function of Q^0 (or the expectation of a concave function of Q^0). These functions are well-behaved representations of "noneconomic" objectives.

1.A.2 Special Cases

A number of applications (chapters 4 and 6–10) deal with randomness. The objective function is the expectation of (A.4) or (A.4′). Save for chapter 9, it is assumed that variation in the marginal utility of income is trivial; hence the objective function is expected surplus. This can be justified on practical grounds in partial equilibrium (the variation in the income focused on is trivial relative to national income). It can also be justified as risk diversification opportunities exist such that consumers can achieve complete smoothing of marginal utility of income over states. Chapter 9 relaxes this assumption to consider a general equilibrium economy with no risk smoothing possibilities for consumers.

Chapters 2, 3, and 5 suppress randomness. In chapters 3 and 5, imports are heterogeneous, so that Q is a vector. In chapter 2, there is one import and one domestic substitute, but a tariff or quota can differ due to shifting the structure of competition between firms; hence the Y choice associated with a given Q depends on the nature of the trade control. In chapter 3, the direct primal method is used to develop the optimal import quota vector; the interested reader can check that the method of this book gives the same optimality conditions (inessentially generalizing the model to include variable production).

The "noneconomic" constraint facing the planner under heterogeneity is often taken to be average imports (chapters 4, 7, and 9), or aggregate imports (chapters 2 and 3). A deeper approach uses employment or average employment (chapters 2, 5, and 6) and considers constraints on the variability of imports (chapter 7) or government price support budgets (chapter 8). In chapter 10, the constraint on variability is assumed to forbid all imports above a target level.

Symbol Table

The following symbols are used throughout the book (other symbols are locally defined as needed):

Q = import demand quantity,

Y = domestic import-competing production quantity,

D = domestic import-competing demand quantity,

Z = exportable good demand quantity,

X = exportable good production quantity,

L = labor demand quantity in import-competing production,

I = consumer income,

R = production revenue,

G = government revenue,

P = domestic price of imports,

P^* = foreign price of imports,

H = price of import-competing good,

W = wage rate,

r = price of exportable good,

$e(\cdot)$ = expenditure function,

E = expectations operator,

$V(\cdot)$ = indirect utility function,

$v(\cdot)$ = reduced form indirect utility function,

$l(\cdot)$ = reduced form labor demand function,

$w(\cdot)$ = reduced form expected surplus function,

C = cost function in import-competing production,

C^* = foreign import cost function,

s = index of the state of nature,

i, j = indices of import good type,

t = specific import tax,

τ = ad valorem import tax,

ρ = coefficient of relative risk aversion.

Conventions

Subscripts denote differentiation unless they equal i or j. In the latter case they denote an import category index.

Prime denotes a particular value of a variable, save when it is used to denote a vector transpose.

A vector such as Q denotes either a row or a column vector, with context determining which. Where necessary for clarity, the row or column identity is made explicit.

log denotes natural logarithm (to the base e).

Notes

1. Strictly, this is true in the broad class of models in which distortions are not too significant or are not perverse in just the right way. Models of the alternative class have structure that seems implausible to most economists. Even when distortions can justify protection, there is generally a superior domestic instrument available. The profession has had near unanimity of opinion for a liberal trade policy for over a century.

2. Conjectural variations are assumptions firms make about their rivals. Firm i assumes that when it raises output by one unit, its rivals will shift output by the "conjectural variation." Cournot behavior is when all firms assume a zero conjectural variation. Market share preservation is implied by an assumed equiproportional conjectural variation. This is cooperative behavior and is equivalent to joint monopoly. Rational, or "consistent," conjectural variations are when the assumed response is correct.

3. One candidate for this type of structure involves "dumping" of the type analyzed by Ethier (1982). Industries with fixed cost facing random shocks to demand or cost may occasionally find it optimal to sell below long-run marginal cost. When this occurs across international frontiers, foreign firms can in essence "export the adjustment cost" to domestic firms. Ethier disavows commercial policy based on his model because it is too rudimentary a basis for a welfare analysis. In a further development it is conceivable that a fixed quota would dominate a fixed tariff, because it is clostly for home firms to deviate from their planned output, which implies rising costs of imports.

4. The empirical example of chapter 3 assumes the size of the support budget is of no concern for dairy products (save as reflected in the aggregate import constraint). That is a natural consequence of the assumed structure of a bureaucrat operating under limited information (not knowing cross-price elasticities), and was reflected in the publicly stated rationale for import quotas (see chapter 8). Nevertheless, for price-supported products, a concern for the support budget is appropriate. Under randomness for a single product, the administrator has better information for judging the relative performance of tariffs and quotas.

5. The same type of reasoning can lead to quota dominance in the "optimal tariff" case where a fixed tariff or quota is implemented to exploit monopoly power in trade.

6. The situation can be either a complete absence of insurance markets or a variety of intermediate cases. In the complete absence of markets for risk sharing, with capital committed in advance of knowing the state of nature, laissez-faire is not the

optimal policy. Second-best policies involve intervention in capital markets, but trade intervention can dominate laissez-faire. With the limited form of stock market analyzed by Helpman and Razin (1978), free trade remains optimal.

7. Their model takes as given a "noneconomic" constraint on average imports. They assume all decisions are taken ex post. This model can readily be extended to cover ex ante capital commitment with a Helpman-Razin stock market. In either case the optimality of free trade holds in the absence of the noneconomic constraint. Given the necessity of intervention, the insurance aspects of trade policy come into play, so long as capital markets are incomplete—do not fully smooth out real income fluctuations.

8. It is useful to relate this to the prices versus quantities literature inspired by Weitzman (1974). In the trade case the social marginal benefit function is given by $P - P^*$, and social cost by a variety of suggested numbers or functions. Picking a Q or a tax instrument always involves hitting a point on the marginal benefit function.

In Weitzman's case, simplifying to make production choice be ex post, the price or quantity instrument selects a point on the social cost function (which gives the producer's supply response). This somewhat alters the analysis, but the result is the same: the preference depends on the relative slope of marginal benefit and marginal cost functions.

In the trade case the point is simply that the steep rise in marginal cost needed for quota preference is implausible.

9. Furthermore, in such a shortage situation, distributive justice considerations among consumers can imply that a quota system without sale of ration coupons is superior to a tax (see Baumol, 1987, chapter 4). In normal times the imposition of quotas or tariffs is not accompanied by such a concern for distributive justice, the import premium being charged to all consumers equally.

VERs *may* be rationalized on distributive-justice-among-suppliers grounds, although this seems farfetched to me. An analysis of VERs along Baumol's "fairness" lines may be an interesting exercise.

References

Anderson, James E. (1985), "The Relative Inefficiency of Quotas: The Cheese Case," *American Economic Review*, 75, 178–190.

Anderson, James E., and Leslie Young (1982), "The Optimality of Tariff-Quotas," *Journal of International Economics*, 13, 337–351.

Baldwin, Robert E. (1982), "The Inefficacy of Trade Policy," Frank Graham Memorial Lecture, Princeton University.

Baldwin, Robert E (1987), *The Political Economy of U.S. Trade Policy*, Cambridge, MA: MIT Press.

Baumol, William J. (1987), *Superfairness*, Cambridge MA: MIT Press.

Bhagwati, Jagdish (1965), "On the Equivalence of Tariffs and Quotas," in *Trade, Growth, and the Balance of Payments*, ed. R. Caves et al., Chicago: Rand-McNally.

Bhagwati, Jagdish, and T. N. Srinivasan (1983), *Lectures in International Trade*, Cambridge, MA: MIT Press.

Buffie, Edward, and Pablo Spiller (1986), "Trade Liberalization in Oligopolistic Industries: The Quota Case," *Journal of International Economics*, 20, 65–82.

Cassing, James H., and Arye L. Hillman (1985), "Political Influence Motives and the Choice between Tariffs and Quotas," *Journal of International Economics*, 19, 279–290.

Deaton, Angus (1979), "The Distance Function and Consumer Behavior with Applications to Index Numbers and Optimal Taxation," *Review of Economic Studies*, 46, 391–405.

Ethier, Wilfred J. (1982), "Dumping," *Journal of Political Economy*, 90, 487–506.

Falvey, Rodney E. (1979), "The Composition of Trade within Import-Restricted Categories," *Journal of Political Economy*, 87, 1105–1114.

Forrester, Jay (1971), *World Dynamics*, Cambridge, MA: Wright, Allen.

Helpman, Elhanan, and Assaf Razin (1978), *A Theory of International Trade under Uncertainty*, New York: Academic Press.

Krueger, Anne O. (1974), "The Political Economy of Rent-Seeking," *American Economic Review*, 69, 291–303.

Rodriguez, Carlos A. (1974), "The Non-Equivalence of Tariffs and Quotas under Retaliation," *Journal of International Economics*, 4, 295–298.

Weitzman, Martin (1974), "Prices vs. Quantities," *Review of Economic Studies*, 41, 50–65.

Young, Leslie (1980), "Optimal Revenue-Raising Trade Restrictions under Uncertainty," *Journal of International Economics*, 10, 425–440.

Young, Leslie, and James E. Anderson (1980), "The Optimal Instruments for Restricting Trade under Uncertainty," *Review of Economic Studies*, 46, 927–932.

Young, Leslie, and James E. Anderson (1982), "Risk Aversion and Optimal Trade Restrictions under Uncertainty," *Review of Economic Studies*, 49, 291–305.

I

Tariff Dominance: Pure Cases

2   Tariffs versus Quotas in Imperfect Competition

In imperfect competition, firms recognize the effect of their actions upon the price they will receive through the reactions of consumers and of their rivals. The marginal benefit to the firm of producing another unit of output is generally below the marginal social benefit; hence output is under-produced. When some firms are foreign, and their shipments are controlled by either taxes or quotas, the effect of the instrument on the degree of underproduction by firms must be considered. This chapter will argue that save for esoteric and implausible cases, quotas enhance the monopoly power of domestic firms relative to tariffs, and make the rate of under-production worse. In doing so they shift rent from foreign to home firms and from home consumers to home firms. The net social impact is nega-tive. The argument is based on proving the proposition for simple cases and then arguing that the results should be robust to a fair degree of generalization.

The reason for tariff dominance is simple: under a quota, the responsive-ness of foreign rivals is more restricted than under a tariff. Bhagwati (1965) showed that under the limiting case of a domestic potential monopoly and a competitive large external market, the quota restriction on foreign rivals converts the potential to an actual monopolist by shifting the demand curve facing the monopolist. Hence the quota is inferior to a tariff that permits the same level of imports. This chapter extends the same reasoning to a broad class of oligopolistic market structures. Quotas present the domestic firm with less elastic demand curves than do tariffs, and hence lead to more monopolistic outcomes.

A key element in the extension is the effect of the shift in instruments upon the firms' perceptions of rivals' reactions to changes in own output or price: their "conjectural variations." These conceivably could be constant with respect to the change in instrument, implying no effect on the perceived demand curve and hence equivalence between tariffs and quotas. It is unlikely that a shift in the nature of the trade restraint would have no effect, however, so a theory of the determination of conjectural variations is needed. The recent theory of "consistent" conjectural variations, which produces conjectural variations with rationality properties, is the natural starting point. Using it, this chapter shows that under the most plausible circumstances, quotas decrease the rivalry between firms as compared to tariffs. This leads to more monopolistic outcomes, which turn out to be welfare-inferior, the profit-increasing aspect being dominated by the consumer-price-increasing aspect. "Perverse" outcomes that reverse the ranking are possible only in association with values of conjectural relations that imply collusion under free trade.[1] It is worth noting, however, that if full collusion (joint profit maximization) is assumed, the tariff and quota are equivalent, the effect of either instrument being confined to a tax or tax-equivalent on output of the foreign plant.

More generally, all consistent conjectural equilibria are the outcome of a noncooperative process. Collusive solutions to the mathematical representation of the process should be regarded as implausible in the absence of more information.

Game theorists have argued along these lines that the conjectural variations approach, "consistent" or not, is a dangerously superficial static representation of a dynamic repeated game. Their point has special force in considering collusive outcomes. What are manifest as conjectures reflect, in a repeated game, consideration by rational agents of a set of credible retaliations in the future by rivals. Collusive equilibria can be sustained if the set of credible penalties is sufficiently harsh; otherwise the equilibrium reverts to a noncollusive form. Consistent conjectural variations equilibria that are collusive are not very believable if the analyst cannot specify the penalties that would enforce such an outcome. This is a telling criticism of the conjectural variations approach, but given the absence of sufficient penalties to enforce collusion, a "consistent" conjectural equilibrium still appears to be the most relevant notion.[2]

Interestingly, the presumptive superiority of the tariff over the quota in consistent conjectural equilibrium holds up whether firms are regarded as price setting or as quantity setting. Both types of behavior do occur, so it is of practical importance to check both cases. Theoretically it is well-known that oligopolistic equilibrium is different in the two cases (unlike the classic monopoly case). Therefore, intuition suggests that the ranking might be different, and perhaps that a price instrument might be better under quantity competition, and a quantity instrument under price competition. Instead, a tariff dominates a quota constrained to achieve either the same quantity of imports or the same price of imports (the latter is a more natural target under price setting).

Section 2.1 sets out the model of static oligopolistic equilibrium. Two differential product oligopolists, one domestic and one foreign, set either quantities or prices to maximize profits subject to a "perceived " demand curve based in part on a conjecture as to their rival's response to marginal changes in "own" output or price. Conjectural equilibrium settings of outputs or prices are a function of the conjectural variations, ranging from competitive to collusive values. Section 2.2 is about formation of consistent conjectural variations, rationalizing them as the reduced form of a dynamic (unspecified) learning process. Trade policy shifts the environment in which the learning occurs and thus the conjectural variations the firms will eventually hold. Section 2.3 builds on 2.1 and 2.2 to show that tariffs are generally superior to quotas in the model.

Section 2.4 develops the case where one or both firms know the government's policy constraint function (such as an employment target) rather than taking the trade policy as given. Tariffs and quotas are then equivalent. An important further implication is that in such a case the government commitment creates a collusive consistent conjectural equilibrium. The chapter concludes with a discussion of some extensions for future work. These include important combinations of asymmetric information and imperfect competition.

2.1 Static Conjectural Equilibrium

Two firms, one domestic and one foreign, set either quantities or prices in the home country markets for the home good and the foreign good. The goods are imperfect substitutes in demand. The firms' choice of quantity or price competition is exogenous to the model (which may be justified if the nature of the good dominates any strategic element in the choice of type of competition). Each maximizes profits based on the perceived demand curve it faces. This in turn depends on the conjectured response of the rival. With the conjectural variations constant, the equilibrium output or price pair is implied by the pair of the firms' first-order conditions (their reaction functions). The dependence of outputs or prices upon the conjectures is implicit in the first-order conditions, and made explicit in comparative static derivatives.

2.1.1 Quantity Competition

Let $P(Y, Q)$ be the inverse demand function for the home good, with Y the output of the home good and Q the foreign firm's sales. Let $P^*(Y, Q)$ be the inverse demand curve for the foreign good. Let $y(Q)$ be the foreign firm's conjecture as to the home firm's output in response to a foreign offer of Q. Symmetrically, let $q(Y)$ be the home firm's conjecture as to the foreign firm's sales in response to a home offer of Y. The "perceived" demand curves are obtained by substitution: $P(Y, q(Y))$ and $P^*(y(Q), Q)$, respectively. These are assumed downward sloping. Let $C(Y)$ and $C^*(Q)$ be the cost functions for the home and foreign firms. The firms' profits are π and π^*, respectively. Subscripts denote partial differentiation throughout.

In quantity-setting conjectural equilibrium, the outputs Y', Q' satisfy the pair of first-order conditions

$$P(Y', Q') + Y'[P_Y(Y', Q') + P_Q(Y', Q')q_Y(Y')] - C_Y(Y') = \pi_Y(\cdot) = 0, \quad (1)$$

$$P^*(Y', Q') + Q'[P_Q^*(Y', Q') + P_Y^*(Y', Q')y_Q(Q')] - C^*(Q') = \pi_Q^*(\cdot) = 0. \quad (2)$$

For constant conjectural variations, q_Y, and y_Q are constants, so the system is reduced to

$$\pi_Y(Y', Q'; q_Y) = 0, \tag{1'}$$

$$\pi_Q^*(Y', Q'; y_Q) = 0. \tag{2'}$$

To be solution values for Y', Q', the system must also satisfy $\pi_{YY} < 0$ and $\pi_{QQ}^* < 0$, the second-order conditions. To be a stable equilibrium (under a "tatonnement" mechanism for quantities), $\Delta = \pi_{YY}\pi_{QQ}^* - \pi_{YQ}\pi_{QY}^* > 0$.

The conjectural variations may be set at various values to obtain familiar results. Cournot equilibrium is obtained when $y_Q = q_Y = 0$. Competitive equilibrium ($P = C_Y$ and $P^* = C_Q^*$, the square bracket terms vanish) involves a negative setting for each ($q_Y = -P_Y/P_Q$ and $y_Q = -P_Q^*/P_Y^*$) under the reasonable hypothesis that the goods are substitutes in demand, P_Q, $P_Y^* < 0$. Collusive behavior in a limiting case satisfies joint profit maximization, and implies positive values of q_Y and y_Q ($q_Y = QP_Y^*/YP_Q$ and $y_Q = YP_Q/QP_Y^*$).

Y' and Q' are implicit functions of q_Y and y_Q via (1') and (2'). The general relation between the settings of the conjectural variations and the outputs is obtained from the comparative static derivatives of (1') and (2'):

$$\begin{pmatrix} dY' \\ dQ' \end{pmatrix} = \frac{1}{\Delta}\begin{pmatrix} \pi_{QQ}^* & -\pi_{YQ} \\ -\pi_{QY}^* & \pi_{YY} \end{pmatrix}\begin{pmatrix} -Y'P_Q\, dq_Y \\ -Q'P_Y^*\, dy_Q \end{pmatrix}, \tag{3}$$

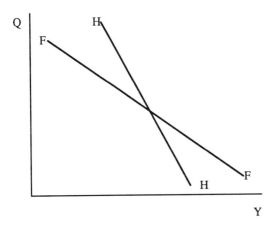

Figure 2.1

where $\Delta = \pi^*_{QQ}\pi_{YY} - \pi_{YQ}\pi^*_{QY}$. From (3), a rise in q_Y will always lower the home output Y', by stability, $\Delta > 0$, and the second order condition $\pi^*_{QQ} < 0$. It will also lower (raise) foreign output as π^*_{QY} is positive (negative). Normally it is assumed that $\pi^*_{QY} < 0$, so that the foreign reaction curve $\pi^*_Q(Y', Q') = 0$ is downward sloping in Q as a function of Y. Then the effect of a rise in q_Y is to raise Q and lower Y. Similar statements go through for the effect of a change in y_Q. It is convenient in what follows to render the implicit functions explicitly as $Y' = f(q_Y, y_Q)$, $Q' = g(q_Y, y_Q)$.

The textbook reaction function diagram, figure 2.1, neatly summarizes the information of the above paragraphs. HH is the home firm reaction function and FF is the foreign firm reaction function. Both curves slope downward under the reasonable restriction that the effect on own marginal profits of a rise in rivals' output is negative. Stability requires that HH be steeper than FF. A rise in q_Y shifts the home firm's reaction function in and leads to a fall in Y and a rise in Q.

2.1.2 Price Competition

Under price setting behavior the reaction functions are in terms of prices, and conjectural equilibrium is defined by

$$Y(P, P^*) + [P - C_Y(Y)]\{Y_P(P, P^*) + Y_{P^*}(P, P^*)p^*_P\} = 0, \tag{4}$$

$$Q(P, P^*) + [P^* - C^*_Q(Q)]\{Q_{P^*}(P, P^*) + Q_P(P, P^*)p_{P^*}\} = 0. \tag{5}$$

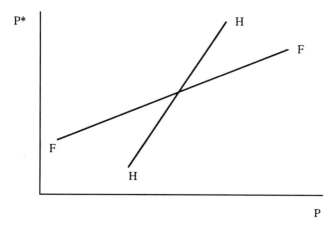

Figure 2.2

p_P^* and p_{P^*} are the conjectural variations on prices. Under the second order conditions and "tatonnement" stability conditions, (4)–(5) yield a reaction function diagram illustrated by figure 2.2. Stability requires the relative slopes shown. Nonnegative conjectural variations under the assumption of linear demand imply positive sloping reaction functions. A rise in p_{P^*} (p_P^*) shifts the foreign (home) reaction function to the left (right) and raises both prices. Bertrand behavior is when p_{P^*} and p_P^* are zero. Competitive behavior is when they are unboundedly negative (allowing $P = C_Y$ and $P^* = C_Q^*$). Collusive behavior is when $[P - C_Y]Y_{P^*}p_P^* = [P^* - C_Q^*]Q_P$ and $[P^* - C_Q^*]Q_P p_{P^*} = [P - C_Y]Y_{P^*}$, which allows joint profit maximization. For the symmetric case of $Y_{P^*} = Q_P$, and equal price/marginal cost margins, the consistent conjectural price variations in elasticity form (e.g., $P_{P_P^*}/P^*$) are unity, as is intuitive.

Entry structures are best understood as applying to reasonably short run analysis, such that entry is impossible. In the long run, entry may occur, in which case a zero profit condition is imposed and the number of firms becomes endogenous. Entry turns out to be essentially irrelevant to the analysis of tariffs versus quotas, so long as it is anticipated by incumbents.

With anticipated entry in the home industry, the home firm knows that there is an infinitely elastic supply of entrants ready to supply at his average cost. The home industry is effectively competitive, as in Baumol-Panzar-Willig's contestable markets. The foreign industry is symmetrically also effectively competitive with entry. Here a possible difference between tariffs and quotas can appear. The quota licenses can be competitively auctioned, in which case entry is free and the tariff and quota have equivalent cost-increasing implications for foreign firms. But it is likely in practice that the quota will be assigned to incumbents, in which case it sets up a barrier to entry and makes the foreign firm a monopolist. This makes the quota welfare-inferior to the tariff that achieves the same quantity of trade.

Entry that is not anticipated appears to be in absurd contrast to "rational" conjectures about incumbent firms' behavior. Thus this case is suppressed.

2.2 The Formation of Conjectural Variations

Conjectural variations have always been understood as the outcome of an unspecified learning process over time. Recently, under the stimulus of the rational expectations hypothesis, the kindred concept of "consistent" conjectural variations has been developed (Bresnahan, 1981; Robson, 1982). While the dynamic learning process is left unspecified, all such processes must, it is argued, pass a rationality test: the conjectures must be confirmed by equilibrium outcomes.

While the consistent conjectural equilibrium can be rationalized as the outcome of a repeated game, it is especially unsuited as a description of collusive outcomes. Rotemberg and Saloner (1986) illustrate the issue nicely. They consider tariffs versus quotas in a dynamic repeated game context, noting that a quota limits the damage the foreign firm can do to the domestic firm, while a tariff does not. Thus it is possible for a tariff to allow enforcement of a collusive outcome under parameter values for which a quota will not. The quota limit, the very factor that makes the home firm's monopoly power more effective in a one-shot game, can reverse its influence in a repeated game. This is a clever point, but of slight practical relevance, since it assumes literally incredible government policy. Their analysis presumes that a government would, under the tariff, permit unlimited market access to a predating foreign firm, and that this would be believed by both foreign and domestic firms. Rational agents will instead anticipate that government policy will shift the tariff in the event of predation to protect firms and employment in the "sensitive" sector. The implication of this point can be pushed to the extreme if agents entirely anticipate the government's policy constraint function, and use it to form conjectures in a consistent conjectural equilibrium. Under such a fully informed rational structure, it is shown in section 2.4 that the tariff is equivalent to the quota. With less full information, it is possible that something like Rotemberg and Saloner's structure can reemerge. This awaits a deeper investigation.

2.2.1 Quantity Competition

The outcome of (1)–(2) satisfies the equilibrium requirement that the anticipated *levels* of outputs are realized [$Y' = y(Q)$ and $Q' = q(Y)$]. On the other hand, generally q_Y and y_Q do not equal the slopes of the other firm's reaction functions, and are thus not "consistent" in the sense of Bresnahan. One can impose that consistency by stipulating that the learning process find the solution (fixed point) of

$$q_Y = -\pi^*_{QY}(f(q_Y, y_Q), g(q_Y, y_Q), y_Q)/\pi^*_{QQ}(f(q_Y, y_Q), g(q_Y, y_Q), y_Q)$$

$$= \phi(q_Y, y_Q), \tag{6}$$

$$y_Q = -\pi_{YQ}(f(q_Y, y_Q), g(q_Y, y_Q), q_Y)/\pi_{YY}(f(q_Y, y_Q), g(q_Y, y_Q), q_Y)$$

$$= \psi(q_Y, y_Q). \tag{7}$$

The theory of consistent conjectural variations to be used in what follows utilizes properties of the solution values of (6)–(7).

Unfortunately, the system is intricate, and economic theory does not fully inform the process of restricting it. A primarily mathematical digression is necessary. A solution to (6)–(7) need not exist without further restrictions. A solution also need not be stable, in the sense that an ad hoc adjustment process need not converge. Thus suppose

$$\dot{q}_Y = \alpha[\phi(q_Y, y_Q) - q_Y], \tag{8}$$

$$\dot{y}_Q = \beta[\psi(q_Y, y_Q) - y_Q] \qquad \text{for} \quad \alpha, \beta > 0. \tag{9}$$

(8)–(9) describe a trajectory of conjectural variations that will locally converge on a solution of (6)–(7) if $\phi_1 - 1 < 0$, $\psi_2 - 1 < 0$, and $(\phi_1 - 1) \times (\psi_2 - 1) - \phi_2\psi_1 > 0$. If these conditions are globally met, existence and uniqueness of a solution is guaranteed. Economic theory does not restrict the ϕ, ψ derivatives, so there are not generally palatable conditions that guarantee existence or uniqueness. Bresnahan (1981) shows that if inverse demand is linear, own effects dominate cross-effects, and that if marginal costs are linear and nondecreasing, then a unique solution is obtained. It may also be shown to be stable. Moreover, most significantly for the comparison of tariffs and quotas, *the consistent conjectural variations are between 0 and* -1.

More generally, Robson (1982) showed that *only* in the Bresnahan case does a fully consistent conjecture exist, in the sense that all higher derivatives, such as q_{yy}, are consistent with the actual behavior. He concluded that the concept of consistent conjectures was of limited usefulness. The concept has nonetheless continued to be used, for two reasons. First, it is a step toward realism from the static Cournot-Nash model. Second, there is small value to more accurate information about rivals' behavior far from equilibrium (which would motivate a search for consistent higher order derivatives). With information costly, it may be rational to have limited consistent conjectural variations.

To proceed, the analyst can either use the Bresnahan assumptions and evaluate the consistent conjectural variations or, alternatively, the multiple solution values of the conjectural variations q_Y' and y_Q' can be examined at critical points in a more general system, and unstable or negative profits points ruled out. Simulation is indicated due to the complexity of the system. But the latter mechanical procedure is potentially misleading, as well as inelegant. Under the Bresnahan assumptions the unique consistent conjectural variations are negative, and lie between the competitive value and the Cournot (0) value. This should be a robust property in learning models in a noncooperative environment, since the underlying structure of substitution in demand makes it implausible that agents should ever believe and act on a conjectural variation that is positive. For a positive value, it is required that agents believe that a cut in output will induce rivals to cut output. Such an own conjecture can only be confirmed by experience if the rival is in fact also acting on a positive conjectural variation. A system that mechanically produces such a solution appears suspect. Credible (to an economist) collusive behavior should only arise from a fully specified repeated game structure, in which penalties enforce cooperation.

2.2.2 Price Competition

Let $h(p_{P^*}, p_P^*)$ and $k(p_{P^*}, p_P^*)$ be the reduced form conjectural equilibrium solutions to (4)–(5). Analogously to (6)–(7), consistency of conjectural variations is imposed by the system

$$p_{P^*} = -\pi_{PP^*}(h(p_{P^*}, p_P^*), k(p_{P^*}, p_P^*), p_P^*)/\pi_{PP}(h(p_{P^*}, p_P^*), k(p_{P^*}, p_P^*), p_P^*), \qquad (10)$$

$$p_P^* = -\pi_{P^*P}^*(h(p_{P^*}, p_P^*), k(p_{P^*}, p_P^*), p_P^*)/\pi_{P^*P^*}^*(h(p_{P^*}, p_P^*), k(p_{P^*}, p_P^*), p_{P^*}). \qquad (11)$$

As with quantity setting in (6)–(7), the behavior of the system (10)–(11) is complex. Under the Bresnahan assumptions (linear inverse demand with own effects dominating cross-effects, and quadratic convex costs), it can be shown that there is a unique stable solution to p_{p^*} and p_P^* that is greater than 0, the Bertrand assumption (see the appendix).

2.3 Tariffs versus Quotas

The oligopoly models of section 2.2 can now be manipulated to consider the effect of tariffs versus quotas on the consistent conjectural equilibria, and then on welfare. With no change in conjectural variations, a quota and a quantity-equivalent tariff are obviously equivalent in all respects (save the distribution of the quota rent), since Y and Q must lie on the unshifting home reaction curve at the quota value of Q.

The essence of the comparison in this chapter is that government policy generally will shift the consistent conjectural variation, hence the home reaction curve. In the specific tariff case with the Bresnahan assumptions the quantity conjectures do not shift at all. To see this, consider (1)–(2) and (6)–(7). A specific tax shifts the constant term of marginal cost of the foreign producer, which appears as an argument in the conjectural equilibrium system (1)–(2) determining (Y', Q'), but not in the consistent conjectures system (6)–(7). Thus the only possible effect of the tax on the conjectures must be indirect, via changes in Y and Q. Under linearity of demand, all terms in π_{YY}, π_{YQ}, π_{QQ}^*, and π_{QY}^* that depend on the conjectural equilibrium quantities Y', Q' vanish. Thus the specific tax does not change the solution values of q_Y, y_Q (see also the formula in Bresnahan, in which the constant term of marginal cost is not an argument). Under the Bresnahan assumptions (linear increasing marginal costs) the conjectural variations shift under an *ad valorem* tax, since the tax-inclusive C_{QQ}^* rises, but remain in the $[-1, 0]$ interval. In the quota case, the foreign quantity is fixed (suppressing nonbinding quotas for simplicity). For quantity-setting behavior, the Cournot assumption is consistent for the home firm. Thus it is less competitive, resulting in lower output of the home good, *ceteris paribus*, than the tariff. Figure 2.3 illustrates this.

For the price-setting case, matters are a bit more involved. The consistent conjecture about the foreign firm held by the home firm under the quota is $p_P^* = -Q_P/Q_{P^*}$, since Q is fixed. This turns out to be greater than the tariff value that solves (8)–(9) under the Bresnahan assumptions, so it is less competitive (results in higher prices), *ceteris paribus*. The foreign firm's consistent conjecture about the home firm also is larger under the quota than under the tariff (see the appendix for details). Thus the conjectural equilibrium outcome for a given quantity of imports will be less competitive, and have higher prices. Figure 2.4 illustrates this. E is the tariff

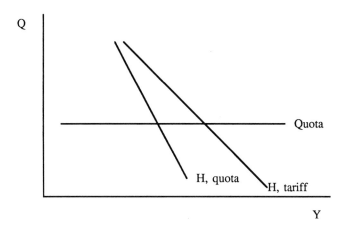

Figure 2.3

equilibrium and E' is the quota equilibrium. The government quota policy creates a function $Q(P, P^*) = Q^0$ facing the rational home firm. This implicitly yields a schedule through E', which is not drawn. It would be positively sloped and steeper than the foreign reaction function.

On the other hand, it may be implausible to suppose that the government target intervention variable would simply be quantity when firms engage in price competition. Oligopolistic industries where this behavior appears to be an issue are subject in the United States to antidumping statutes that provide for countervailing duties, which bring the U.S. price up to a foreign base price. A limiting case example of explicit price fixing is the U.S. steel reference price system of the 1970s, which required all sellers to mark up to a calculated cost based on Japanese data. The natural measure of equivalence of instruments under price setting might thus be better expressed in terms of price. If this is so, then with a target domestic price for the import good understood, the home firm's consistent conjectural variation (CCV) for the foreign firm is 0, the Bertrand value under either the tariff or the quota. The equilibrium prices P_e^* and P_e are the same under a tariff or a quota. In a diagram like figure 2.3 they are found at the intersection of the home reaction function given Bertrand behavior with a horizontal line at the target price P_e^*.

The tariff and quota need not be equivalent, however, since the foreign firm's conjectural price variation affects the size of potential home government quota rent or tariff revenue captured. The foreign firm's CCV under the quota has two possibilities. First, if the target price forecast is also understood by the foreign firm then the tariff and quota instruments are equivalent, since the foreign firm understands that whatever the trade

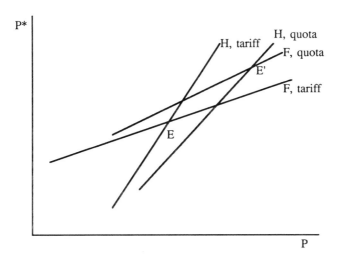

Figure 2.4

instrument, the home price of the foreign good is fixed. The foreign firm's maximization problem is degenerate and p_{P^*} assumes the value needed to assume $\pi_{P^*}^* = 0$ at P_e^*, P_e. Alternatively, if under the quota the target price is not understood, the foreign firm's CCV about the home firm under the tariff falls below its quota value. This arises because (10) implies that p_{P^*} is a decreasing function of p_P^*. The switch from a tariff to a quota lowers p_P^*, hence raises p_{P^*}. These results are symmetric to those for quantity setting (policy creates a consistent Cournot or Bertrand conjectural variation for the home firm).[3] A final (implausible) possibility is that neither firm understands the government constraint, in which case the quota analysis reverts to the quantity constraint case above and both tariff regime CCVs lie below their quota regime values. In no case can the quota cause lower consistent conjectural price variations than the tariff.

One extra peculiarity of the price-setting model is that it might be necessary to use variable levies to implement the target price regime if the target price is not understood. Thus the comparison is no longer between a pure quota and a pure tariff. But the variable levy is precisely the form the home government's trade policy takes in the antidumping cases where the price-setting model applies.

Welfare Evaluation: Quantity Setting
The simplest case to analyze is one in which the oligopolistic sector has no effect on other prices in the economy. This partial equilibrium analysis has a general equilibrium equivalent if (i) relative prices in the (competitive) rest

of the domestic economy are fixed (so that all other goods form a composite exportable),[4] and (ii) government revenue is lump sum redistributed such that changes in revenue due to changes in the firms' decision variables do not affect the perceived elasticity of the demand functions.[5] Under these assumptions, let indirect utility for the representative consumer be $V(P, P^*, I)$, where I denotes income. The consumer receives the profits of the home duopolist, $\pi(Y, Q)$. This element makes necessary a full welfare analysis, since a quota policy that increases the advantage of the home firm over the foreign firm might conceivably take away enough rent from the foreigner to compensate for the effect of lower output upon the consumer. Assume first that all tariff revenue or quota rent (denoted "revenue") is captured by the government and returned to the consumer. The alternative case in which all revenue goes to the foreign firm will also be developed. Revenue is

$$G(Y, Q) = Q[P^* - C_Q^* + Q(P_Q^* + P_Y^* y_Q)],$$

where the expression in square brackets equals the gap between marginal revenue and marginal cost, the tax or tax equivalent of the quota facing the foreign producer, using his first-order condition. Then $I = I^0 + G(Y, Q) + \pi(Y, Q)$. Substituting this expression and the inverse demand functions into the indirect utility function yields $V(P(Y, Q), P^*(Y, Q), I^0 + G(Y, Q) + \pi(Y, Q)) = v(Y, Q, y_Q)$. Conjectural equilibrium implies that the solution value of Y is dependent on q_Y, y_Q: $Y = f(q_Y, y_Q)$. Under either regime, however, Q is constrained to the same value Q^0. This implies that y_Q is no longer of significance in determining home output, and $Y = f'(q_Y, Q^0)$ from the home producer's first order condition. Substituting, the *reduced form indirect utility function* is

$$v'(q_Y, y_Q, Q^0) = v(f'(q_Y, Q^0), Q^0, y_Q). \tag{12}$$

The welfare analysis of the tariff versus the quota proceeds by recognizing that the instrument choice is tantamount to shifting the conjectural variations in (12). One further step simplifies the analysis by recognizing that with q_Y parametric, y_Q depends on q_Y. Examining (7) in the linear case of demand, y_Q is increasing in q_Y:

$$y_Q = -P_Q/[2P_Y - C_{YY} + P_Q q_Y] \qquad \text{and}$$

$$dy_Q/dq_Y = \{P_Q/[2P_Y - C_{YY} + P_Q q_Y]\}^2 > 0.$$

The effect of the difference in regimes comes down to the evaluation of the difference (rise) in q_Y under the quota. From the derivation of (12), its derivative with respect to q_Y is, using Roy's identity and the structure of G

and π,

$$dv'/dq_Y = -V_I Y P_Y f'_{q_Y} - V_I Q P^*_Y f'_{q_Y}$$
$$+ V_I Y P_Y f'_{q_Y} \qquad\qquad + V_I (P - C_Y) f'_{q_Y} \qquad\qquad (13)$$
$$+ V_I Q P^*_Y f'_{q_Y} + V_I Q^2 P^*_Y \, dy_Q/dq_Y,$$

where the first line gives the terms via the price arguments of V, the second line gives the terms via home firm profits π, and the third line gives the terms via revenue G. This simplifies to

$$dv'/dq_Y = V_I (P - C_Y) f'_{q_Y} + V_I Q^2 P^*_Y \, dy_Q/dq_Y < 0. \qquad (13')$$

The sign of $(13')$ follows from using $f'_{q_Y} < 0$ and $P^*_Y < 0$. Then the quota is inferior to the tariff in welfare terms.

The alternative revenue capture assumption is that all revenue goes to the foreign firm, which implies that the third line of (13) is deleted. The simplified expression for the welfare change is

$$dv'/dq_Y = V_I (P - C_Y) f'_{q_Y} - V_I Q P^*_Y f'_{q_Y} < 0. \qquad (13'')$$

The sign follows under the same assumptions. If instead the tariff policy allows revenue capture at home while the quota policy does not (which seems likely), the tariff is preferred *a fortiori*. The results are summarized as follows:

PROPOSITION 1   Under consistent conjectural variations with quantity-setting duopolists, under the Bresnahan assumptions, quotas are inferior to quantity-equivalent tariffs.

Note that the contradiction of proposition 1 must necessarily involve a "collusive" (i.e., q_Y, $y_Q > 0$) consistent conjectural equilibrium in the absence of a tariff or quota. These are mathematically possible when non-linearity is permitted in inverse demand, but have an air of implausibility when derived as the outcome of a noncooperative game. Proposition 1 should hold under a much wider range of structure than the linear demand-quadratic cost assumptions of Bresnahan.

Welfare Evaluation: Price Setting
The representative consumer's indirect utility function is $V(P, P^*, I^0 + \pi'' + G'')$ under home revenue capture, where

$$\pi'' = Y(P, P^*)P - C(Y(P, P^*)),$$

$$G'' = (P^* - C^*_Q)Q + Q^2/[Q_{P^*} + Q_P p_{P^*}].$$

The revenue expression is based on embedding a specific tax or tax equivalent of a quota into the foreign firm's first order condition (5).

In consistent conjectural equilibrium, P and P^* are functions of p_{P^*} and p_P^*, $h(p_{P^*}, p_P^*)$, and $k(p_{P^*}, p_P^*)$, respectively. A reduced form indirect utility function dependent on the conjectural variations is obtained by substituting $h(\cdot)$ and $k(\cdot)$ for P and P^*. Denote it $v''(p_{P^*}, p_P^*)$. The welfare effect of the change in instruments is evaluated via its effect on the conjectural variations. By previous steps, the quota (weakly) increases the solution values for p_{P^*} and p_P^* as compared to the specific tariff under government (price) quantity targetting. Welfare is weakly reduced by use of the quota if v'' is decreasing in p_{P^*} and p_P^*. This remains to be shown.

Using Roy's identity and the definitions of G'' and π'', under home revenue capture

$$v''_{p_{P^*}} = -V_I(Y - Y)\partial h/\partial p_{P^*} - V_I(Q - Q)\partial k/\partial p_{P^*}$$

$$- V_I Q^2 Q_P/[Q_{P^*} + Q_P p_{P^*}]^2 + V_I(P - C_Y)dY/dp_{P^*},$$

where

$$dY/dp_{P^*} = Y_P \partial h/\partial p_{P^*} + Y_{P^*} \partial k/\partial p_{P^*}.$$

It is a routine exercise in algebra to show that $dY/dp_{P^*} < 0$ rather generally, with the result assured if $Q_P - Y_{P^*} \geqslant 0$. Intuitively, both prices rise, but P^* rises relatively more, by figure 2.2. The product group Q, Y substitutes against all other goods, however, and with own effects dominating cross-effects, and cross-effects not too different, Y must fall. Thus $v''_p < 0$ if the goods are substitutes. Similarly,

$$v''_{p_P^*} = V_I(P - C_Y)dY/dp_P^* < 0.$$

The proof that $dY/dp_P^* < 0$ is simple, since the reaction curve diagram, figure 2.2, shows that a rise in p_P^* will raise P proportionately more than P^*. Both substitution against other goods and substitution against Q reduce Y.

For the case of foreign rent capture the analogous expressions are

$$v''_{p_{P^*}} = -V_I Q \partial k/\partial p_{P^*} + V_I(P - C_Y)dY/dp_{P^*} < 0,$$

$$v''_{p_P^*} = -V_I Q \partial k/\partial p_P^* + V_I(P - C_Y)dY/dp_P^* < 0.$$

Thus as in the home revenue capture case, the derivatives are negative. The regime with lower conjectural variation has higher welfare.

The results are summarized as follows:

PROPOSITION 2   For price-setting duopolists in consistent conjectural equilibrium, a (price-equivalent) quantity-equivalent quota is (weakly) inferior to a tariff in the linear demand/quadratic cost model.

Two definitions of equivalence are provided for completeness, since the quantity definition may not be relevant under price competition. Price equivalence is not an entirely natural base of comparison either, which leads to another reason for the necessity of investigating a deeper base for equivalence.

2.4 Anticipation of Government Policy

Suppose that the target level of imports in sections 2.1–2.3 is a proxy for some deeper target for which imports are instrumental. The most appealing simple target is domestic employment. It stands in for a wide variety of other possible targets (wages, profits, the utility of workers, etc.), in which more home output is good and more foreign sales displace home sales, hence are "bad." If trade policy is the only instrument and the employment target is a binding commitment, then firms will learn that trade policy will react to their actions. Consistent conjectural variations must rationally incorporate this new information. Under these circumstances, the tariff is equivalent to the quota because the CCVs are invariant to the mode of intervention.

How likely is a full anticipation? It depends on the circumstances under which protection is obtained. Baldwin (1984) has divided cases of protection into two groups for the United States. First, by the *administrative route* interested parties can appeal to the appropriate federal agencies and possibly receive protection via application of statutory principles, a favorable case finding by the ITC, and assent by the president. Such cases are cheap to bring and largely out of the hands of the firms to influence. Previous models apply. Most cases under this heading involve competitive industries. The second, *political, route* may follow a loss on the first route and involves a substantial commitment of resources to create a political majority coalition in favor of protection. The president then assents to negotiation by the USTR (the U.S. Special Trade Representative) of VERs to "head off protectionist pressure." It is less clear then that previous models apply, since administering the VER system involves continuous tinkering in the presence of the political lobbies that have been created by the campaign to obtain protection. Many cases arrived at by this route involve oligopolistic industries (e.g., steel, autos). Thus a model of anticipation, possibly even full anticipation, may apply. It is worthwhile to initiate a formal treatment.

The simplest model of employment policy is based on a Keynesian labor market. The home firm hires labor so that the fixed wage equals its marginal revenue product. At the target level of employment, with other factors fixed, the marginal physical product of labor is fixed. The employment policy then reduces to control of trade so that a target marginal revenue for the domestic firm is attained:

$$P(Y, Q) + YP_Y(Y, Q) + YP_Q q_Y = \mu. \tag{14}$$

Equation (14) holds only for those values of Q for which the foreign firm earns nonnegative profits. It is assumed that the feasible set of such Q values is large enough (or μ is small enough) so that an interior solution will be possible. (14) implies a policy function $Q(Y)$, the permitted level of imports given what government anticipates home output to be.

$Q(Y)$ is the upper bound on imports and it is possible that it will not bind. In this case the standard conjectural equilibrium analysis holds. The new case is where $Q(Y)$ binds. Then Y and Q are determined entirely by the game between the home firm and the government. Given the outcome of the game, the foreign firm's best move, by the assumption that $Q(Y)$ binds, is $Q = Q(Y)$.

There are three possible ways the game between the home firm and the government can be played. If government assumes the home firm will not react to changes in Q, under the Bresnahan assumptions, the slope of its reaction function is $Q_Y = -[2P_Y + P_Q q_Y]/P_Q$. This structure implies that the government has a Stackelberg follower position relative to the home firm; i.e., it moves first under the assumption that the home output is fixed. The home firm is able to play leader and shift the permitted level of imports by taking advantage of the government commitment to employment protection. It is also possible that the government and the home firm are engaged in a noncooperative learning game similar to the home and foreign firms in preceding parts. Then the government has a conjecture y_Q^G to be determined in a consistent fashion, simultaneously with q_Y. It can be shown that in both cases the CCVs for the home firm and the government are usually positive; i.e., the anticipation of government policy creates a collusive consistent conjectural equilibrium. This is intuitive from the nature of the government policy, since the home firm knows it can use the government to impose output curbs on its foreign rival. A cut in home firm output will induce the government to reduce the permitted level of imports to achieve the employment target. Correct anticipation by the home firm implies a collusive CCV. Finally, the home firm can be a follower and the government a Stackelberg leader. This simply returns the analysis to the previous case, where the firms know only the trade policy, and the CCVs are negative for a tariff or free trade. The essential technical point is that the game between the home firm and the government (in the two new cases) completely determines the relevant conjectural variations, given the feasibility of the implied trade policy.

There are two cases of firms' anticipation of government to consider. If the policy function is known to both home and foreign firms, then it is intuitively obvious that the form of intervention will be irrelevant; tariffs, quotas, and any mixture of them will all be equivalent. More formally, for the firm-leader/government-follower case, the home firm will have consistent conjectural variation $q_Y = Q_Y = -P_Y/P_Q$, and the foreign firm will have consistent conjectural variation $y_Q = -P_Q/[2P_Y + P_Q Q_Y]$. Under either form of revenue distribution, the tariff and quota give identical results. The alternative case is when the home firm knows the government policy function but the foreign firm does not. The home firm has consistent conjectural variation $q_Y = Q_Y$ under either instrument. The foreign firm's CCV is the correct slope of the home firm reaction function, $y_Q = -P_Q/[2P_Y + P_Q Q_Y]$, so again the consistent conjectural equilibrium is invariant to the form of the intervention. As before, tariffs and quotas are welfare equivalent.

The same proposition goes through for price-setting behavior, as should be clear from the structure of the above argument. Essentially what runs the propositions is that the government's intervention policy is no longer a pure trade policy, but an industrial policy. This being correctly anticipated determines the consistent conjectural variations, hence the *form* of the trade intervention no longer matters.

More intricate and realistic cases of incomplete and asymmetric information can doubtless yield a richer menu of results as above at the cost of a higher level of complexity. Information that is sufficiently incomplete involves a breakdown of equivalence, and in some measure a return to the models of the previous section. Quotas should be presumptively inferior. It is possible, however, that government lack of information could be so severe as to imply an "inappropriate" target variable. In this case the quota could dominate. Also, it is possible that under such circumstances, the point raised by Rotemberg-Saloner could become practically relevant. Specifically, in the absence of monopoly power, a tariff could be a superior means of reaching a target; but the necessary binding of trade policy under imperfect competition could mean that the tariff allows the enforcement of collusion while a quota would not. There would then be an interesting trade-off. As a related part of this research it should be useful to model the lobbying game that creates the government constraint imposed in the output/trade restriction game. Intuition suggests that the more profitable (via collusive outcomes or other factors) the constraint, the more resources the firm will devote to obtaining the constraint in the first stage game. This is a rich agenda for future research.

Appendix 2.A

The price-setting consistent conjectural variations are solved from

$$
\begin{bmatrix} p_{P\cdot} \\ p_P^* \end{bmatrix} = \begin{bmatrix} -Y_{P\cdot}/[2Y_P + Y_{P\cdot}p_P^* - C_{YY}Y_P(Y_P + p_P^*Y_{P\cdot})] \\ -Q_P/[2Q_{P\cdot} + Q_P p_{P\cdot} - C_{QQ}^* Q_{P\cdot}(Q_{P\cdot} + p_{P\cdot}Q_P)] \end{bmatrix}.
\tag{A.1}
$$

This is a quadratic in the conjectural variations and solves for

$$
p_{P\cdot} = -\frac{Q_{P\cdot}}{Q_P}\left[\frac{(1 + m_Q)(1 + m_Y) + m_Q Q_P Y_{P\cdot}/Y_P Q_{P\cdot}}{(1 + m_Y)m_Q}\right] \pm \left[\frac{-Q_{P\cdot}}{Q_P}\right]\text{radical}, \tag{A.2}
$$

where $m_Y = 1 - C_{YY}Y_P \geq 1$ and $m_Q = 1 - C_{QQ}Q_{P\cdot} \geq 1$. Under the demand assumptions the square bracket exceeds 1. The radical is positive and less than the first term. By examining the first-order condition for the foreign firm, it is immediately obvious that $p_{P\cdot} \geq -Q_{P\cdot}/Q_P$ does not permit nonnegative profits at nonnegative output. The negative root is ruled out. Thus the economically relevant value of $p_{P\cdot}$ is less than $-Q_{P\cdot}/Q_P$. Substituting into (A.1), and noting that p_P^* is an increasing function of $p_{P\cdot}$,

$$
p_P^* < -Q_P/Q_{P\cdot}. \tag{A.3}
$$

Since the right-hand side of (A.3) is the quota value of the consistent conjectural variation, the tariff value is smaller.

Notes

1. That is, positive conjectural variations; home firm behavior that assumes that rival firms will cut output or raise price equiproportionately as the home firm cuts output or raises price.

2. See section 2.2 for discussion of whether a quota or tariff has different implications for enforcement.

3. A further symmetry arises when under quantity-setting behavior the government announces a home firm quantity target. The choice of trade instrument then has no influence on the consistent conjectural variations.

4. This arises if (i) the technology outside the Y sector has constant returns to scale, (ii) at least as many traded goods face fixed international prices as there are domestically mobile factors, and (iii) only the Y sector has a specific factor.

5. The first assumption means that the marginal cost of Y in preceding sections is a general equilibrium marginal cost equal to the marginal rate of transformation.

The second assumption with the first means that the general equilibrium consumer income argument of the demand functions is irrelevant to the conjectural equilibrium. The general equilibrium production income is the sum of all factor payments plus profits, where the latter term potentially offers a complication which disappears due to maximization.

To see how this can be so, let the consumer's income be $I = I^0 + \pi + R$, where R is the lump sum redistribution of government revenue, and π is profit of the home firm. I^0 is the sum of all factor payments in the economy, which is constant under the assumption of frozen relative prices (which includes factor prices) and full employment in the competitive equilibrium of factor markets. For the price setting case the home demand function is $Y(P, P^*, I)$. The home firm reaction function for price setting is $\pi_P = Y + (P - C_Y)[Y_P + Y_{P^*}p_P^*] + (P - C_Y)Y_I \pi_P$, or $0 = Y + (P - C_Y)[Y_P + Y_{P^*}p_P^*]$, just as above. Similarly in the quantity setting case the inverse demand function is $P(Y, Q, I)$ and the reaction function of the home firm is $\pi_Y = P - C_Y + Y[P_Y + P_Q q_Y] + YP_I \pi_Y$, or $0 = P - C_Y + Y[P_Y + P_Q q_Y]$, as above. The foreign firm reaction functions are similarly unaffected once the first order conditions are imposed. This means that the income linkage of home firm profits to the demand function does not affect the conjectural equilibrium, nor the consistent conjectural variations. If on the other hand the firms are allowed to see through to the dependence of R on the strategic price or quantity variables (violating the lump-sum assumption), then the change in R with respect to the strategic variables enters the demand functions changes in similar fashion to π_P or π_Y. This in turn makes the reaction functions nonlinear, which does not permit the Bresnahan solution of consistent conjectural variations as the roots of a quadratic.

References

Baldwin, R. E. (1984), "The Changing Nature of U.S. Trade Policy since World War II," in *The Structure and Evolution of Recent U.S. Trade Policy*, R. E. Baldwin and A. O. Krueger, eds., Chicago: NBER, pp. 5—27.

Bhagwati, J. N. (1965), "The Nonequivalence of Tariffs and Quotas," in *Trade, Growth, and the Balance of Payments*, R. E. Baldwin et al., eds., Amsterdam: North-Holland.

Bresnahan, T. (1981), "Duopoly Models with Consistent Conjectures," *American Economic Review*, 71, 934—945.

Robson, A. (1982), "Existence of Consistent Conjectures: Comment," *American Economic Review*, 73, 454—456.

Rotemberg, J., and G. Saloner (1986), "Quotas and the Stability of Implicit Collusion," NBER Working Paper No. 1948.

3   The Relative Inefficiency of Quotas: The Cheese Case

The nonequivalence of tariffs and quotas under a wide variety of circumstances is well established in economic theory. This chapter considers heterogeneity as a source of nonequivalence and demonstrates its practical importance. Where restriction is inevitable, the bias of economists in favor of price instruments is not thoroughly grounded; this chapter should help provide a foundation.

The point of departure from the equivalence model is differentiation of products. In practice, almost any quota system will be applied to what is in fact a commodity group. Legislators or chief executives restrict total imports of a group, possibly due to either lack of information or lack of a model that would allow a basis for derivation of a more detailed set of restrictions. Quota system administrators by default have wide authority to allocate trade within the group. Distribution of quota licenses in this case involves substantive resource allocation.

It is shown below that optimal allocation of quota licenses subject to a group total import constraint will produce uniform rent on use for each member of the group. This is equivalent to a uniform specific import tax save for revenue distribution. Administrators typically do not have competitive auctions in licenses, which would accomplish the same end, but use simple rules like base year quantity or value proportions to hand out licenses, which are type and country-of-origin specific. Provided resale is frustrated, the allocation will be inefficient. Section 3.1 sets out the simple analytics of optimal and quantity proportion quota allocations and discusses factors influencing the size of inefficiency.

The purpose of this chapter is to provide a case study of an import quota system with essentially the characteristics noted. Section 3.2 briefly discusses the U.S. dairy quota system. Section 3.3 reviews the econometric model of cheese demand used to calculate welfare effects. The results in section 3.4 demonstrate that the inefficiency loss is indeed substantial. The estimated AIDS (Almost Ideal Demand System) model of the U.S cheese quota system (see Anderson, 1983) is used to calculate the welfare costs of the quota compared to an efficient tariff that produces the same aggregate quantity of cheese imports in the constrained categories. The analysis shows added cost amounting to over 15% of base expenditure on the constrained categories. Another revealing way of scaling the welfare cost compares the quota inefficiency loss with the total welfare loss from not having free trade. Switching from the quota to an efficient tax that yields the same quantity of imports gets us nearly a third of the way back to free trade. Or, the quota distribution inefficiency adds nearly 50% to the unavoidable loss due to the constraint on imports.

Sections 3.2 and 3.3 discuss the considerable difficulties encountered in building an econometric model of the cheese quota system. The results of section 3.4 thus are subject to considerable bias, especially from aggregation, when regarded as a realistic account of the costs of the U.S. cheese quota system. This is unfortunate, but does not detract from the main point of this chapter, which is to show a presumption that quota systems in practice are inefficient. The results of section 3.4 can be interpreted as plausible simulations of a quota system not unlike the U.S. cheese quota system. The size of the welfare loss together with the difficulties experienced in carrying on the study of quota incidence suggest that economists are on firm ground in opposing the trend toward use of quantity restrictions. Failing a return to price instruments we should advocate data collection in a manner that makes incidence analysis easier.

The results here are related to general propositions suggesting that aggregation seriously understates the deadweight loss of tax systems since aggregation reduces both estimated elasticities of substitution and estimated average taxes (see Dixon, 1978). The disaggregation of the model here avoids the type of bias Dixon studied, but in addition disaggregation by cheese type and countries uncovers a new source of loss worth over 15% of base expenditure on the restricted cheese categories. And even these results are based on a (forced) considerable aggregation of cheese types. Thus, painful as it is, disaggregation is strongly indicated for tax incidence problems.

3.1 Efficient Quotas on Commodity Groups

We assume that political pressures result in an import quota to be applied to an aggregate commodity group. This takes the form of what Bhagwati and Srinivasan (1983) call a "non-economic" constraint. Administration of the quota system is left to civil servants, who will typically use simple rules to allocate licenses under the constraint. While political interests build around the allocation systems, we regard these as second-order effects. They can be disregarded by an enlightened administrator who must nevertheless obey the legally mandated aggregate quota.

The optimal allocation is, intuitively, going to equalize rent on quota licenses across members of the group. This would be the equilibrium outcome of a competitive auction of licenses, and the inefficiency of any other allocation is seen to be a foregone arbitrage gain. The optimum can automatically be achieved by a uniform tax.[1]

Under alternative noneconomic constraints, a quota thus allocated "efficiently" can be inferior to, for example, an *ad valorem* tariff. The substitution toward higher value categories that reaps an arbitrage gain can also conflict with a noneconomic constraint on employment or revenue (see Baldwin, 1982, and Dixit, 1983). The issue of what constraint is appropriate is serious. It is always necessary to specify as closely as possible the deeper variable targeted by the political economic process and its relation to the trade control. Once this is done, ignorance of detailed elasticities and/or absence of a complete model will often necessitate an aggregate trade control.[2]

For example, consider the case of dairy quotas. They arose out of a desire to limit domestic price support payments (see section 3.2). This might imply a deeper noneconomic constraint on disturbing the subsidy budget by no more than a given amount. Possibly revenue raised on imports might also be relevant. Nevertheless it is reasonable to use an aggregate import constraint for two reasons. First, the stated objective of administrators was to place quotas on substitutable categories so that total annual imports of dairy products did not exceed a given milk equivalent tonnage, this being instrumental in limiting support payments to domestic producers (see section 3.2). This effectively translates into a simple aggregate quantity constraint. Presumably, administrators chose this objective because they were ignorant of demand elasticities when formulating quotas. By default all cheeses in a substitutable category were made identical. Second, optimizing the price support (possibly plus dairy import restriction revenue) subsystem is of dubious relevance when we observe that subsidy payments come from the general government revenue with little evidence of concern for magnitude as coverages change and when licenses are given away. Consideration of optimal fiscal systems, if it can be done sensibly at all, must be made a much bigger project. The simple noneconomic constraint is the natural primal analogue to partial equilibrium analysis.

Proceeding formally, we set out a simple analysis of a small trading country subject to a noneconomic constraint on aggregate imports within some group. The vector of import quantities in the constrained group is $Q = (Q_1, \ldots, Q_n)$. The vector of trade quantities in the other commodities is x (which contains positive elements for imports and negative elements for exports). Nontraded goods are irrelevant to the point we make, so are suppressed. External prices of Q are given by the vector P, and external prices for the vector x are given by s. Allocation of production (if any in given categories) is irrelevant, so we assumed fixed endowments of goods that are produced: Z_1 for the constrained goods and Z_2 for unconstrained goods.

The enlightened civil servant must choose a trade vector (Q, x) to maximize utility of the representative consumer subject to the balance of trade constraint and the noneconomic constraint. Thus he solves the program

$$\max_{Q,x} U(Z_1 + Q, Z_2 + x):$$

$$(\lambda) \quad P \cdot Q + s \cdot x \leqslant 0, \tag{1}$$

$$(\mu) \quad \iota \cdot Q \leqslant \bar{Q},$$

where Z_1, Z_2 are constant production vectors, μ and λ are Lagrange multipliers, and ι is the vector of ones.

The first-order conditions are sufficient with concave utility, and yield in terms of a numeraire from the unconstrained group

$$\frac{1}{U_{2n}} U_1 = P + (\mu/\lambda)_\iota,$$

$$\frac{1}{U_{2n}} U_2 = s, \tag{2}$$

where $U_{2n} = \partial U / \partial x_n =$ marginal utility of the numeraire good,

$U_1 = \partial U / \partial Q,$

$U_2 = \{\partial U / \partial x_i\}, i \neq n.$

The conditions (2) immediately imply that the unique global optimum can be decentralized with a uniform specific tax $= \mu/\lambda$ on every element of Q, the tariff proceeds being lump-sum redistributed to the representative consumer. Equivalently, quota licenses can be competitively auctioned with redistribution of the proceeds.

In practice, quota licenses are usually distributed according to a simple rule, like quantity proportions in a base year. We now briefly consider theoretical factors affecting the magnitude of inefficiency created by such rules. With Leontief-type utility functions and endowments that grow radially (neutral growth), quantity rules will attain the optimal allocation in problem (1). Nonneutral growth of the Zs has an obvious effect. Less obviously, as the elasticity of substitution rises, two counteracting forces mediate the inefficiency of the rule. General analytical results are not attainable, but these forces are clear. First, the higher the elasticity of substitution, the less the harm associated with a given configuration of nonuniform taxes (equivalent to a quota distribution), since it is easier to substitute away from expensive categories. But second, the lower the elasticity of substitution, the less far the rule-given quantity restriction is from the optimal quantity change.

In simulation of the dairy quota system using a CES (Constant Elasticity of Substitution) utility function and methods analogous to those of section 3.4, the first effect predominated in a reasonable range of elasticity values (from 0.10 to 3), based on welfare loss relative to base expenditure. The second effect showed up when the inefficiency loss was scaled relative to the unavoidable inefficiency due to the constraint. This measure of relative inefficiency rose with the elasticity of substitution, but much more gently than the relative-to-base-expenditure measure fell. The latter typically dropped by a factor of 10 in the range of elasticity values 0.10–1.0.

Similar exercises can be done for other rules or other utility functions. These results point to the sensitivity of empirical findings to the elasticities used, and thus emphasize the need for sound empirical work. The results of section 3.4 show large welfare losses; this and the theoretical analysis above indicate how easily a quantity rule can err badly.

3.2 The U.S. Dairy Industry and the Quota System

We first consider the institutional and legal structure of dairy import controls and then the resulting market structure we assume. We aim to justify our use of (1) the simple form of "noneconomic" import constraint and (2) a partial equilibrium model.

The U.S. dairy quota system originated as a by-product of the dairy price support system. The main element is support of a manufacturing grade milk price, but there are also butter and American type cheese support prices. At various times, beginning in 1937, quotas have been imposed on a variety of cheeses, as well as butter, nonfat dry milk, substances high in nonfat dry milk or butterfat, and other milk products. The president has very broad authority to proclaim, raise, or suspend these trade controls,[3] but in practice revision has been limited.

In the timeless model of section 3.1, the quota allocation problem is faced once for all. In practice, the set of dairy quotas reflect an evolution of broadening the scope of coverage as more products appear to be sufficiently substitutable with domestic products to warrant control. Thus the date of inception and benchmark period (upon which proportionate allocations are based) differ for different cheeses and other products. The spirit of the quota system is, however, to set detailed levels of imports on a basis consistent with historic proportions. The presidential authority does not stipulate that this principle is to be carried through to allocation by country of origin, but the administrators have so proceeded. An important implication of the evolving nature of the quota system is that the administrators help create the marginal changes in the system issued by the president. Significantly, they appear to regard their objective as a target level of milk equivalent tonnage in groups identified as substituting for domestic milk products (see, for example, Emery, 1969, pp. 9–11). Thus both the history of quota setting and the stated objective of the quota administrators support a noneconomic constraint of the simple form in (1). We assume that any second-order political interests do not create binding constraints.

On the other hand, the current allocation system does apparently create *economically* binding constraints. The U.S.D.A. (U.S. Department of Agriculture) quota system administrators develop license allocation by commodity by country from base year allocations in the legally mandated categories. They claim to have effective auditors who implicitly frustrate resale of licenses. Measured differences in average quota rent margins, reported below, bear out the claim. This creates the basis for our study of efficient alternative dairy product import controls.

Butter and other milk product quotas are ignored in the study on the grounds that they are rather simple undifferentiated products with low elasticity of substitution with cheese or with each other. On prior reasoning, the quota allocations in these categories might be reasonably appropriate. The group of cheese controls appears to represent a much closer approximation to the theoretical model above. Cheese is a highly differentiated product with fairly high within-group elasticities of substitution. The Census trade data have nine commodity categories of continuously imported cheese plus a catch-all, with six of the nine plus a part of the catch-all category subject in part or whole to quota constraint. This creates the circumstances for a case study of quota inefficiency when we convert the quota constraints into an overall constraint on the six categories. Inefficiency will arise due to (1) inefficient allocation by country within the same cheese type (a matter of administrative discretion) and (2) inefficient allocation over types (partly mandated in current presidential proclamations, but presumably easily changed within the spirit of the presidents' previous exercises of authority).

We now rationalize a partial equilibrium approach to the market for imported cheese. The United States is a small consumer of foreign cheese; hence foreign price of foreign cheese is reasonably taken to be exogenous. Domestic price in quota constrained categories is of course endogenous. U.S. consumption of cheese is a tiny fraction of total food consumption, so ignoring spillover effects onto noncheese prices may be reasonable. Domestic price of domestic cheese is endogenous save when the government is maintaining a floor price through large purchases. Endogenous prices are fitted to an implicit reduced form in the econometric work reported below.

In principle, it is possible to model the supply side of the domestic cheese industry. Domestic cheese production and sale is dominated by the government's milk, cheese, and butter price supports, but not wholly so. Successful dealing with these markets probably requires a model of how the government sets its supports. The highly politicized process attending this in the '70s is common knowledge. An attempt to deal with modeling domestic cheese supply was dropped at an early stage because in the welfare (as opposed to econometric) analysis it is permissible to treat the U.S. price of U.S. cheese and related dairy products as exogenous to import policy changes, being separately set by the government and maintained by price support purchases. This is effectively true in a large part of the sample (1964–1979), particularly in the later years. The displacement effect of foreign price changes on domestic cheese categories can be calculated using the demand functions for imported cheese and relying on the symmetry implied by demand theory. The implied change in price-support-purchases of domestic cheese is carried through as part of the analysis.

We now consider briefly problems of aggregation. With the data available it proved to be impossible to match exactly the quota constraints with the commodity categories. Our solution was to aggregate. Quota authority lies with the U.S.D.A. and with different statistical codes from the Customs (TSUS) code, which are different still from the Census (SITC) codes. Country level quota information was available but attempts to build a complete model of import supply were frustrated by aggregation problems and complexities in how quota licenses are used (see the appendix to Anderson, 1983, for more detail). The econometric model used in the next sections glosses over quota system complications by assuming that for each of the six categories constrained by quota, the entire set of members is treated uniformly. Foreign price of any cheese is exogenous, but domestic price of domestic cheese and all quota constrained cheese is endogenous and fitted to an implicit reduced form. This creates aggregation bias of unknown sign and magnitude. Similarly, the welfare analysis is biased as a "true" account of the cost of U.S. quota system inefficiency.

3.3 The Model of U.S. Imported Cheese Markets

The preceding section essentially justifies a partial equilibrium approach to modeling the effect of switching from quotas to tariffs. The U.S. domestic cheese prices are assumed to be made exogenous by government price support, other food prices are not affected, and the U.S. is a small customer in world dairy markets—hence foreign prices are exogenous. For the welfare evaluation, the endogenous variables are assigned their sample mean values in the quota regime.

For econometric modeling, U.S. domestic cheese prices are made endogenous (since they are at least some of the time) and the U.S. price of quota constrained foreign cheese is also endogenous. We thus evade modeling domestic supply of both foreign and domestic cheese except as it is embedded in an implicit reduced form. We do require a set of demand functions for imported cheese.

A nine-equation model of imported cheese demand is estimated for the years 1964–1979. A food and beverage expenditure function is assumed to exist for a representative U.S. consumer identifiable in the aggregate data (see Anderson, 1983, for discussion of the implied assumptions). The AIDS expenditure function is used, with the further wrinkle that only a tiny portion of total food and beverage consumption is estimated—that for nine imported cheeses (see Deaton and Muellbauer, 1980a, b, for a general treatment of AIDS). AIDS is used because it is a flexible functional form with particularly simple capability for allowing nonhomothetic preferences while permitting exact linear aggregation.

The AIDS expenditure function is defined as

$$\log(P_1, \ldots, P_n, u) = \sum_{i=1}^{n} \alpha_i \log P_i + \frac{1}{2} \sum_{i=1}^{n} \sum_{j=1}^{n} \gamma_{ij} \log P_i \log P_j$$

$$+ u\beta_0 \prod_{j=1}^{n} P_j^{\beta_j},$$

(3)

where u = utility indicator, $e(\ )$ = expenditure function, and P_i = price of good i. Shepard's lemma implies the compensated demand functions: $\partial e/\partial P_i = c_i(P_1, \ldots, P_n, u)$. It is more convenient to place these in compensated expenditure share form: $w_i = (P_i/e)(\partial e/\partial P_i)$, where w_i is the share of expenditure on i. Next, (3) can be solved for u using $e = y$, expenditure = income. The resulting indirect utility substituted into the compensated share equations yields the uncompensated expenditure share equations:

$$w_i = \alpha_i + \sum_{j=1}^{n} \gamma_{ij} \log P_j + \beta_i \log(y/P), \tag{4}$$

where P is the true cost of living index defined by

$$\log P = \sum_j \alpha_j \log P_j + (1/2) \sum_i \sum_j \gamma_{ij} \log P_i \log P_j. \tag{5}$$

Deaton-Muellbauer argue that P is usually closely approximated by standard indices. The restrictions implied by consumer theory are

$$\gamma_{ij} = \gamma_{ji} \quad \text{(symmetry)}, \tag{6}$$

$$\sum_{i=1}^{n} \alpha_i = 1, \quad \sum_{j=1}^{n} \gamma_{ij} = 0, \quad \sum_{j=1}^{n} \beta_j = 0 \quad \text{(homogeneity)}, \tag{7}$$

$$\{k_{ij}\} = \{-\delta_{ij} w_i + w_i w_j + \beta_i \beta_j \log y/P\}, \quad \text{negative semidefinite} \tag{8}$$

$$\text{(concavity).}$$

In (8), δ_{ij} is the Kronecker delta. The matrix $k = \{k_{ij}\}$ is a simple transform of the Slutsky matrix, with the same properties.

Equation (4) in its stochastic form is fitted to 1964–1979 U.S. quarterly data. A nine-equation set of w_is is fitted to the logs of a set of 15 cheese prices (including domestic types), a general price index for good, and a "real food and beverages" expenditure term y/P. It is very convenient to normalize the price data by division by the arithmetic mean. The transformed log price data is then all zero at the point of arithmetic means. In our base case estimation, symmetry and homogeneity are imposed on (4). Concavity (for the nine imported cheese prices) is imposed at the point of means and holds in a small region about it as discussed in Anderson (1983). The results are reasonably "good." The main sources of possible specification error are in aggregation over consumers and over cheeses. The data do not permit an attack on these problems. To give some feel for the demand structure that results, appendix table 3.A1 presents point estimates of compensated price elasticities. They are defined by

$$e_{ij} = -\delta_{ij} + w_j + \frac{\gamma_{ij}}{w_i} + \frac{\beta_i \beta_j \log y/P}{w_i}, \tag{9}$$

where δ_{ij} is the Kronecker delta. The elasticities are evaluated at the point of means of the shares. A reader skeptical of the econometric methods used is free to regard these and the underlying parameters as plausible guesses to be used in simulation.

The estimated imported cheese demand functions and the symmetry restrictions of the expenditure function $(\gamma_{ij} = \gamma_{ji})$ permit a complete account of the effect of a change in import policy. All relevant parameters of the expenditure function are known, as are the relevant cheese demand parameters. The analysis of section 3.1 derives the efficient policy as being a uniform tax that would achieve the same aggregate quantity of constrained cheese. The estimated demand functions evaluated at the point of means can be used to solve for the efficient tax. A welfare analysis can then be carried through, based on the consequences of the change in the vector of constrained imported cheese prices.

3.4 The Welfare Loss of Inefficient Dairy Quotas

The model used to evaluate the welfare effects of the change from quotas to the efficient tax system is standard. The changes are measured in (1) the representative (hence aggregate) consumer's expenditure,[4] (2) the government's tax receipts, and (3) the quota license holder's loss of rent. Ordinarily, we would need to add in the change in income from production, but we assume domestic product prices are constant. For noncheese products, this is because we assume the changes in imported cheese prices have negligible effect on demand. For all domestically produced cheese, we assume for convenience that the government supports the price by purchases.

In practice government price support is given only for American-type cheese. The effect of assuming support for non-American-type cheese is to wash out some second-order effects on welfare via domestic product price changes. These have negligible first-order effect, since with supply = demand, the expenditure effect and production revenue effect cancel. We make this assumption to avoid what might be an inappropriate use of the implicit model of domestic supply. We report below on both American-type and total support payment changes.

Formally, the expenditure function may be written as $e(P, s, u)$, where P is the vector of domestic prices for constrained goods, s is the vector of domestic prices for unconstrained goods, and u is the parameter utility level. The vector s is made parametric by either (a) the small country assumption for traded goods other than cheese, (b) standard partial equilibrium "smallness" arguments with respect to nontraded goods, or (c) government floor price support purchases for domestic cheese products displaced by import price changes. The vector P is built up from foreign prices:

$$P = P^* + \text{(margins)} + t, \tag{10}$$

where P^* is the parametric foreign price vector, (margins) is the assumed parametric vector of distribution margins, and t is the tax-cum-quota-rent vector. If P^0 and P^1 are two vectors created by alternative restriction policies, the change in expenditure is

$$\Delta e = e(P^1, s, u) - e(P^0, s, u). \tag{11}$$

The change in quota rent is simply the original demand times the quota rent: $\partial e / \partial P \cdot t$ in the case where there was no initial tax on imports. In practice, there is in fact a portion of t that is a tax, t_g, so the actual rent lost is

$$\Delta \text{rent} = \frac{\partial e(P^0, s, u)}{\partial P} \cdot (t - t_g). \tag{12}$$

Now we account for government support payments. The displaced domestic demand is replaced by government purchases. Let s_d denote the supported products price vector, where s_d is composed of some element of s. The change in support payments is

$$\Delta \text{support} = \left[\frac{\partial e}{\partial s_d}(P^1, s, u) - \frac{\partial e}{\partial s_d}(P^0, s, u) \right] \cdot s_d, \tag{13}$$

where $\partial e / \partial s_d$ is the compensated demand vector for supported products. Below we present two measures for (13). One is the American-type cheese support payments—the only cheese so supported in reality. The other is the assumed support payments for all domestic cheese in the quota protected categories.

The first variant on (13) is a lower bound for actual support payment changes, since additional small changes in demand for other supported dairy products might be expected. The second minus the first is an upper bound for additional welfare loss, due to changes in other domestic cheese prices, since cheeses other than American-type are not supported. It should ordinarily far exceed the actual small secondary effect we are neglecting.

Finally, we account for changes in tariff revenue. On the group of constrained cheeses, the revenue is based on the common scalar efficient tax t^* solved for to satisfy the constraint

$$\frac{\partial e}{\partial P}(P^* + (\text{margins}) + t^* \iota, s, u) \cdot \iota = \bar{Q}, \tag{14}$$

where ι is the vector of ones. Revenue is collected in the amount $t^* \cdot \bar{Q}$. From this must be deducted the revenue previously collected by the government with its taxes on this group of cheese: $\partial e/\partial eP \cdot t_g$, where t_g is the initial specific tax vector (converted from the *ad valorem* actual tax at the point of mean prices). Thus the change in revenue is

$$\Delta\text{revenue} = t^*\bar{Q} - \frac{\partial e}{\partial P}(P^0, s, u) \cdot t_g. \tag{15}$$

We may note that (15) neglects the change in tariff revenue on the non-quota-constrained imported cheeses. This is done on the principle that the government budget constraint is supposed to be irrelevant, although we have kept track of Δsupport.[5] The amounts involved are small, in any case.

We report two welfare measures below. Gross welfare is the logically consistent measure corresponding to the theoretical model. It neglects Δsupport:

$$\Delta\text{gross welfare} = -\Delta e - \Delta\text{rent} + \Delta\text{revenue}. \tag{16}$$

Net welfare subtracts from this the change in support payments on American-type cheese.

The efficient tax and its welfare consequences in (12)–(15) are calculated using the parameter estimates detailed in Anderson (1983). The procedure can be performed at any data point. We restrict our attention primarily to the point of sample means, but discuss briefly the evaluation of extremal values. In the estimated AIDS system (4), the income terms β_i are effectively zero, so that we may impose homothetic preferences for evaluation purposes.[6] The uncompensated share equations (4) are equal in this case to the compensated share equations. We solve them for quantity demanded in the six quota constrained categories. The government's noneconomic constraint is to hold aggregate imports across the six cheeses to the given sample mean quantity. We know the efficient solution requires a uniform specific tax t. The new domestic price for import i will be $\hat{P}_i + t^*$, where $\hat{P}_i$ is the margin augmented foreign price, or free trade price. We solve for the optimal tax t^* in

$$\bar{Q} = y \sum_{i \in QR} \frac{1}{\hat{P}_i + t} \left\{ \alpha_i + \sum_{k \in QR} \gamma_{ik} \log((\hat{P}_k + t)/P_k^0) \right\}. \tag{17}$$

The term in curly brackets is the new expenditure share for import i, $i \in QR$. QR is the index set for constrained cheeses. $\bar{Q}$ is the given sample mean aggregate quantity. Operations outside the curly brackets convert shares to quantities, and aggregate. Inside the brackets, P_k^0 is the sample mean (quota regime) price. Its presence is necessitated by the econometric procedure of using sample-mean-scaled prices. The great convenience of this method is that other arguments of (4) are zeroed out in evaluation at the sample mean [all right-side data are scaled by the sample mean and $\log(x/\bar{x}) = 0$ at $x = \bar{x}$].

(17) is well behaved as a function of t at the sample means point, and Newton's method converged very quickly. For evaluation away from the point of means, (17) is somewhat more complex in form, and for extremal values of P_k has possible multiple roots (one case was discovered). This difficulty is related to the problem of nonconcavity of the estimated $e(P, u)$ at extreme values of P.[7] We restrict primary attention to the point of means for this reason, but report results at other data points because the extremal price distortions are precisely where the quota inefficiency ought to be greatest.

From evaluation of (17), the resulting new domestic price vector $\{\hat{P}_i + t^*\}$ for six categories is then plugged into the expenditure function (3). The relative change in expenditure is obtained by subtracting the log expenditure at the initial point from that at the new point, then exponentiating. The absolute size is obtained by multiplying by base expenditure. Making use again of the zeroing-out property of evaluation at the point of means we report the application of (11):

$$\Delta e = y \cdot \exp \left[\sum_{i \in QR} \left\{ \alpha_i \log((\hat{P}_i + t^*)/P_i^0) \right. \right.$$

$$\left. \left. + (1/2) \sum_{k \in QR} \gamma_{ik} \log((\hat{P}_i + t^*)/P_i^0) \log((\hat{P}_i + t^*)/P_k^0) \right\} \right]. \tag{18}$$

Government tax revenue is lost by doing away with the existing *ad valorem* taxes, and gained by the new specific tax. The new revenue for the six categories is $t^* \cdot \bar{Q}$. The revenue lost is subtracted from this, so the application of (15) is

$$\Delta \text{revenue} = t^* \bar{Q} - y \sum_{i \in QR} \frac{\tau_i}{1 + \tau_i + \text{cif}_i + \text{whl}} \alpha_i, \tag{19}$$

where $\tau_i = ad\ valorem$ tariff rate on i, and other variables are cif and wholesale margins, respectively. In (19) we make use of evaluation at the point of means, so α_i is the relevant share of imported cheese. We divide by 1 + the tax rate plus the cif % markup (cif) + the wholesale % markup (whl) to convert the domestic value in α_i into a foreign f.o.b. value.

We calculate Δsupport, the application of (13), using evaluation at the sample mean, as

$$\Delta\text{support} = y \sum_{j \in S} \sum_{k \in QR} \gamma_{jk} \log((\hat{P}_k + t^*)/P_k^0)], \tag{20}$$

where S is the set of supported cheeses and other variables are previously defined.

Below, the gross welfare measures represent the pure logic of quota inefficiency measurement; the net measures have increases in cheddar support payments subtracted out. These overestimate the change the government would actually experience, since aged cheddar is not supported. We also report a support payment change on the assumption that *all* domestic cheese displaced must be purchased by the government.

The net welfare figure presented below is biased very far downward; the gross welfare figure is biased somewhat upward by its failure to account for the displaced domestic cheese not subject to support payments. Presumably this will cause changes in the price of domestic cheese, the welfare consequences of which will have to be traced through. For the efficient tax solutions the bias is very minor, since the displacement is under 3% of the total market in each cheese. For the free trade solutions the case is more serious (displacement of 9% and 19% in the two cases below), and for cheddar in particular the bias will be substantial (displacement of 19% and 39%). In the absence of a model of domestic cheese production there was little to be done about this. It was not significant to the study, since the free trade solutions are produced primarily to scale the efficient tax solutions of interest.

The final category in the welfare calculation is the loss of quota rent. The entire rent change is treated as a loss, though some rent probably goes to foreigners or is dissipated in rent-seeking activity.

Two cases are detailed below. In one, the allocation of country imports does not shift to low cost producers; in effect there is only one representative exporter for each cheese. The average based period f.o.b. unit value is thus used to form $\hat{P}_i$. The other case uses a conservatively picked lower cost producer as the importer. The new import price was far from the lowest and came from a supplier with deep markets and substantial share

Table 3.1
Mean policy distortions on imported cheese, 1964–1979[a]

	Tariff	Quota, ad valorem equivalent
Blue	.15	.025
Cheddar	.15	.33[b]
Edam-Gouda	.15	.33
Romano, etc.	.20	.14
Swiss	.11	.20
Gruyere	.11	.33[b]

a. Aggregating biases these estimates downward.

b. No domestic price of imported cheese is available. Estimate is constructed by applying the mean of markups of a large number of components from other categories.

already (e.g., New Zealand or West Germany). The new lower $\hat{P}_i$ then serves as the base for recalculating all previous steps. This procedure inevitably has considerable danger of (dis)aggregation bias. For the composite SITC 0240025, Romano-Parmesano-Provolone, etc., no such reallocation is allowed. For the other categories, the gain in realism appears worthwhile. For one category, Swiss, we have domestic price series for Finnish, Austrian, and Swiss origin. The latter commands about a 10% premium. The cif import unit values in these categories diverge by 30% or more. Thus there is clearly a country reallocation gain to be reaped.

As a basis for the commodity reallocation gains, table 3.1 presents the sample mean *ad valorem* tariff rates and the mean *ad valorem* equivalent quota margins for the six constrained categories. The sample mean foreign port values of the various imported cheeses range from .6 to 1.6, so table 3.1 obviously implies an inefficient specific tax equivalent. At most data points, the quota margins show *much* wider variation over categories than at the point of means shown in the table, so greater efficiency gains can be expected.

The results of efficiency allocation are in tables 3.2 and 3.3. Table 3.2 has the optimal specific tax [the solution of (17)], and the unscaled amounts (in millions of base dollars). A negative sign is a fall in the category whether increasing or decreasing welfare. Since imported cheese is small relative to GNP or even advanced war equipment, the numbers in table 3.2 are not impressive. They are supplied mainly to allow alternative treatment by the reader of dubious categories like support and rent.

Scaling the absolute magnitude of changes is critical to seeing their importance. One scale used is base expenditure on the six imported con-

Table 3.2
Effect of switch to efficient tax on constrained cheese (sample mean points, in millions of dollars)

	Tax ($/1b)	(a) Expenditure	(b) Rent	(c) Tax revenue	(d) American support	(e) All support	(f) Gross welfare [−(a) − (b) + (c)]	(g) Net welfare [−(a) − (b) + (c) − (d)]
No supply reallocation	.224	−.942	15.52	14.98	25.14	27.45	.402	−24.7
Supply reallocation	.405	−.80	15.52	36.3	51.95	392.13	21.58	−30.3

Table 3.3
Scaled welfare changes of efficient tax and free trade in cheese

	Gross welfare/ base expenditure		Net welfare/ base expenditure		Relative inefficiency (1)/(2)
	(1) Efficient tax	(2) Free trade	(3) Efficient tax	(4) Free trade	(5)
No supply reallocation	.0028	.087	−.17	−1.70	.103
Supply reallocation	.152	.497	−.21	−3.27	.306

strained cheeses. The other scale used is the welfare change implied by going to free trade (redo the calculations above with $t = 0$).

Two appropriate scales are in table 3.3. The first four columns express the savings as a proportion of base expenditure on the six cheeses. Columns 2 and 4 contain the net and gross welfare proportionate changes implied by free trade. The percentages in columns 1 and 2 are fairly impressive. Our best guess is that at the point of means, an efficient tax saves us over 15% of base expenditure (row 2, column 1 of table 3.2). Standard triangle welfare loss measurement seldom turns up relative gains of more than 1%.

Perhaps the most revealing measure of relative inefficiency of the quota is in column 5, the result of dividing column 1 by column 2. For the two cases shown, the number says that efficient taxation takes us 10% and 30%, respectively, of the way back to free trade.

Table 3.4 contains percentage changes in imported cheese consumption in the efficient tax solutions. Short of implementing an efficient tax, the figures in table 3.4 could be used to guide a reallocation of quota licenses. Quota administrators might in fact not be surprised at the numbers in table 3.4, since they are linked to the size of current sample mean quota margins and tariffs—compare tables 3.4 and 3.1. In the more extreme data points the quota margin variations cause less obvious substitution patterns to be optimal.

The most "disappointing" result of tables 3.2 and 3.3 is the small gross welfare gain derived by going to the efficient tax without supply realloca- tion. This is the "pure-differentiated-product" effect (though the gain from country reallocation operates partly through the differentiated product effect). Only about 1/4 of 1% of base expenditure is saved by efficient

Table 3.4
Changes in cheese consumption in efficient tax solution (%; % changes in consumption)

	(1) No supply reallocation	(2) Supply reallocation	(3) Base food expenditure share × 10^9
Blue	−.123	−.126	32,092
Cheddar	.292	.619	94,767
Edam-Gouda	.216	.474	81,898
Romano, etc.	−.022	−.159	80,587
Swiss	−.023	−.067	270,110
Gruyere	.120	.158	88,780

allocation. If evaluation is done at other data points, however, this figure rises to over 2% at the maximum. The mean of all gross welfare efficient tax gains (as a percent of base expenditure) is .0044, with a standard deviation of .0043. Over 10% of the evaluations yield gross welfare savings in excess of 1% of base expenditure. Interestingly, extreme data points also frequently change the sign of net welfare changes. The reason is that support payments often drop rather than rise due to substitution effects. The mean net welfare change as a percent of base expenditure is .012 with a standard deviation of .14. The maximal value of the relative net welfare change is .41 and the minimal value −.39. More could be made of these extreme values were it not for doubts about their reliability due to the estimated demand system being moved outside the reasonable approximation region.

This brings up the important general issue of sensitivity of results to the estimation of the demand system, especially to the "concavifying" restrictions. As discussed in Anderson (1983), concavity was imposed by setting linear constraints that were incrementally tightened. Tables like 3.2 and 3.3 were generated automatically for a large number of "concavifying" restriction values. The numbers in especially the first three rows of table 3.3 were highly robust with respect to these changes. It is notable that this statement applies even to evaluations where concavity at the point of means was not attained. Another check on sensitivity is afforded by using the Cobb-Douglas limiting case of the AIDS. The Cobb-Douglas parameters are the mean shares. It implies price elasticities that differ substantially from the point estimates of AIDS elasticities at the point of means. Compare the first nine rows and columns of table 3.A1 with minus the identity matrix, which closely approximates the compensated Cobb-Douglas price elasticity matrix given the smallness of shares. Net and gross welfare changes are approximately equal for the Cobb-Douglas, so we check the sensitivity of gross welfare changes to the functional form. When analogous calculations are carried through to produce the upper left cell of table 3.3, gross welfare inefficiency relative to base expenditure, with no supply reallocation, the corresponding number is .0013, versus the table's .0028. With reallocation, the Cobb-Douglas gain is .147 of base expenditure versus .152 in table 3.3. The data reject the Cobb-Douglas model very strongly (the equation R^2s in the AIDS average over .50). Nevertheless, the Cobb-Douglas is so familiar and easy to use that it makes a convenient benchmark. A bias factor so small when even so gross a misfit as the Cobb-Douglas is imposed suggests that the underlying inefficiency is indeed substantially accurately measured by the methods of this study at the point of means. Something like this relationship is maintained even at more extreme values of the data.

The impressive magnitudes in tables 3.3 and 3.4 validate the main proposition of this study: Quota systems on heterogeneous commodities are likely to add substantially to the inefficiency of protection. Subsidiarily, the results bear out claims that any welfare loss measure will be greater the greater the disaggregation. Painful as it may be, commodity detail is strongly indicated for studies of protection. Finally, the results, together with difficulties experienced in achieving comparability of data, argue strongly that government statistical bureaus should collect data on quota categories automatically in the form required to assess incidence.

Appendix 3.A: Price Elasticities at the Point of Means

Table 3.A1
Price elasticifies at point of means

	Blue	Cheddar	Edam-Gouda	Roquefort	Romano, etc.	Swiss	Gruyere	Grating Pecorino	Nongrating Pecorino
Blue	−1.22567044	−0.36196737	−0.00008190	−0.00002466	0.2979905	−1.46954474	0.00008878	−0.19759316	0.00006180
Cheddar	−0.12363571	−6.38763977	−0.24473892	−0.07932095	−0.3825105	0.00027011	0.00008878	0.00013060	0.09562920
Edam-Gouda	0.00003209	−0.28271565	−1.77124995	0.00002466	0.0000805	0.00027011	−0.94083556	0.00013060	0.03080344
Roquefort	0.00003209	−0.41988079	0.00008190	−0.84767953	0.0462413	0.00027011	0.05061753	0.70071737	0.53713195
Romano, etc.	0.11871424	−0.44639119	0.00008190	0.01020211	−1.4208345	0.00027011	0.00008878	0.00013060	0.10335093
Swiss	−0.17431817	0.00009477	0.00008190	0.00002466	0.0000805	−2.03426124	−0.73051634	0.07559175	0.00006180
Gruyere	0.00003209	0.00009477	−0.86768188	0.01019569	−0.0000805	−2.23981415	−1.70398023	0.54818688	0.00006180
Grating Pecorino	−0.04844285	0.00009477	0.00008190	0.09507469	0.0000805	0.15623685	0.36952309	−1.01506819	0.60988780
Nongrating Pecorino	0.00003209	0.14574259	0.04064101	−0.15465579	0.1349808	0.00027011	0.00008878	1.29433575	−1.23172324

Notes

1. Formally, the analysis has much in common with Young and Anderson (1980, chapter 4). There the product differentiation is by states of nature. They analyze optimal quota allocations across uncertain states subject to an average import constraint, and show the optimum is reached with a uniform tax. Anderson and Young (1982, chapter 7) consider constraints on other portions of the probability distribution of imports under uncertainty and are able to rationalize tariff quotas, in which the tariff rate steps upward with import volume. In the present context of differentiated products this translates into other constraints on distribution within the group besides the aggregate one. Again, analogous to Anderson and Young (1982), this will imply an optimum in which rents are equalized within subgroups.

We should also note that everything said about quantitative restrictions and uniform specific taxes has immediate analogy with foreign exchange revenue restrictions and uniform *ad valorem* taxes. An inefficiently distributed quantity quota can, however, achieve higher welfare than an *ad valorem* tax in the achievement of a quantity constraint.

2. This can have a variety of forms. For example, an efficiently applied constraint on foreign exchange value is indicated if employment is more closely linked to value than to quantity. Using the analysis above, this is readily seen to be equivalent to a uniform *ad valorem* tariff.

3. Presidential authority for the quota is drawn from section 22 of the Agricultural Adjustment Act of 1933 (originally added in 1935 and subsequently revised extensively). It directs the Secretary of Agriculture to advise the president whenever he has reason to believe any article is imported in such conditions and such quantities as (1) to render or tend to render inefficient or materially interfere with any price support or stabilization program relating to agricultural commodities or (2) to reduce substantially the amount of any product processes in the United States from any agricultural commodity with respect to which any such program is being undertaken. If the president agrees there is reason for such belief, he directs the U.S. International Trade Commission to conduct an investigation and submit a report. The president is authorized, based on such findings, to impose such fees or quotas in addition to the basic duty as he shall determine necessary. The president may designate the affected article by physical qualities, value, use, or upon such other basis as he shall determine. The president may revise or suspend any previously proclaimed fee or quota. Any decision by the president as to the facts under this authority is final.

4. A superior alternative is available. (3) can be solved for u with $e = y$, with u now indirect utility. The result can be substituted back into (3), which now becomes the (log of) income compensation function, or (log of) the money metric of utility change, $\log e(P^0, u(P, y))$, where P^0 is a base price vector and P is an alternative price vector. This is the ideal welfare measure. For the case studied, movement of u is guaranteed to be trivial and it is simpler to keep it constant. Thus we use the expenditure function (3) as the basis of welfare calculations (which corresponds to use of compensating rather than equivalent variations).

5. If government revenue is made to matter, a revenue constraint is added to the problem, and in the optimal solution a Ramsey-price element is added to the uniform part of the optimal tax, as noted in section 3.1.

It should be noted that another version of the problem kept the existing *ad valorem* taxes as given politically, and optimized the quota system analogously to the procedure above. This procedure worked nearly as well as the solution reported. This is not surprising in view of the low level and low dispersion of the *ad valorem* tariffs.

6. One income elasticity differs statistically significantly from unity in the third place to the right of the decimal point.

7. The efficient quota problem (1) has a unique global optimum defined by equations (2), the first-order conditions. Equation (17) is the sum of the rows of the inverse of system (2), hence need not yield a unique t^*. Among its solutions must lie the optimal tax. We may note that the derivative of (17) with respect to t is ordinarily negative, the more so as own effects predominate. "Good behavior" has the derivative negative in the relevant range, thus yielding a unique solution. Nonconcavity evidently exacerbates the "bad behavior" problem, since it is associated with prominent cross-effects.

References

Anderson, James E. (1983), "An Econometric Model of Imported Cheese Demand," mimeo.

Anderson, James E., and Leslie Young (1982), "The Optimality of Tariff-Quotas under Uncertainty," *Journal of International Economics*, 13, 337–352.

Baldwin, Robert E. (1982), "The Inefficiency of Trade Policy," Essay in International Finance No. 150, Princeton University.

Bhagwati, Jagdish N., and T. N. Srinivasan (1983), *Lectures on International Trade*, Cambridge, MA: MIT Press, Chap. 24.

Deaton, Angus, and John Muellbauer (1980a), *Economic Theory and Consumer Behavior*, Cambridge: Cambridge University Press.

Deaton, Angus, and John Muellbauer (1980b), "An Almost Ideal Demand System," *American Economic Review*, 70, 312–326.

Dixit, Avinash (1985), "Tax Policy in Open Economies," in *Handbook of Public Economics*, Alan Auerbach and Martin Feldstein, eds., Amsterdam: North-Holland.

Dixon, Peter (1978), "Economies of Scale, Commodity Disaggregation, and the Costs of Protection," *Australian Economic Papers*, 70, 312–326.

Emery, Harlan (1969), *Dairy Price Support and Related Programs, 1949–1968*. Agricultural Economic Report No. 165, U.S. Department of Agriculture.

Young, Leslie, and James E. Anderson (1980), "The Optimal Policies for Restricting Trade under Uncertainty," *Review of Economic Studies*, 46, 927–932.

4   The Optimal Policies for Restricting Trade under Uncertainty

4.1 Introduction

A basic theme of microeconomics is the equivalence of price and quantity controls under certainty. The welfare comparison of these two control modes under uncertainty has been undertaken recently in two different contexts. Weitzman (1974) initiated the comparison of these two modes in the context of a planning authority that faces uncertainty about the costs and benefits of producing a particular good. It chooses between controlling quantities and setting a price for producers. His analysis has been developed by Laffont (1977), Ireland (1977), Malcomson (1978), Weitzman (1978), and Yohe (1978). A second area of analysis, to which this chapter contributes, is the welfare comparison of the two control modes in the context of international trade under uncertainty. In this context, prices are determined by market choices by both sellers and buyers but the government intervenes in the market, e.g. through a quota or a tariff. Fishelson and Flatters (1975) and Young (1979a) have compared the use of quotas and *ad valorem* tariffs by a large country to improve its terms of trade. For a small country, Dasgupta and Stiglitz (1977) and Young (1980) have compared the two instruments when they are constrained to raise a fixed expected tariff revenue; Pelcovits (1976) has compared the two instruments when they are constrained to yield a fixed level of expected imports. Anderson (1978) has shown that, for a small country, a specific tariff yields higher domestic expected consumer's surplus than the mean-equivalent import quota. For a large country, he showed that a specific tariff yields higher world expected consumer's surplus than the mean-equivalent quota.

It is natural to compare the welfare effects of quotas, *ad valorem* tariffs,

Reprinted, with changes, by permission from *Review of Economic Studies* (1980), XLVI, 927–932. © 1980 The Society for Economic Analysis Limited.

and specific tariffs under uncertainty because there are the most widely used and easily administered instruments for restricting trade. However, none of the above authors have considered what policy would be *optimal* for the objective that they consider. This paper shows that the answer to this question can be surprisingly simple and general. Our results should be compared to Weitzman's recent results (1978) on the optimal form of controls for a planning authority.

For the small country case we have

THEOREM 1   Suppose a country faces a random world price for a good and has a random excess demand function that decreases with price. The policy that maximizes domestic expected consumer's surplus subject to a ceiling on expected imports of the good is a fixed specific tariff on imports.

THEOREM 2   Under the assumptions of theorem 1, the policy that maximizes domestic expected consumer's surplus subject to a ceiling on the expected foreign exchange expenditure on the good is a fixed *ad valorem* tariff on imports.

For the large country case we have

THEOREM 3   Suppose a country faces a random foreign supply function that increases with price and has a random excess demand function that decreases with price. The policy that maximizes world expected consumer's surplus subject to a ceiling on expected imports is a fixed specific tariff on imports.

The proofs of these results are generalizations of arguments developed by Anderson (1978). Moreover, his interpretation of a tariff as a set of state-contingent quotas arbitraged across states can be used to give an intuitive interpretation of the results.

In the above cases the importing country need not monitor the state of the world in order to implement the optimal policies: the fixed parameter policies cannot be improved upon even by state-contingent policies. Young (1979a, b) obtains further results of this type for a large country seeking to improve its terms of trade and for a country seeking to raise a fixed expected tariff revenue from trade restrictions.

4.2 The Small Country Case

Let $P^*(\theta)$ be the world price of the good in question. This can be contingent on θ, the random variable denoting the state of the world. Let $P(Q, \theta)$ be the domestic inverse excess demand function where Q is the quantity imported. This function can also be state dependent. The consumer's surplus given imports Q is

$$\int_0^Q P(v, \theta)\, dv - P^*(\theta)Q, \tag{1}$$

i.e., the area under the demand curve to the left of Q less the foreign exchange expenditure on Q.[1] We follow previous writers in the area in using expected consumer's surplus as our welfare criterion.[2,3]

Every policy f for restricting imports defines, for each state of the world, an equilibrium quantity of imports $Q_f(\theta)$ and a domestic equilibrium price $P_f(\theta) \equiv P(Q_f(\theta), \theta)$. If the state of the world is θ, then by (1) the consumer's surplus from a policy g exceeds that from policy f by

$$\Delta(\theta, g, f) \equiv \int_{Q_f(\theta)}^{Q_g(\theta)} P(v, \theta)\, dv - P^*(\theta)\{Q_g(\theta) - Q_f(\theta)\}.$$

Theorems 1 and 2 follow from the following lemma:

LEMMA 1   If the domestic excess demand function is downward sloping, then

$$\Delta(\theta, g, f) \geqslant \{P_g(\theta) - P^*(\theta)\}\{Q_g(\theta) - Q_f(\theta)\}.$$

Proof   Since $P_g(\theta) \equiv P(Q_g(\theta), \theta)$,

$$\Delta(\theta, g, f) - \{P_g(\theta) - P^*(\theta)\}\{Q_g(\theta) - Q_f(\theta)\}$$

$$= \int_{Q_f(\theta)}^{Q_g(\theta)} \{P(v, \theta) - P(Q_g(\theta), \theta)\}\, dv.$$

But $P(v, \theta)$ is a decreasing function of v so this expression is nonnegative whether $Q_g(\theta) \geqslant Q_f(\theta)$ or $Q_g(\theta) < Q_f(\theta)$.   QED

Proof of Theorem 1   If policy g is the specific tariff s that leads to the ceiling level of expected imports, then

$$P_g(\theta) - P^*(\theta) = s.$$

Therefore

$$E[\{P_g(\theta) - P^*(\theta)\}\{Q_g(\theta) - Q_f(\theta)\}] = sE[Q_g(\theta) - Q_f(\theta)].$$

If policy f leads to expected imports not greater than the ceiling, then the expression is nonnegative and lemma 1 implies that

$$E[\Delta(\theta, g, f)] \geqslant 0.$$

Thus the specific tariff is the optimal policy given a ceiling on expected imports.   QED

Proof of Theorem 2   If policy g is the *ad valorem* tariff a that leads to the ceiling level of expected foreign exchange expenditure, then

$P_g(\theta) - P^*(\theta) = aP^*(\theta)$.

Therefore

$E[\{P_g(\theta) - P^*(\theta)\}\{Q_g(\theta) - Q_f(\theta)\}] = aE[P^*(\theta)Q_g(\theta) - P^*(\theta)Q_f(\theta)]$.

If policy f leads to a foreign exchange expenditure not greater than the ceiling, then this expression is nonnegative and lemma 1 implies that

$E[\Delta(\theta, g, f)] \geqslant 0$.

Thus an *ad valorem* tariff is the optimal policy given a ceiling on expected expenditure of foreign exchange.   QED

It is clear that if a policy f has a positive probability of leading to imports that differ from those under the optimal policy g, then f is strictly inferior to g. For example, theorem 2 implies that an *ad valorem* tariff is strictly superior to a quota that leads to the same expected foreign exchange expenditure.

Lemma 1 also enables us to compare two policies, both of which are suboptimal. For example, suppose policy g is a specific tariff s and policy f is a fixed quota q. If these two policies lead to the same expected expenditure of foreign exchange, then, since $P^*(\theta)$ and $Q_g(\theta)$ are negatively correlated,

$E[P^*(\theta)]E[Q_g(\theta)] > E[P^*(\theta)Q_g(\theta)] = E[P^*(\theta)]q$.

Therefore

$E[Q_g(\theta)] > q$.

But by lemma 1

$E[\Delta(\theta, g, f)] \geqslant sE[Q_g(\theta) - q] > 0$.

Thus a specific tariff is superior to the quota leading to the same expenditure of foreign exchange. However, it is not generally true that an *ad valorem* tariff is superior to a quota that yields the same expected imports—unless world prices are fixed (see Anderson, 1978, p. 15, and Pelcovits, 1976, p. 387).

Following Anderson (1978) we can give an intuitive explanation of theorems 1 and 2. Any policy f restricting trade is equivalent to a set of quota licenses $Q_f(\theta)$ that are contingent on the state of the world. If there is a ceiling q on expected imports, then the quota q must be arbitraged across states. Under a specific tariff, the rent on a unit of contingent quota licenses (i.e., $P_g(\theta) - P^*(\theta)$) is the same in all states of the world. Hence there is optimal arbitrage of the implicit quota licenses.[4,5]

Any policy f restricting trade is also equivalent to a set of state-contingent quota licenses $P^*(\theta)Q_f(\theta)$ on foreign exchange expenditure on the good. If there is a ceiling e on foreign exchange expenditure, then the quota e must be arbitraged across states. Under an *ad valorem* tariff the rent on a unit of foreign exchange quota licenses, i.e.,

$$\{P_g(\theta) - P^*(\theta)\}/P^*(\theta),$$

is the same in all states of the world. Hence there is optimal arbitrage of the implicit foreign exchange quota licenses.

4.3 The Large Country Case

If the importing country is large, then the world price of imports will depend on the policy f that it adopts. Let $P_f^*(\theta)$ be the price paid to foreigners under state θ and let $P^*(Q, \theta)$ be the foreign inverse excess supply function. Under policy f the sum of domestic and foreign consumer's surplus is

$$\int_0^{Q_f(\theta)} \{P(v, \theta) - P^*(v, \theta)\}\, dv,$$

i.e., the area between the domestic demand curve and the foreign supply curve to the left of $Q_f(\theta)$ (netting out domestic payments for imports). If the state of the world is θ, then world consumer's surplus from a policy g exceeds that from policy f by

$$\Delta'(\theta, g, f) \equiv \int_{Q_f(\theta)}^{Q_g(\theta)} \{P(v, \theta) - P^*(v, \theta)\}\, dv.$$

LEMMA 2   If both the domestic and the foreign excess demand functions are downward sloping, then

$$\Delta'(\theta, g, f) \geqslant \{P_g(\theta) - P_g^*(\theta)\}\{Q_g(\theta) - Q_f(\theta)\}.$$

Proof   Since $P_g(\theta) \equiv P(Q_g(\theta), \theta)$ and $P_g^*(\theta) \equiv P^*(Q_g(\theta), \theta)$,

$$\Delta'(\theta, g, f) - \{P_g(\theta) - P_g^*(\theta)\}\{Q_g(\theta) - Q_f(\theta)\}$$

$$= \int_{Q_f(\theta)}^{Q_g(\theta)} \{P(v, \theta) - P(Q_g(\theta), \theta) + P^*(Q_g(\theta), \theta) - P^*(v, \theta)\} \, dv.$$

Since $P(v, \theta)$ is a decreasing function of v and $P^*(v, \theta)$ is an increasing function of v this expression is nonnegative whether $Q_g(\theta) \geqslant Q_f(\theta)$ or $Q_g(\theta) < Q_f(\theta)$.   QED

Proof of Theorem 3   If policy g is the specific tariff s that leads to the ceiling level of expected imports, then

$$P_g(\theta) - P_g^*(\theta) = s.$$

Therefore

$$E[\{P_g(\theta) - P_g^*(\theta)\}\{Q_g(\theta) - Q_f(\theta)\}] = sE[Q_g(\theta) - Q_f(\theta)].$$

If policy f leads to expected imports not greater than the ceiling, then this expression is nonnegative and by lemma 2

$$E[\Delta'(\theta, g, f)] \geqslant 0.$$

Thus the specific tariff maximizes world expected surplus subject to a ceiling on expected imports.   QED

We cannot extend theorem 2 in the way that theorem 3 extends theorem 1. If the policy g is the *ad valorem* tariff a leading to the ceiling level of foreign exchange expenditure, then

$$E[\{P_g(\theta) - P_g^*(\theta)\}\{Q_g(\theta) - Q_f(\theta)\}] = aE[P_g^*(\theta)Q_g(\theta) - P_g^*(\theta)Q_f(\theta)].$$

In general, the foreign price under policy g differs from the foreign price under policy f so it does *not* follow that the above expression is non-negative for any policy f leading to a foreign exchange expenditure not greater than the ceiling. Hence in general we *cannot* conclude that an *ad valorem* tariff maximizes expected world surplus subject to a ceiling on expected foreign exchange expenditure.

To derive the optimal policy for this case we must solve the constrained maximization problem explicitly. The problem is equivalent to choosing a set of contingent quotas $Q(\theta)$ for the problem

$$\max_{\{Q(\theta)\}} E\left[\int_0^{Q(\theta)} \{P(v, \theta) - P^*(v, \theta)\} \, dv\right] \quad \text{subject to} \quad E[P^*(Q(\theta), \theta)Q(\theta)] \leqslant e.$$

Form the Lagrangean:

$$E\left[\int_0^{Q(\theta)} \{P(v, \theta) - P^*(v, \theta)\}\, dv - \lambda\{P^*(Q(\theta), \theta)Q(\theta) - e\}\right],$$

where λ is a Kuhn–Tucker multiplier. The Kuhn–Tucker equations are

$$P(Q(\theta), \theta) - P^*(Q(\theta), \theta) = \lambda\{P^*(Q(\theta), \theta) + Q(\theta)\, \partial P^*(Q(\theta), \theta)/\partial Q(\theta)\}.$$

If $\eta(\theta)$ is the elasticity of supply in state θ, then

$$\frac{P(Q(\theta), \theta) - P^*(Q(\theta), \theta)}{P^*(Q(\theta), \theta)} = \lambda\left\{1 + \frac{1}{\eta(\theta)}\right\}. \tag{2}$$

The left-hand side of (2) is just the rent on a license for a unit of foreign exchange expenditure on the good. (2) implies that, at an optimum, this rent should be lower in states θ where the supply elasticity $\eta(\theta)$ is high. The rationale is that state-contingent dollar quotas should be greater (*ceteris paribus*) in those states where marginal purchases cause proportionately less deterioration in the terms of trade and hence less foreign exchange losses. (2) implies that the optimal policy would be a fixed *ad valorem* tariff only if the supply elasticity were identical in all states, i.e., if the foreign supply function were of the form $g(\theta)(P^*)^{\bar{\eta}}$, where $g(\theta)$ is a function of θ and $\bar{\eta}$ is a fixed number.[6]

4.4 Conclusions

Under broad conditions we have shown that the optimal policy subject to a ceiling on expected imports is a specific tariff and the optimal policy subject to a ceiling on expected foreign exchange expenditure is an *ad valorem* tariff. The widely held presumption that, under uncertainty, tariffs are preferable to quotas as instruments for restricting trade is vindicated— and sharpened since we now see that different constraints require different forms of tariff.

In the General Agreement on Trades and Tariffs, tariffs are the only generally acceptable form of trade restriction. The most important excep- tion [article XII : 2(a)] is that a country may impose quantitative restrictions "to forestall the imminent threat of, or to stop, a serious decline in its monetary reserves." Theorem 2 implies that, within our model, quantitative restrictions would be inferior to an *ad valorem* tariff as an instrument for conserving foreign exchange. Hence this GATT concession only expands the range of wilfully suboptimal national policies.

Helpful comments from Peter Hammond and a referee are gratefully acknowledged.

Notes

1. This expression equals the usual expression for consumer's surplus plus the tariff revenue

$$\{P(Q, \theta) - P^*(\theta)\} Q.$$

2. We thereby assume that (1) distributional considerations can be ignored; (2) the market price $P(v, \theta)$ represents the social demand price ("shadow price") of the good in question; (3) in the region of interest, the marginal utility of income is constant and independent of the state of the world. If these assumptions are violated, then it is possible to construct examples where the conclusions of our theorems are no longer valid. See Anderson (1978, p. 20) for such an example and Anderson (1979) for a discussion of the use of expected consumer's surplus as a welfare criterion.

3. Our results are derived for a one-good partial equilibrium model. However, as Anderson (1978, fn. p. 6) has argued, the model can also be interpreted as a general equilibrium model of single market distortion in a purely competitive economy with many goods—provided that the excess demand function is interpreted as the general equilibrium excess demand function.

4. If the maximization of expected surplus subject to a constraint on expected imports or on expected import expenditure is carried out explicitly, then this fixed rent emerges as the Lagrange multiplier or dual variable associated with the constraint in question; cf. section 4.3.

5. By contrast, state-contingent policies are required if the government wishes to impose a ceiling, not on *expected* imports but on the imports in each state θ. This is because the former leads to a linear constraint linking imports in all states while the latter leads to a separate constraint for each state. Similar remarks hold for ceilings on foreign exchange.

6. This result also holds in the large country case if the objective function is *domestic* expected surplus. Moreover, it can be shown that if the foreign supply function has multiplicative uncertainty, then, in the large country case, the optimal trade restriction given either objective function and either constraint is a fixed schedule of tariffs depending only on world price (see Young, 1979b, for the reasoning).

References

Anderson, J. E. (1978), "Specific Taxes Are Usually Preferred to Mean Equivalent Quantitative Restrictions Under Uncertainty," Boston College.

Anderson, J. E. (1979), "On the Measurement of Welfare Cost under Uncertainty," *Southern Economic Journal*, 45, 1160–1171.

Dasgupta, P., and J. E. Stiglitz (1977), "Tariffs vs. Quotas as Revenue-Raising Devices under Uncertainty," *American Economic Review*, 67, 975–981.

Fishelson, G., and F. Flatters (1975), "The (Non-)Equivalence of Optimal Tariffs and Quotas under Uncertainty," *Journal of International Economics*, 5, 385–393.

Ireland, N. J. (1977), "Ideal Prices vs. Prices vs. Quantities," *Review of Economic Studies*, 44, 183–207.

Laffont, J. J. (1977), "More on Prices vs. Quantities," *Review of Economic Studies*, 44, 177–182.

Malcomson, J. M. (1978), "Prices vs. Quantities: A Critical Note on the Use of Approximations," *Review of Economic Studies*, 45, 203–208.

Pelcovits, M. G. (1976), "Quotas vs. Tariffs," *Journal of International Economics*, 6, 363–370.

Weitzman, M. L. (1974), "Prices vs. Quantities," *Review of Economic Studies*, 41, 50–65.

Weitzman, M. L. (1978), "Optimal Rewards for Economic Regulation," *American Economic Review*, 68, 683–691.

Yohe, G. W. (1978), "Towards a General Comparison of Price Controls and Quantity Controls under Uncertainty," *Review of Economic Studies*, 45, 229–238.

Young, L. (1979), "Ranking the Optimal Tariff and Quota for a Large Country under Uncertainty," *Journal of International Economics*, 9, 249–264.

Young, L. (1980), "Optimal Revenue-Raising Trade Restrictions under Uncertainty," *Journal of International Economics*, 10, 425–440.

Young, L. (1980), "Tariffs vs. Quotas under Uncertainty: "An Extension," *American Economic Review*, 70, 522–527.

Suppose that some domestic target (e.g., real income of a "sensitive" group) or domestic distortion (e.g., a labor market distortion) must be dealt with by international trade instruments applied to a heterogeneous group of imports. What form should protection take to efficiently deal with the problem? In chapter 3, it is shown that with an external quantity target (an aggregate import constraint) the optimal instrument is a uniform specific tax. In chapter 4 it is shown that with an external average quantity (value) constraint under uncertainty, the optimal instrument is a uniform specific (*ad valorem*) tax. In this chapter it is shown that under the restriction of weak separability in preferences or technology, the optimal trade instrument for domestic sectoral targets is a uniform *ad valorem* tax. For revenue targets the same proposition holds under the additional stipulation that the within-group expenditure pattern of imports be invariant to the aggregate level of import expenditure. Technically, the subutility function for imports must be homothetic.

The results are closely related to those of chapter 4. Weak separability is imposed with respect to the partition between imports and domestic goods. The weak separability assumption turns out to imply that the link between internal and external variables reduces to targeting an aggregate external value of imports. *Arbitrage efficiency* then requires uniformity of the *ad valorem* tariff. The results are not identical, however, since in the case of uncertainty, under the expected utility axioms (additive separability across states), the weak separability restriction is violated, so what follows must be interpreted as applying strictly only to cases where uncertainty is unimportant; the dimension of heterogeneity is product type.

The weak separability restriction covers most of the cost-of-protection empirical studies ever performed (in their certainty-equivalent form), still allows for a variety of substitutability and nonhomotheticity patterns among imports, and is an intuitively appealing base case in the absence of a strong prior belief to the contrary. Thus it is a very useful result in creating a presumption in favor of the *ad valorem* tariff. If nonseparability is suspected, and confirmed by investigation, then the optimal instrument is a separate tax rate for each separable group of imports. For the general case, second-best theorems ranking uniform *ad valorem* tariffs versus other instruments are provided. They illuminate further the presumption in favor of *ad valorem* tariffs.

The results are directly applicable to the concern among policymakers about the change in the mix of imports subsequent to the imposition of VERs. In the U.S. case this has found expression in the concern over *quality upgrading*: a protection-induced shift in the mix of imports toward more expensive varieties. For example, the Japanese auto VERs apparently caused an increase in the average quality of Japanese autos imported into the United States. Most policymakers seem to believe that quality upgrading reduces the efficacy of protection. Economists have been more cautious, though Baldwin (1982) suggests the bureaucrats may be right. I have not seen the reasoning laid out, but it appears to be a folk theorem based on the notion that high quality imports will be closer substitutes (have higher cross-price elasticities) with domestic goods. On the other hand, the same reasoning applied to an import-substituting developing country implies that quality upgrading means less effective competition for the (assumed) low quality protected sector, thus enhancing the effectiveness of the quota instrument. The relative efficiency of the two instruments appears to depend upon the details of production structure and demand structure.

The issue is ubiquitous, because protection is almost always erected against a heterogeneous group of foreign products. Profit-seeking agents respond by shifting the mix of imported goods to substitute away from the taxed attribute.[1] Even if the tax cannot be evaded, uniform specific taxes cause economic agents to substitute away from quantity toward higher unit value: quality upgrading. Uniform *ad valorem* taxes are neutral in this respect. Falvey (1979) provides a theoretical analysis of the tendency to upgrade quality based on the generalized substitution effect (the Slutsky matrix). Aw and Roberts (1986) demonstrate the quantitative importance of quality upgrading in U.S. footwear imports, and Feenstra (1984) does so for Japanese autos. These authors assume that quota systems are equivalent to a uniform specific tariff, which requires that quota license rents be arbitraged across types through resale markets.

The optimality of the *ad valorem* tax under separability is intuitive. Trade controls achieve domestic targets (for example, on employment) by shifting up the price of substitutes for the domestic target. Under weak separability, a price index exists for the import group, and controls are effective through raising the index by the required proportion. In the subsidiary problem of import type choice, it is efficient to preserve the free trade equality between marginal rates of substitution and external price ratios within the import group. In terms of the arbitrage efficiency analysis of chapter 1, the domestic sectoral target induces a constraint on the external price value of aggregate imports; the *ad valorem* tariff achieves *arbitrage efficiency* relative to any other allocation of imports by type.

Under general structure, two second-best ranking theorems are provided, giving sufficient conditions for the dominance of either the *ad valorem* or specific tax instrument in the case where imports are final goods. These can be interpreted as partial validation of the folk theorem: loosely speaking, *ad valorem* tariffs dominate as expensive imports are quantity substitutes for the domestic import-competing good. Specific tariffs can dominate if expensive imports are quantity complements for the domestic good. An example is provided. A similar pair of second-best theorems can no doubt be developed for the case where imports are intermediate goods. The interested reader is left this as an exercise.

The motivating example of a domestic distortion in the sectoral labor market apparently leaves open the significant question of whether the optimality of a uniform *ad valorem* tariff extends to the case where tariffs must be used to raise revenue. This is an important revenue source for LDCs and historically was for all countries. It turns out that under weak separability and import-group homotheticity, the optimal revenue tariff is uniform. Another method of neutralizing income effects is to assume lump-sum compensation is paid. Under weak separability and homotheticity, the optimality of the uniform tax holds, which parallels a well-known result in public finance (Atkinson and Stiglitz, 1980).

Another significant complication is imperfect competition. For a foreign multiproduct monopoly it is shown that the *ad valorem* tariff is again optimal under weak separability. The result also extends to Cournot duopoly.

The results create a presumption in favor of the *ad valorem* tariff in the absence of uncertainty. Weak separability is the baseline case for which *ad valorem* tariffs are optimal. Nonseparability can enhance the advantage of the *ad valorem* tax, or reduce it. To reverse it, under competition just the right pattern of external prices and demand structure must coincide, with the substitution effects sufficiently strong. Under imperfect competition anticipations of rivals' actions must assume the right values. Where such "perverse" patterns are suspected, it would pay to depart from a uniform tax and respect the heterogeneity of the product group. Reverting to the tariff versus quota question, *ad valorem* tariffs must be presumed to dominate either proportionately distributed or auctioned quotas in the presence of quality differentiation.

Section 5.1 lays out the basic model. Section 5.2 presents the main proposition, and section 5.3 presents the second-best results for the final good imports case. Section 5.4 derives the parallel results for the intermediate good imports case. Section 5.5 returns to the final goods case and develops the optimality of the uniform *ad valorem* tariff for the case of a revenue constraint. Section 5.6 extends the analysis to a monopoly foreign producer of the import product line. Section 5.7 concludes with some further reflections.

5.1 The Model

A representative consumer[2] economy in general competitive equilibrium must respect a target in a "sensitive" sector, and must use protection in some form. No other distortions are relevant (save as distortions dual to the target may be introduced to motivate protection of the target). There is a group of imports that substitute in consumption for the domestic product, and that are supplied at fixed foreign prices. Their convenient small-country assumption avoids consideration of the well-understood terms-of-trade effects in forming the optimal protection.

For simplicity, there is one domestic import-competing good, and one export good, which may be thought of as a composite with externally fixed prices. Additional import-competing goods do not add anything important to the analysis, so long as there is some type of aggregate sectoral target. Also, as will be shown, it makes no difference to the analysis whether the target is for output or employment (or indeed returns to any specific factor, or a utility function of some of the above arguments). Sectoral employment is usually used below, for convenience.

Extensive use is made of inverse demand functions. Despite Deaton and Muellbauer (1980), their use is relatively unfamiliar, so some care is taken to develop them. A reduced form inverse demand function in terms of a set of import quotas is developed.

The reduced form inverse demand functions are then substituted for prices in the representative consumer's indirect utility function. The consumer's income in general equilibrium equals production income plus rent from quota licenses,[3] all of which depend on the reduced form prices.

With the substitution of the reduced form for income into the indirect utility function, the *reduced form general equilibrium* indirect utility function is defined. This will then be maximized over the settings of the quotas, subject to the employment constraint. The great advantage of working with *reduced form primal* functions is that (i) the first-order conditions are in terms of prices, hence are readily interpretable (see Deaton (1979) for a general advocacy of this method), and (ii) the prices are *market* prices, hence allow interpretation away from the optimal point.

5.1.1 The Inverse Demand Functions

The first task is to define the inverse demand functions. Let Q be a vector of import quantities, D be the quantity consumed of the domestic import-competing good, and Z be the quantity consumed of the export good. The representative consumer's utility is $U(Q, D, Z)$. Let Y be the quantity produced of the import-competing good. $Y = D$ is required in equilibrium, hence the equilibrium utility is

$$U^0 = U(Q, Y, Z). \tag{1}$$

Let the export good be the numeraire.

The inverse demand functions are defined by the marginal rates of substitution. Let subscripts denote differentiation. Let P be the domestic price vector of imported goods, and H be the price of the import-competing good. The (uncompensated) inverse demand functions are

$$U_Q(Q, Y, Z)/U_Z(Q, Y, Z), \tag{2}$$

$$U_Y(Q, Y, Z)/U_Z(Q, Y, Z). \tag{3}$$

These equal P and H, respectively, when (Q, Y, Z) are at their realized levels.

5.1.2 Reduced Forms

The representative consumer's indirect utility is

$$V(P, H, I), \tag{4}$$

where I is numeraire income. Reduced forms for the arguments of V in terms of Q must be constructed.

Let P^* be the foreign price vector for imports, and let all quota rent be redistributed back to consumers. The rent is $[P - P^*]Q$. Under the balanced trade (no borrowing) assumption, the remainder of income comes from production. This depends on price as follows. Efficient production in an undistorted economy implies that production income is give by the *revenue function* (see Dixit and Norman, 1980) $R(H, K)$, where K is a vector of fixed factor endowments. The consumer's income is thus

$$I = [P - P^*]Q + R(H, K). \tag{5}$$

Now consider reduced forms for prices. By the envelope theorem for efficient production,

$$R_H(H, K) = Y. \tag{6}$$

The budget constraint for the economy in internal prices is

$$R(H, K) + [P - P^*]Q = HY + PQ + Z. \tag{7}$$

Combining (6), (7), with (2), (3) creates a system with Z, Y, P, H determined by K, Q, P^*. This allows definition of the *reduced form inverse demand functions*:

$$P(Q, K, P^*), \tag{8}$$

$$H(Q, K, P^*). \tag{9}$$

The *general equilibrium indirect utility function* is defined by

$$V(P, H, [P - P^*]Q + R(H, K)). \tag{10}$$

The *reduced form general equilibrium indirect utility function* is defined by substituting (8)–(9) into (10), deleting the (P^*, K) arguments in reduced form prices for clarity:

$$v(Q) = V(P(Q), H(Q), [P(Q) - P^*]Q + R(H(Q), K)). \tag{11}$$

This function looks hopelessly convoluted, hence useless for analysis. The envelope property in fact cleans it up remarkably, so that it is very useful.

5.1.3 Reduced Form Properties

The first derivative of v is

$$\begin{aligned} v_Q &= V_I\{-QP_Q - DH_Q\} \\ &\quad + V_I\{[P - P^*] + QP_Q + R_H H_Q\} \quad \text{(using standard properties)} \\ &= V_I[P - P^*] \quad \text{[using (6) and } Y = D\text{]}. \end{aligned} \tag{12}$$

(12) is a simple expression in the import (specific) tariff, and justifies the effort involved in getting to it.

The second derivative matrix of v, v_{QQ}, is of interest to ensure that the second-order conditions for maximization are met and, more significantly, to allow second-best statements.

LEMMA   Under risk aversion,[4]

$$V_{II} \leqslant 0,$$
$$V_{QQ} \leqslant 0. \tag{13}$$

Proof   See appendix 1.A.

5.1.4 The Constraint Function

In Section 5.2, $v(Q)$ is maximized over Q subject to a constraint on sectoral activity sensitive to Q. Usually this is interpreted below as sectoral employment. In fact, however, it stands in for a verity of plausible targets, or distortions dual to those targets. So long as the linkage of Q to those targets or distortions is via H or its dual Y, the formal analysis is identical for final demand imports. For the case where there is also a linkage of Q to the constraint function via P (as when a representative worker's utility function is constrained), the analysis is essentially the same provided the restrictions applied to the consumer's preferences are also applied to the worker's preferences.

The remainder of this section develops a general equilibrium reduced form for the sectoral employment function. Generally, for nonjoint production, employment demand in the sensitive Y sector is $L(W, Y)$ using the standard partial equilibrium cost-minimizing framework. Sectoral employment is presumably of interest due to specific human capital. W is the vector of factor prices. In the general equilibrium, W is a function of (H, K), the arguments of the revenue function, as is Y. Then using the reduced form for $H(Q)$ the *general equilibrium reduced form employment function* is

$$l(Q) = L(W(H(Q), K), R_H(H(Q), K). \tag{14}$$

In Section 5.2, $l(Q)$ is required to be no less than a target L.

The dual to this case, which illustrates the applicability of the analysis to domestic distortions, is one in which an element of W is fixed exogenously, as in a sectoral version of the Keynesian labor market. Assume that unemployed labor has no alternative value. National income is then "profits," the maximum value of output of the two goods, plus the wage bill,

$$R'(H, K, W) + WR'_W(H, K, W) = R'(H, K, W) + WL(W, R'_H(H, K, W)).$$

Employment creating trade policy then arises endogenously, since for this case

$$v_Q = V_I\{[P - P^*] + WR'_{WH}H_Q\},$$

with $v_Q = 0$ defining the optimal policy settings of Q. For the purposes of this chapter the two structures differ only inessentially, with equivalence when the target L is at the proper value. Thus for simplicity the sectoral Keynesian case is suppressed.

$l(Q)$ bounds a convex set if it is concave, which cannot generally be assured, so second-order conditions are again of concern.

The first derivative of $l(Q)$ is

$$l_Q = \{L_W W_H + L_Y R_{HH}\}H_Q = l_H H_Q. \tag{15}$$

The second derivative matrix is

$$l_{QQ} = l_H H_{QQ} + l_{HH}H_Q H'_Q. \tag{16}$$

If $l_{HH} < 0$, and H is concave in Q, then l_{QQ} is negative semidefinite. Both hypotheses are problematic, with the first somewhat less so. $l_{HH} < 0$ essentially implies diminishing marginal employment effects of rises in product price, which is intuitively appealing as a plausible condition. The structure of convex technology does not, however, guarantee it.[5] In what follows, it is assumed that solutions for Q are found where $l(Q)$ is locally concave.

5.2 Optimal Trade Policy

The optimal trade policy is the solution to

$$\max_{Q, \lambda} v(Q) + \lambda[l(Q) - L^0]. \tag{17}$$

It is assumed that L^0 is feasible and that the constraint binds, and that v and l are locally concave in Q in the relevant region. The first-order conditions then characterize the optimum:

$$V_I[P - P^*] = -\lambda l_H H_Q. \tag{18}$$

To see the intuition of (18), note that the left-hand side is the marginal net benefit of another unit of imports, positive if trade is restrained. The right-hand side is the marginal cost in terms of the employment constraint. λl_H is constant across the varieties of imports, so the only source of variation in the optimal rate of specific taxation arises from $-H_Q$.

Now consider H_Q. The reduced form $H(Q)$ is defined from (3) and (6)–(7). From (7),

$$Z = R(H, K) - HR_H - P^*Q \qquad \text{using (6) to substitute } R_H \text{ for } Y. \qquad (7')$$

Substituting (7') and (6) into (3), and differentiating with respect to Q_i,

$$H_{Qi} = (1/\Delta)\{\partial(U_Y/U_Z)/\partial Q_i - P_i^*\partial(U_Y/U_Z)/\partial Z\}, \qquad (19)$$

where $\Delta = 1 - R_{HH}\{\partial(U_Y/U_Z)/\partial Y + H\partial(U_Y/U_Z)/\partial Z\} > 0$ under the assumption of diminishing marginal rate of substitution. Alternatively,

$$H_{Qi} = (1/\Delta)\{H_{Qi}^u - P_i^*H_Z^u\}, \qquad (19')$$

where the u superscript denotes the uncompensated inverse demand function [see (2)–(3)], and $H_Z^u > 0$ is assumed.

(19') could have either sign, though a negative effect is intuitive and motivates protection in the first place. Special cases of (19') are now developed to allow the main results. Preferences are weakly separable with respect to the partition between imports and domestic goods [i.e., $U(Q, Y, Z) = U(\phi(Q), Y, Z)$ for some quasiconcave monotonic increasing function ϕ], if and only if $\partial(U_Y/U_Z)/\partial Q_i = H_{Qi}^u$ is proportional to P_i.[6] Specifically, using weak separability and (2)–(3), $\partial(U_Y/U_Z)/\partial Q_i = U_Y/U_Z[U_{Y\phi}/U_Z - U_{Z\phi}/U_Z]\phi_{Qi}$. Noting that $P_i = U_\phi\phi_{Qi}/U_Z$ and substituting in the previous expression,

$$H_{Qi}^u = P_iH[U_{Y\phi}/U_\phi - U_{Z\phi}/U_\phi], \qquad (19'')$$
$$-H_{Qi} = P_i^*\{H_Z^u - (1 + \tau_i)H[U_{Y\phi}/U_\phi - U_{Z\phi}]\}/\Delta,$$

where τ_i is the *ad valorem* tariff on import i. The term in square brackets is negative if imports are quantity-substitutes for Y, as is most likely for protection to be considered at all. Then $-H_{Qi}$ is proportional to P_i, where the positive proportionality factor does not depend on i, save as τ_i might vary. Then substituting (19'') into (18) it is seen that τ_i must be constant:

THEOREM 1   For preferences weakly separable with respect to the partition between imports and other goods, the optimal trade policy for protecting employment is a uniform *ad valorem* tariff.

The theorem is an instance of a "piecemeal" second-best structure (Davis and Whinston). The marginal rates of substitution between import pairs remain equal to the external price ratios with an *ad valorem* tariff just as in the unconstrained situation. This is optimal when preferences are weakly separable with respect to the partition between imports and domestic goods because shifts in the mix of imports serve no useful purpose along the constraint, trade policy being effective by shifting the index $\phi(Q)$. The optimal mix remains determined by the same considerations as in the unconstrained case: the ratios of external prices.

Note that nothing in the structure of the argument involves knowing which goods are more expensive, have higher quality. Also, weak separability is general enough to allow nonuniform cross-price elasticities of demand for the Y good with respect to imports, and nonhomotheticity of the subutility function defined on the Q_i, and of preferences between imports and the domestic goods (see Deaton and Muellbauer, 1980, for a full treatment).

Weak separability encompasses nearly all empirical studies of protection (in their certainty equivalent form), but there may sometimes be reason to split imports into two or more weakly separable groups. The methods above easily extend to show

COROLLARY   For weakly separable groups of imports, the optimal instrument is an *ad valorem* tariff schedule with one rate for each group.

Proof   Suppose there are two groups, with subutility functions $\phi_1(Q_1)$ and $\phi_2(Q_2)$. The new version of the steps above leading to theorem 1 is

$$-H_{Qi} = P_i^* \{ H_Z^u - (1 + \tau_i) H [U_{Y\phi k}/U_{\phi k} - U_{Z\phi k}/U_{\phi k}] \} / \Delta, \qquad (19''')$$

for $k = 1, 2$ and i a member of group k. Substitution of (19''') into (18) yields an optimal two step *ad valorem* tariff.   QED

One interesting implication of theorem 1 is that proportionately distributed quotas (i.e., licensing with no resale of imports in proportion to base year proportions) can achieve the optimum under weak separability and the added restriction that ϕ be homothetic in Q. The result is less attractive for advocates of quotas than at first appears, however, because nonhomotheticity (nonunitary expenditure elasticities) is utterly compelling at a fine level of disaggregation. The representative U.S. consumer's food-expenditure elasticity of demand for meals at a popular Mexican restaurant far exceeds his food-expenditure elasticity of demand for bulk dried beans. Furthermore, even with homotheticity, preserving the optimality of quotas involves greater complexity than with the tariff, since shifts in P^* and K must shift the appropriate base for the proportional distribution.

5.3 Second-Best Rankings

Returning to the more general case of (19′) in (18), the optimal specific tax on i is positively proportional to P_i in one term, and negatively proportional to H^u_{Qi} in the other. This structure motivates a discussion of second-best comparisons of fixed specific and *ad valorem* tariffs. Let the index i be arranged so that P^*_i rises as i rises. In contrast to the optimum, a fixed specific tax does not vary over i in response to either term. A fixed *ad valorem* tax has specific tax equivalent which is proportional to P^*_i. If tax settings are all such that the employment constraint is met, a comparison can be made. So long as H^u_{Qi} rises as P^*_i rises, it appears that the *ad valorem* tariff has a specific tax equivalent that responds in the right direction as i rises. If it does not go too far, it should dominate the specific tariff. On the other hand, if H^u_{Qi} falls as i rises, it is possible that the *ad valorem* tariff moves in the wrong direction as i rises. Then the specific tariff should do better. These conjectures can be verified in essence. The methods developed below are used for the two natural comparisons of specific and *ad valorem* tariffs, but are applicable to any comparison of allocations.

Note that the admissible trade control systems must all obey $l(Q) = L^0$. $l(Q)$ is assumed to be a concave function in the relevant region. Let Q^s denote the specific tax import vector and Q^a denote the *ad valorem* tax import vector. By the mean value theorem for a concave function,

$$l_Q(Q^s)[Q^a - Q^s] \geqslant l(Q^a) - l(Q^s) = 0 \geqslant l_Q(Q^a)[Q^a - Q^s]. \tag{20}$$

The right-hand inequality with (15) implies

$$-H_Q(Q^a)[Q^a - Q^s] \geqslant 0. \tag{21}$$

Combining (21) with (19′) the restriction implied by meeting the constraint is

$$\{P^*H^u_Z - H^u_Q\}'[Q^a - Q^s] \geqslant 0, \tag{22}$$

or

$$H^u_Z P^{*\prime}[Q^a - Q^s] \geqslant H^{u\prime}_Q[Q^a - Q^s]. \tag{22′}$$

The objective function is concave in Q and changes by

$$v(Q^a) - v(Q^s) \geqslant V_I(Q^a)\tau P^{*\prime}[Q^a - Q^s] \tag{23}$$

using the mean value theorem as above and (12) for v_Q evaluated at the *ad valorem* tariff solution, τ.

Comparing (22′) and (23), the *ad valorem* tariff yields higher welfare so long as $H_Q^w[Q^a - Q^s] > 0$. The change in Q depends on the difference in the instruments and their effect on Q via the substitution effects matrix. Compared to the *ad valorem* tariff the specific tariff raises the price of cheap goods relatively more, inducing substitution toward more expensive goods (see Falvey, 1979, for a thorough development of the two-good case). As more expensive goods tend to raise H relatively more via H_Q^u, this will make the right-hand side of (22′) positive.

This is more meaningfully and formally expressed with a formula for the change in Q. First, note that $\Delta H = 0$ in order to meet the constraint. Now consider the effect of the difference in import prices on the compensated demand for Q given the $v(Q^a)$ level of utility. Use of compensated demands permits an intuitive analysis that is correct so long as income effects are not too strong. See Falvey (1979) for the same analysis and a defense. Based on the compensated demand system, by the mean value theorem, evaluating the Slutsky matrix S in its reduced form dependence on Q at $Q^0 = \beta Q^a + (1 - \beta)Q^s$ for some β between 0 and 1,

$$Q^a - Q^s = -S(Q^0, v(Q^a)))[t - \tau P^*]. \tag{24}$$

S is negative semidefinite and thus has characteristic form $D'\Lambda D$, where Λ is diagonal, D is the (orthogonal) matrix of characteristic vectors, and the characteristic roots on the diagonal of Λ, λ_i, are all nonpositive. Then the condition for *ad valorem* tariff dominance is

$$-[D(H_Q^u)]'\Lambda[D(t - \tau P^*)] = -\sum H_{Qi}^u \lambda_i (t - \tau P_i^*) \geqslant 0. \tag{25}$$

(25) expresses the precise sense in which increases in the relative price of cheap goods via the specific tax, $t - \tau P_i^* > 0$, act to lower their consumption, and raise H via H_Q^u so long as cheapness and H_Q are positively associated. Note that

$$[D(H_Q^u)]'[D(t - \tau P^*)] = H_Q^w(t - \tau P^*), \qquad \text{by} \quad D'D = I.$$

It is tempting to conclude that $H_Q^w(t - \tau P^*) > 0$ guarantees that (25) is met, but this is not sufficient unless the λ_i are nearly equal. What is sufficient is that every element of the sum, $H_{Qi}^u(t - \tau P_i^*)$, be nonnegative. This is summarized as

THEOREM 2   *Ad valorem* tariffs are superior to specific tariffs if increases in the consumption of (less) more-expensive-than-average imports (raises) lowers consumer's willingness to pay for the domestic good.

The theorem is expressed in terms of "willingness to pay," H, in terms of the numeraire. The intuition of the sufficient condition of theorem 2 is that the substitution toward more expensive goods under a specific tariff is more inefficient as more expensive imports tend to quantity substitute ($H_Q^u < 0$) for the domestic import substitute, and cheap imports tend to quantity complement the domestic import substitute ($H_Q^u > 0$).[7] This intuition shows that there is a nugget of truth in the popular perception that quality upgrading is inefficient as the changing mix of imports increases the degree of their closeness of substitution with domestic goods.

To illustrate the robustness of the presumption in favor of *ad valorem* tariffs, it is useful to consider what is needed for dominance of the specific tariff. Using the same reasoning as in (23),

$$v(Q^s) - v(Q^a) \geqslant v_Q(Q^s)[Q^s - Q^a] = V_I(Q^s)t[Q^s - Q^a]. \tag{26}$$

Using (20), the constraint implies the admissible imports satisfy

$$l_Q(Q^a)[Q^s - Q^a] \geqslant 0. \tag{27}$$

From (15), $l_Q = l_H H_Q$. Dividing through the irrelevant positive constant l_H and substituting for H_Q using (19′) evaluated at the *ad valorem* tariff solution, and $P = P^* + t$, (27) becomes

$$t[Q^s - Q^a] \geqslant \{P - H_Q^u/H_Z^u\}[Q^s - Q^a], \tag{28}$$

where H_Q^u/H_Z^u is evaluated at Q^a. Dominance of the specific tax is guaranteed if the right-hand side of (28) is nonnegative. By the same steps as in (24) and (25) this becomes

$$\sum \{-P_i + H_{Qi}^u/H_Z^u\}\lambda_i'(t - \tau P_i^*) \geqslant 0, \tag{29}$$

where $\lambda_i' \leqslant 0$. Rearranging (29) to isolate two key components, the condition is

$$-\sum P_i\lambda_i(t - \tau P_i^*) + [1/H_Z^u]\sum H_{Qi}^u\lambda_i(t - \tau P_i^*) \geqslant 0. \tag{30}$$

The first term of (30) is usually negative. Most simply this arises in the separable case because expenditure minimization implies $[P^* + t]'[Q^s - Q^a] \leqslant 0$ on the right-hand side of (28). It is legitimate to use the expenditure function property under the compensated demand structure used in moving from (28) to (29). With separability, the second term is zero, so (30) cannot be met. More generally, with nonseparable structures, the first term is $-\sum w_i(P_i^* + t)(\tau P_i^* - t)$, where t may be understood as an intermediate value in the range of τP_i^*, and $w_i > 0$. As t is near the weighted mean of τP^*, the term is negative, by the standard algebra of covariance. Negativity should hold for a reasonable range of other values of t in the range of τP^*.

Essentially the first term represents the *arbitrage efficiency* of the *ad valorem* tariff: for a given total value of imports, the cheapest distortion to achieve it is uniform *ad valorem*. The second term of (30) is negatively proportional to (25), the sufficient condition for *ad valorem* tariff dominance. Thus reversing the sign of the second term opens the way to possible specific tariff dominance. Its reversal involves, for sufficiency, $H^u_{Qi}(t - \tau P^*_i) < 0$ for all i. Essentially, the substitution toward more expensive goods can lead to specific tariff dominance if these goods quantity complement the domestic import substitute. (30) reveals that this alone will not suffice: the strength of the opposite effect must be strong enough to overcome the first, *arbitrage efficiency*, term of (30), the effect that makes *ad valorem* tariffs dominate in the absence of effects via H^u_Q. This discussion can be summarized in

THEOREM 3   Specific tariffs dominate *ad valorem* tariffs if the substitution toward higher priced goods under the specific tariff increases the consumption of goods that complement the domestic import substitute sufficiently strongly.

Note that the structure of theorems 2 and 3 can be used to construct conditions on welfare-improving partial reform for any pair of policies Q^a, Q^s and their associated Ps. Thus a reform moving *toward* the *ad valorem* solution can be evaluated.

   To check on the reasoning behind theorem 3 and demonstrate that the set of preferences it covers is not empty, it is convenient to produce an example in which the specific tariff dominates.

5.3.1 A Specific Tariff Dominance Example

Let utility be $U = Q_1 + Z^\alpha + Q^\beta_2 Y^{1-\beta}$, where $0 < \alpha, \beta < 1$. The target employment implies a target output of the sensitive good, Y^0, and a target price, H^0. Then the marginal rates of substitution conditions are

i. $U_{Q1}/U_Z = 1/\alpha Z^{\alpha-1} = P_1$,

ii. $U_{Q2}/U_{Q1} = \beta Q^{\beta-1}_2 (Y^0)^{1-\beta} = P_2/P_1$,

iii. $U_Y/U_Z = (1 - \beta)Q^\beta_2 (Y^0)^{-\beta}/\alpha Z^{\alpha-1} = H^0$.

Note that $H^u_{Q1} = 0$, $H^u_{Q2} = H^u \beta/Q_2 > 0$; so the example has the potential for either ranking, depending on the correlation of H^u_{Qi} with P^*_i.

   (i) and (ii) may be solved for Z and Q_2 as functions of P_1 and P_2/P_1, respectively;

$$Z = (\alpha P_1)^{1/(1-\alpha)} \qquad \text{and} \qquad Q_2 = Y^0(\beta P_1/P_2)^{1/(\beta-1)}.$$

Substituting these into (iii) yields a reduced form relation for P_2/P_1 as a function of P_1 and H^0:

iv. $P_2/P_1 = k(H^0)^{(\beta-1)/\beta}P_1^{(1-\beta)/\beta} = k'P_1^{(1-\beta)/\beta}$, where $k > 0$ is a parameter.

Trade must balance in external prices; hence

v. $Q_1 = -(P_2^*/P_1^*)Q_2 + (1/P_1^*)[X^0 - Z]$,

where $X^0 =$ output of the export good, fixed by $H = H^0$.

Now (i) and (ii) may be inverted with (iv) substituted into the inverse of (ii). The resulting expressions for Z and Q_2, with (v) for Q_1, may be substituted into the utility function to give a reduced form in terms of P_1. The result is

vi. $w(P_1) = X^0/P_1^* - (P_2^*/P_1^*)k'^{1/(\beta-1)}P_1^{-1/\beta}[\beta^{1-\beta}]Y^0 - (1/P_1^*)(\alpha P_1)^{1/(1-\alpha)}$

$+ (\alpha P_1)^{\alpha/(1-\alpha)} + k'^{\beta/(\beta-1)}[\beta^{1-\beta}]Y^0/P_1$.

The first derivative is

vii. $w_{P_1} = (1/P_1)\{P_2^*Q_2/\beta P_1^* - Q_2^\beta(Y^0)^{(1-\beta)}$

$- Z/(1-\alpha)P_1^* + Z^\alpha \alpha(1-\alpha)\}$.

w_{P1} evaluated at the *ad valorem* solution is negative, using (i)–(ii).[8] Assuming the sign of w_{P1} does not change in the interval,[9] the *ad valorem* tariff is superior (inferior) to the specific tariff as $\{P_1^a - P_1^s\} < (>)0$.

Finally, note that (iv) can be solved for the value of P_1 consistent with the constraint. For an *ad valorem* tariff, $P_2/P_1 = P_2^*/P_1^*$, while for a specific tariff, $P_2P_1 = (P_2^*/P_1^*)[(1 + t/P_2^*)/(1 + t/P_1^*)]$. Then

viii. $\{P_1^a - P_1^s\} = (H^0/k)[P_2^*/P_1^*]^{\beta/(1-\beta)}\{1 - [(1 + t/P_2^*)/(1 + t/P_1^*)]^{\beta/(1-\beta)}\}$.

(viii) is positive (negative) as $P_2^* > (<)P_1^*$. Combining the information of (vii)–(viii),

The specific tariff dominates if $P_2^* > P_1^*$.

Note that in this case (see note 9) it can be shown that $w_{P1} < 0$ at the specific tax solution, so the derivative assumption is guaranteed. The intuition is that for this case Q_2 quantity complements Y ($H_{Q2}^u > 0$), while Y is quantity independent of Q_1 ($H_{Q1}^u = 0$). The condition of theorem 3 is met, H_Q^u and P^* are positively correlated. If $P_2^* > P_1^*$, the substitution toward the expensive import induced by the specific tariff is efficient. Reversing the ranking of the prices reverses this effect, and meets the condition of theorem 2 and

The ad valorem tariff dominates if $P_1^* < P_2^*$.

The optimal trade instruments are implied by solving (vii) for the value of P_1 for which the derivative is zero (w is concave in P_1, at least in the neighborhood of the *ad valorem* tariff[10]). Then (iv) implies the tax on import 2. Whether the optimal specific tax on 2 lies above or below that on 1 is given by considering (vii) essentially as in the second-best rankings.

5.4 Intermediate Product Imports

There are two reasons for developing a separate treatment of intermediate input trade. First, much of world trade is in fact in intermediate products. Second, trade policy discussions about manufactured goods industries often involve the location of stages of production. Employment in the auto industry may be increased or reduced by protection as home firm managers decide whether to import or produce parts.[11]

A minimal model in which to study such issues has a composite export good, a domestic good, and a vector of imported inputs. Essentially, imports switch from the demand side to the supply side of the economy in the simplest possible way. The formal analysis permits the two domestically produced goods to be intermediate goods as well as final goods, but this interpretation is not explicitly developed below.

Suppose the domestic consumption of the export good is Z, the production of it is X, and the production and consumption of the domestic good is Y. The vector of imported inputs is Q, available in infinitely elastic supply at foreign price P^*. Employment in a "sensitive" sector is to be constrained with trade policy the only available instrument. It is convenient to make the Keynesian assumption that labor of the constrained type is infinitely elastically supplied at wage rate W, and that such labor has opportunity cost equal to W.[12] Essentially all the value of labor is specific human capital. As in the preceding section, a general equilibrium structure will be reduced to depend only on Q, presenting both a reduced form utility function and constraint function.

Let the concave product transformation curve be $T(X, Y, Q; L, K) = 0$. Assume for simplicity it is twice differentiable. The supply side of the Keynesian competitive economy is represented by a restricted concave product transformation curve $T(X, Y, Q; W, K)$. It is the result of wage bill minimizing employment choice:

$$B(X, Y, Q; W, K) = \left\{ \min_L WL \text{ subject to } T(X, Y, Q; L, K) = 0 \right\}.$$

By the envelope theorem, $B_W(\cdot) = L(X, Y, Q; W, K)$. T follows from substitution of $B_W(\cdot)$ into T. As might be expected, weak separability in production involves the restriction $T(X, Y, Q; L, K) = T(X, Y, \phi(Q); L, K)$, and is sufficient for the optimality of ad $valorem$ tariffs. Import controls advance employment through their direct effect on L, $L_Q = -T_{LQ}/T_{LL}$, and through their indirect effect on X and Y operating on L. The dependence of Y and X on Q in the general equilibrium reduced form is developed in parallel with section 5.1.

The system of inverse demand and supply functions is

$$T_Y/T_X = H, \tag{31}$$

$$-T_Q/T_X = P, \tag{32}$$

$$U_Y/U_Z = H. \tag{33}$$

The model is completed by the internal and external budget constraints

$$HY + Z = HY + X + [P - P^*]Q, \tag{34}$$

$$Z = X - P^*Q. \tag{35}$$

(31)–(35) implicitly determine H, P, X, Y, Z as functions of Q and the exogeneous P^*, W, K.

The first step in the reduction of the system is to use $T(X, Y, Q; W, K) = 0$ to solve for $X = x(Y, Q; W, K)$. By concavity, $x(\cdot)$ exists. $x_Q = P$ by (32), and $x_Y = -H$ by (33). Now substitute $x(\cdot)$ into (35) and (31), and from (35) into (33)

$$U_Y/U_Z(Y, x(Y, Q; W, K) - P^*Q) = T_Y/T_X(Y, x(Y, Q; W, K), Q; W, K). \tag{36}$$

This general equilibrium reduced form equation solves for Y in terms of Q and the exogenous P^*, W, K: $Y = y(Q; P^*, W, K)$. Substituting in $x(\cdot)$ yields the reduced form dependence of X on Q: $X = x(y(Q; P^*, W, K), Q; W, K) = x'(Q; P^*, W, K)$.

The derivative properties of the reduced form are needed for the welfare analysis. Differentiating (36) totally with respect to Q, using the derivative properties of $x(\cdot)$, and solving for the reduced form derivative of Y with respect to the vector Q,

$$y_Q = (1/\omega)\{-[P - P^*]\partial(U_Y/U_Z)/\partial Z$$
$$+ P\partial(T_Y/T_X)/\partial X + \partial(T_Y/T_X)/\partial Q\}, \tag{37}$$

where

$$\omega = [\partial(U_Y/U_Z)/\partial Y - H\partial(U_Y/U_Z)/\partial Z] - [\partial(T_Y/T_X)/\partial Y$$
$$- H\partial(T_Y/T_X)/\partial X].$$

Convex structure (i.e., convex preferences and technology) assures that $\omega < 0$. For weakly separable production, the third term in curly brackets vanishes. Then the elements of the vector are proportional to prices, and under a uniform *ad valorem* tariff they are proportional to P^*. The general equilibrium reduced form derivative of X with respect to Q is

$$x'_Q = x_Q + x_Y y_Q = P - Hy_Q. \tag{38}$$

Under the separability restriction, with a uniform *ad valorem* tariff, (38) is proportional to P^*.

Indirect utility is $V(H, I)$. General equilibrium indirect utility is $V(H, R(H, P, W, K) + [P - P^*]Q)$, where $R(\cdot)$ is the maximum value-added function:

$$R(\cdot) = \{\max HY + X - PQ \text{ subject to } T(X, Y, Q; W, K) = 0\}.$$

As previously, rent or revenue is redistributed to the representative consumer. If W exceeds the opportunity cost of labor W^0, income includes an additional term $(W - W^0)L$. Using the reduced form price functions that can be derived from substituting the various quantity reduced forms such as (36) into the inverse demand functions, the general equilibrium reduced form indirect utility function $v'(Q)$ can be derived. As in section 5.1, it simplifies due to the envelope property in V and r:

$$v'_Q = V_I[P - P^*].$$

$v'(Q)$ is concave under the same circumstances as $v(Q)$.

Finally, consider the employment constraint function. $L(x'(Q), y(Q), Q) = l'(Q)$ is the general equilibrium reduced form for employment (omitting the exogenous P^*, W, K). $l'(Q)$ is concave under strong assumptions that involve third-derivative terms.

As in section 5.2 the policy problem is to maximize $v'(Q)$ subject to an employment constraint on $l'(Q)$. Optimal policy at an interior maximum requires v'_Q proportional to l'_Q. An interior maximum may not exist, but I assume that it does.

THEOREM 4   With weakly separable imported intermediate inputs as instruments, the optimal employment protecting instrument is a uniform *ad valorem* tariff.

Proof   The theorem follows if l'_Q is proportional to P^* under separability and *ad valorem* tariffs.

Using T and L properties,

$$l'_Q = -T_{LQ}/T_{LL} - (T_{LX}/T_{LL})x'_Q - (T_{LY}/T_{LL})y_Q. \tag{39}$$

Note first that the bracketed derivatives are the same across elements of the vector l'_Q and that x'_Q and y_Q are proportional to P^*. Second, under the separability hypothesis, $-T_{LQ} = -T_{L\phi}\phi_Q = PT_Z T_{L\phi}/T_\phi$ using (32). Then the first term of (39) is proportional to P^* under an *ad valorem* tariff.   QED

Depending on the nature of the substitution structure embedded in the abstract technology $T(\cdot)$ it could of course be that the optimal tariff is negative. It is also possible that no interior solution exists, or indeed that the feasible set is empty.

It is possible to use the structure of this section to develop second-best ranking theorems to parallel theorems 2 and 3. This is left as an exercise for the reader. Cases of quantity complementarity between high quality imports and domestic labor, which should tend to favor the specific tariff, may sometimes be quite defensible.

5.5 Optimal Revenue Tariffs

Less developed economies often rely heavily on trade taxation for government revenue. Presumably this choice is explained by collection costs. What is the optimal revenue tariff structure? If imports enter preferences (or technology) in weakly separable fashion, a uniform *ad valorem* tariff is optimal under homotheticity (constant returns to scale).

To see this, reinterpret $l(Q) - L^0$ in (17) as a revenue constraint $g(Q) - G^0$, where $g(\cdot)$ is the government trade distortions revenue function, $g(Q) = [P(Q) - P^*]Q$. The representative consumer's indirect utility is $v(Q) = V(P(Q), H(Q), R(H(Q)))$, since revenue is no longer redistributed. Then optimality is determined by $v_Q + \lambda g_Q = 0$:

$$-V_I[P_Q]'Q + \lambda[P - P^*] + \lambda[P_Q]'Q = 0,$$

or

$$P - P^* = \alpha[P_Q]'Q.$$

The optimality of the *uniform ad valorem* tariff follows as $[P_Q]'Q$ is proportional to P. This follows under weak separability and homotheticity of the subutility function $\phi(Q)$. Thus

THEOREM 5   The optimal revenue tariff is uniform *ad valorem* under weak separability and import subutility homotheticity.

Proof   First, rewrite (2) using the weakly separable form:

$$P = (U_\phi/U_z)\phi_Q = m\phi_Q,$$ (2')

where $m(\cdot)$ is the marginal rate of substitution between imports as a group and the exportable good. Using the reduced form general equilibrium supply functions $Y(H(Q)) = R_H(H)$ and $X(H(Q))$ for the import substitute and export goods, and imposing the external price trade balance constraint to solve for exportable consumption,

$$P = m(\phi(Q), Y(H(Q)), X(H(Q)) - P^*Q)\phi(Q).$$ (2'')

The general equilibrium reduced form derivative P_Q follows from differentiating (2''):

$$P_Q = (1/m)P\{m_\phi\phi'_Q + m_Y Y_H H'_Q + m_Z(x_H H'_Q - P^*)\} + m\phi_{QQ}.$$

Under weak separability, H_Q is proportional to P^*; hence under a uniform *ad valorem* tariff, all terms in $\{\ \}$ are proportional to P. Under homotheticity of $\phi(Q)$, ϕ_{QQ} is proportional to $\phi_Q\phi'_Q$, hence to PP'. Then $P'_Q Q$ is proportional to P. QED

Theorem 5 neutralizes income effects via homotheticity. A less attractive method found in the public finance literature neutralizes them through lump-sum compensation. This is awkward, since the motivation for distortionary revenue taxation in the first place is the absence of lump-sum taxation. It is straightforward to verify that in this model, weak separability plus compensation also suffices for the optimality of the uniform *ad valorem* tariff.

5.6 Quality Upgrading, Imperfect Competition, and Optimal Trade Policy

A significant element of the concern over quality upgrading shown by policymakers has to do with imperfect competition. The Japanese auto VER system apparently resulted in quality upgrading. In a competitive market, this is an inefficient method of protecting employment. What can be concluded about the case of a small number of auto producers?

This section shows that essentially the same insight carries through for a foreign monopoly producer: *ad valorem* tariffs are optimal under weak separability and homothetic cost functions for the multiproduct foreign producer. The latter assumption is needed to assure that the external relative cost structure is not altered by the constant-import-mix trade policy (which is automatically assured in the small country case of the previous analysis).

The foreign producer is permitted full use of his knowledge of cross-price elasticities and his control of his entire product line. Domestic producers behave competitively and the foreign producer has rational expectations—is assumed to be able to see through to the full general equilibrium reduced form dependence of import price on import quantity. On the other hand, the foreign producer takes the government's actions as given.

Two potentially important limitations of the analysis should be emphasized. First, the domestic rivals are assumed to behave competitively. An alternative that produces the same qualitative results is to assume the home and foreign firms are a Cournot duopoly. Under consistent conjectural variations, however, it appears to be possible that strategic linkages of the rival firms can destroy the weakly separable structure that suffices to establish *ad valorem* tariff dominance. A detailed investigation is needed to see if it is possible for consistent conjectural variations to lead to the dominance of a specific tariff under separable demand structure.[13]

Second, the design of products is taken as given (as it implicitly was in the previous analysis), so that quality upgrading means substitution within the given mix. Design costs limit product innovation, but in both competitive and monopolistic markets, a response to taxation will eventually be to redesign the product line. In terms of the present analysis, the added element is that new products can enter (or old ones leave). For monopolistic markets especially, the analysis of alternative trade policies in this context is complex. See Krishna (1984) for a beginning. The analysis of this paper is valid in the short run, and as the valuation of marginal products is small relative to the given product line.

5.6.1 The Model

Suppose that a foreign monopoly producer sells a vector Q of imports in the domestic market. These have domestic price P and are produced with a joint cost function $C^*(Q)$. The standard joint product profit maximizing behavior by the monopolist is assumed. When trade policy is in place, two alternative rent capture assumptions are developed. First, the monopolist is assumed to get all the rent from quotas or any other intervention. This is the simplest and perhaps most plausible case for quotas, especially when they are VERs. The alternative is when all the rent is captured by the domestic government and redistributed to the representative consumer. The remainder of the structure is identical to section 5.1.

Formally, the monopolist selects Q under free trade such that

$$P(Q) - C^*_Q(Q) = -QP_Q(Q), \tag{40}$$

where $P(Q)$ is the monopolist's perceived inverse demand function. In rational expectations equilibrium, this will coincide with the general equilibrium reduced form inverse demand function of the representative consumer, derived essentially as in section 5.1.

Now consider constrained trade. There are two cases, one for each of the rent assumptions. Denote the inverse demand function in the home rent capture case as $P'(Q)$ and in the foreign rent capture case as $P(Q)$; and similarly for $H'(Q)$ and $H(Q)$. When the Q vector is quota constrained, the left-hand side of (40) becomes $P - t - C^*_Q$, where t is the shadow price vector on the Q constraints.

The general equilibrium reduced form utility function of the representative consumer is

$$w(Q) = V(P(Q), H(Q), R(H(Q))) \qquad \text{for foreign rent capture,}$$

$$w'(Q) = V(P'(Q), H'(Q), R(H'(Q))) + [P'(Q) - C^*_Q(Q)]Q$$
$$\text{for home rent capture.}$$

By standard steps the first derivatives are

$$w_Q = -V_I Q P_Q = V_I[P - t - C^*_Q] \qquad \text{using (40),} \tag{41}$$

$$w'_Q = V_I[P' - C^*_Q] - V_I Q C^*_{QQ}. \tag{42}$$

Comparing the two, the effect of home rent capture in (42) is that the familiar optimal tariff structure is added: $w'_Q = 0$ solves for the *ad valorem* tariff inverse elasticity formula.

Optimal quota policy involves government selection of Q such that w_Q or w'_Q is proportional to the reduced form labor demand derivatives l_Q, as in section 5.1. Under weak separability these are proportional to P. With marginal costs C^*_Q constant, and rent captured by foreigners, the structure is essentially as in section 5.1. A quota structure such that t is proportional to C_Q^* is optimal. Thus theorem 1 holds: *ad valorem* tariffs are the optimal instruments for protecting employment.

This can be generalized to variable marginal cost when C^* is homothetic. Examining (40), an *ad valorem* tariff is equivalent to an equiproportional rise in C_Q^* across the product group. The optimal response to this is an equiproportionate reduction in Q if C^* is homothetic and P is based on weakly separable preferences. Then the optimal response in turn shifts C_Q^* equiproportionately in (41), which is consistent with a uniform *ad valorem* tariff.

For the case of home rent capture, the "optimal tariff" term in (42) is proportional to C_Q^* under the homotheticity restriction on C^*. Thus the monopolist's first-order condition (40) and the planner's proportionality of w_Q' can both be achieved with a uniform *ad valorem* tariff. Formally:

THEOREM 5   A uniform *ad valorem* tariff is the optimal instrument for protecting employment from a foreign joint product monopolist under weak separability and homothetic costs.

5.7 Conclusions

Theorems 1–4 formalize a presumption in favor of *ad valorem* tariffs over other forms of protection in the presence of quality heterogeneity. Weak separability is a natural null hypothesis on the form in which imports enter preferences or technology. When no contrary information is known, neutrality (an *ad valorem* tariff) is the indicated policy, and assures an *arbitrage efficiency* gain.

With nonseparability, one form reinforces the advantage of the *ad valorem* tax, while a restrictive form of preferences coincident with price structure is needed to reverse the ranking and overcome the *arbitrage efficiency* property of the tariff. If such a possibility is suspected, it would be worthwhile to depart from a uniform tax for the group, and incur the added administrative expense of a differentiated tax.

Imperfect competition opens a variety of complex channels that possibly could lead to reversal of the presumption. These must be the subject of further research. But for foreign monopoly or Cournot duopoly under fixed product design, the optimality of *ad valorem* tariffs under weak separability holds. The structure of the argument shows that a reversal of the ranking due to imperfect competition must depend on rather esoteric mechanisms.

An earlier version of the chapter was delivered to the May 1987 meeting of the Midwest International Economics Group. Helpful comments from the group, especially by Raymond Riezman and Peter Neary, have improved this draft. They should be absolved from complicity in any errors or obscurities.

Notes

1. Sometimes substitution can go so far as to escape restraint entirely, as when high sugar content products not covered by the Customs' definition of "sugar" were imported into the United States to evade the sugar quota.

2. The representative consumer assumption is for convenience. So long as there are no significant distributional effects arising from the difference in instruments, which seems plausible, the assumption is harmless.

3. The lump-sum redistribution assumption is reasonably innocuous in this analysis. For the typical protection case study, the amount of revenue involved is trivial as a fraction of national income. The effect of the assumption is to wash out of the analysis some inconvenient effects whose magnitude is very small.

4. The hypothesis of risk aversion is not strictly necessary for the results.

5. Examining (15), $l_{HH} < 0$ requires additional curvature conditions on output supply, sectoral labor demand, and the wage rate function. The latter can be met under the constant returns nonjoint production case of the technology. Economic theory does not meaningfully restrict the former.

6. This is the well-known Goldman-Uzawa theorem (see Deaton and Muellbauer, 1980).

7. The terminology is based on Hicks as cited in Deaton and Muellbauer (1980, chap. 2). The compensated inverse demand functions have a derivative matrix known as the Antonelli matrix. Hicks suggested quantity complements as the label for positive off-diagonal elements, and quantity substitutes as the label for negative off-diagonal elements. The compensated inverse demand derivative is related to the uncompensated form used in theorem 2 in the same way the Hicksian and Marshallian derivatives are related. Thus $H_Q^u = H_Q^c - PH_u^c$, where H^c denotes the compensated inverse demand. As is well-known (see Deaton and Muellbauer, 1980), the definitions of Antonelli substitutes and complements are invariant to monotonic transformations, as are the uncompensated forms. They are not generally equivalent to the Hicksian and Marshallian definitions. The Antonelli and Hicks-Slutsky matrices are generalized inverses of one another.

8. To see this note that at the *ad valorem* tax, $P_2/P_1 = P_2^*/P_1^* = \beta[Y^0/Q_2]^{1-\beta}$. Thus Q_2 is invariant to the tax rate. Utility is affected by $P_1 = P_1^*(1 + \tau)$ only through changes in $Z = [\alpha P_1]^{1/(1-\alpha)}$. The relevant portion of the reduced form utility function is $-Z/P_1^* + Z^\alpha$. This can be shown to be downward sloping in $P_1^*(1 + \tau)$ since $\alpha < 1$.

9. The assumption will be met if P_1^* and P_2^* are close together. Also, if $P_2^* > P_1^*$, it

can be shown that the assumption holds for any specific tariff value satisfying the employment constraint. More generally, it appears possible to violate the assumption with a fixed specific tax.

10. Concavity more generally is messy.

11. An interesting case that combines elements of the analysis of sections 5.2 and 5.3 is when the vector of imports contains both intermediate and final goods. Then foreign firms can choose to export either final goods or parts.

12. A variety of labor market distortions or "noneconomic" constraints will produce essentially the same structure so far as comparing the efficacy of trade instruments is concerned.

13. Under Cournot behavior, quotas and specific tariffs are equivalent in output effects, as are *ad valorem* tariffs under constant marginal cost. It is straightforward to obtain the dominance of *ad valorem* tariffs under weak separability using this structure. Under consistent conjectural variations, all will differ generally. More significantly, there is no reason to suppose that the interaction with rivals that firms anticipate will settle at a value such that the key reduced form derivative H_{Qi} [see (19')] remains proportional to P_i. See chapter 2 for discussion of the formation of consistent conjectural variations.

References

Anderson James E. (1985), "The Relative Inefficiency of Quotas: The Cheese Case," *American Economic Review*, 75, 178–190.

Anderson James E. (1986), "The Relative Inefficiency of Quotas: Employment Protection," manuscript.

Atkinson, Anthony B., and Joseph E. Stiglitz (1980), *Lectures on Public Economics*, New York: McGraw-Hill.

Aw, Bee Yan, and Mark Roberts (1986), "Measuring Quality Change in Quota-Constrained Import Markets: The Case of U.S. Footwear," *Journal of International Economics*, 21, 45–60.

Baldwin, Robert E. (1982), "The Inefficacy of Trade Policy," Frank Graham Memorial Lecture, Princeton University.

Bond, Eric (1987), "Optimal Commercial Policy with Quality Differentiated Products," Penn State University, mimeo.

Deaton, Angus (1979), "The Distance Function and Consumer Behavior with Applications to Index Numbers and Optimal Taxation," *Review of Economic Studies*, 46, 391–405.

Deaton, Angus, and John Muellbauer (1980), *Economics and Consumer Behavior*, Cambridge: Cambridge University Press.

Dixit, A., and V. Norman (1980), *The Theory of International Trade*, Cambridge: Cambridge University Press.

Falvey, Rodney E. (1979), "The Composition of Trade within Import-Restricted Categories," *Journal of Political Economy*, 87, 1105–1114.

Feenstra, Robert (1984), "Voluntary Export Restraint in U.S. Autos, 1980–81: Quality, Employment, and Welfare Effects," in *The Structure and Evolution of Recent U.S. Trade Policy*, R. E. Baldwin and A. O. Krueger, eds., Chicago: NBER.

Krishna, Kala (1984), "Tariffs vs. Quotas with Endogenous Quality," mimeo, presented to NBER Summer Institute.

II

Tariff Dominance: Impure Cases

6   Employment Protection under Uncertainty

It is common knowledge among theorists that tariffs and quotas are not equivalent. See, for example, Bhagwati and Srinivasan (1983, chap. 10). Nevertheless, in dealing with nonspecialists, nonequivalence is treated as a minor and esoteric matter. For example, undergraduate texts commonly devote a page or two to a demonstration of equivalence, then a line or two to sources of nonequivalence. Perhaps more significantly, government cost-of-protection studies are always done under assumptions that rule out nonequivalence. Convenience may partly explain this behavior, but I suspect it is also based on a guess that non-equivalence is empirically unimportant. My research is aimed at examining this hypothesis. I show that quotas are significantly more inefficient.

Most economists display a prejudice for tax interventions over quantity interventions, commonly expressed in statements such as "A tariff is more flexible than a quota." Probing further, the preference for tariffs can be founded on Adam Smith's invisible hand theorem. A group of heterogeneous (almost always) import goods is to be limited. A bureaucratic allocation of permitted trade over members of the group usually results in premia (of domestic above foreign price) that vary. A specific tariff on the group, in contrast, automatically has identical premia over the members, and thus effectively finds a competitive equilibrium in import licenses. That is, tariffs implicitly attain efficient arbitrage in the presence of heterogeneous goods. In the absence of any other qualifying effects, this must create gains over alternative allocations.

The purpose of this chapter is to examine the ranking of instruments in the presence of an important qualifying effect: employment. The theoretical section develops a qualitative ranking. The applied section reveals the magnitude of inefficiency found in simulation of a representative case.

6.1 General Discussion

An important dimension of heterogeneity is randomness.[1] Theoretical work by Young and Anderson (1980, chapter 4) and Anderson and Young (1982, chapter 7) has revealed the validity of the above argument in this case.

Nevertheless, the greater arbitrage efficiency of tariffs in the allocation of imports over random events may trade off against a poorer performance in other relevant dimensions. So too, the original invisible hand theorem is qualified in the presence of "distortions" such as externalities. The most practically important of these (in the sense of occasioning most intervention in developed countries at least) is probably employment. There may be reason to believe that quotas more certainly hit employment targets than do tariffs. This at least is a claim that is made on behalf of quotas. There is thus a potential conflict in the greater power of the tariff in easing the burden on consumers versus the greater power of the quota in hitting an employment target.

A theoretical analysis of efficient and "second-best" protection of average employment presented below shows some presumption in favor of a tariff (indeed, for the linear case, the specific tariff is optimal), but also that the ranking can go either way. The structure of the optimal policy is a revealing combination of an arbitrage component (favoring tariffs) and an employment effect component (which can favor quotas, though it need not).

The only satisfactory resolution of the theoretical ambiguity is through detailed examination of cases. Furthermore, even with a tariff presumption, it is important to be able to tell policymakers how much difference it makes.

A particularly suitable candidate for a case study is the textile industry of the United States (SIC 22). This industry is an important recipient of quota protection motivated by employment concerns. Furthermore, the econometric model used as a basis (Pelzman and Martin, 1981) is representative of those used in cost-of-protection studies generally. The results should turn out to be representative.

The simulation study shows that the quota costs an additional 11% of import expenditure relative to the tariff when the objective is a 10% increase in average employment in the base case. An alternative scaling method is to take the added cost relative to the unavoidable loss of welfare caused by using the tariff to hit the employment target. The tariff is on average 30% more efficient than the quota in hitting an average employment target in the base case. The specific tariff almost always dominates the *ad valorem* tariff by 1–2% and is dominated by the optimal (but infeasible) state contingent tariff or quota system by 3–6%. Thus the tariff comes close enough to the optimum so that further refinements are not necessary. The ranking results turn out to be robust with respect to varying the key parameters of the model. Even the relative inefficiency magnitudes are fairly robust. Finally, the added variability of employment under the tariff is trivial in impact, being swamped by a factor of thousands by the consumer welfare effect.

Based on these results for the textile industry, the arbitrage efficiency of tariffs is the dominant factor in selecting an efficient instrument to protect employment. The same proposition applies to "voluntary" export controls. It is much worse for the United States to transfer rent to foreigners than to use import control, but export taxes by foreigners dominate export quotas. VERs are popular because they allow compensation to foreign producers for loss of markets. Presumably their governments would be equally happy to receive tax revenue, and use it to compensate producers. The simulations below show that VERs cost an additional 40% of base expenditure on textile imports over the equivalent employment creating "voluntary export tax."

Recently, U.S. policymakers have shown interest in auctioning quota licenses. This reverses the rent transfer feature of VERs and solves the product-type heterogeneity inefficiency problem (Anderson, 1985a, chapter 3), but it cannot solve the inefficiency due to randomness. This would require auction of *state-contingent* quota licenses, which is infeasible.

Section 6.2 briefly outlines the general economic theory behind the relative efficiency of tariffs and quotas in meeting average employment targets. Two propositions are offered, giving circumstances in which alternately a tariff dominates a quota, and a quota dominates a tariff. Section 6.3 describes the textile model and the random environment that are the basis of the case study. Section 6.4 presents the results. Section 6.5 makes some concluding observations on the implications for commercial policy and for future work. The appendix contains proofs of the two propositions discussed in section 6.2.

6.2 Employment Protection: Theory

This section first describes the economic environment in which employment protection occurs. Then a simple welfare measure is derived in which welfare is dependent on the quota level. The welfare maximizing quota system is then characterized. A modification of its properties suggests the two propositions that rank tariffs relative to quotas.

A single industry in partial competitive equilibrium is a candidate for protection to raise its average employment level. Imports are a (less than perfect) substitute for domestic output. Domestic market clearance imposes a link between imports and domestic output, and labor market clearance imposes a link between domestic output and employment. Randomness enters the model via shifts in the foreign price as well as exogenous shift terms in the import demand, labor demand, and domestic goods demand and supply functions. Such factors as harvest yields, strikes, national income movements, exchange rate movements, and technological change may be embedded, as well as the usual "all-other-factors" disturbance terms. I denote its presence with a function argument s, indexing the state of the world. A shift in s means a shift in the set of exogenous variables indexed by s. Its net effect on the function depends on the set of partial derivatives as well as the covariation of the variables.

Welfare evaluation of alternative trade control instruments involves tracing their implications for prices and incomes through a quasi-general (not fully general because other prices are held constant) equilibrium structure, then evaluating the resultant indirect utility values at various points. This rather formidable complexity is fortunately reduced to elegant and compact expressions by repeated use of the envelope theorem. I shall eventually propose a welfare measure based solely on expected consumers' surplus in the import market. The derivation is not familiar, so it deserves elaboration.

6.2.1 The Welfare Measure

The representative consumer has indirect utility function $V(P, H, r, I)$, where P is the domestic price of imports, H is the price of the import substitute, r is the price vector for other goods (held constant by the partial equilibrium assumption), and I is the consumers' income. By Roy's identity, $V_P = -V_I Q$ and $V_H = -V_I D$, where Q and D are import and import-competing consumption, and subscripts denote differentiation.

I is the sum of national income and tariff or quota revenue (assuming redistribution). National income in a competitive economy is $R(H, r) = \max_{Y,Z}\{HY + r \cdot Z \mid (Y, Z) \in T\}$, where T is the technologically feasible set. By the envelope theorem, $R_H(H, r) = Y(H, r)$. Tariff or quota revenue is $(P - P^*)Q$, where P^* is the foreign price of imports. $I = R + (P - P^*)Q$.

The market for import substitutes must always clear, so $-V_H/V_I = R_H$. Also, with the permitted import Q being regarded as the control variable, $-V_P/V_I = Q$. This is a two-equation system that implicitly defines $P =$

$P(Q, P^*, r)$ and $H = H(Q, P^*, r)$. Substituting back into the indirect utility function, I define the *reduced form* indirect utility function:

$$v(Q, P^*, r) \equiv V(P(Q, P^*, r), H(Q, P^*, r), r, R(H(Q, P^*, r), r)$$

$$+ (P(Q, P^*, r) - P^*)Q).$$

It is a partial equilibrium concept due to the assumed exogeneity of r; otherwise it incorporates general-equilibrium-type linkages.

The key welfare derivative is

$$v_Q = - V_I Q P_Q + V_I Q P_Q + V_I(P - P^*)$$

$$- V_I D H_Q + V_I Y H_Q$$

$$= V_I[P(Q, P^*, r) - P^*].$$

Nontraded goods market clearance guarantees that the welfare measure is based on the import market alone. Constancy of V_I, imposed for convenience, allows focus on consumer's surplus, norming V_I at unity. This is justified if variation in consumer real income over states of the world is too small to matter or, more justifiably, if the variations are smoothed out by a sufficiently rich portfolio of assets (see Young and Anderson, 1982, chapter 9, for analysis of the case where trade policy is directed at smoothing V_I).

A final formal note is necessary on the use of the envelope theorem in production in the context of a possible labor market distortion. If there is a fixed money wage, R can be redefined to be profit in the Y industry plus income in production elsewhere. The envelope theorem is then properly used, understanding that one of the rs is now minus the fixed wage.[2] The full income measure should now include the net benefit of the employment change, the difference between the fixed wage and the value of labor in household or best alternative production times the employment change. Such refinements are unnecessary for present purposes, since in all cases the protection instruments are constrained to yield the same volume of employment, hence the same increment to welfare on this account.[3] (The same argument permits suppression of effects via wage and profits taxes.)

6.2.2 The Welfare Maximizing Trade Instruments

The optimal employment protection structure can now be analyzed. The government attempts to maximize the representative consumer's expected welfare which, under the above derivation, is

$$W = E\left[\int_0^{Q(s)} \{P(v,s) - P^*(s)\}\, dv \right],$$ (1)

where $Q(s)$ is imports in state s, $P(Q(s), s)$ is the domestic price of imports in state s, and $P^*(s)$ is the foreign price of imports in state s. This formulation suppresses the explicit effect of P^* on P via the income effect, for simplicity. In the (infeasible) full optimum, the government has control of imports in each state s. With downward sloping demand, (1) is concave in $Q(s)$.

(1) is maximized subject to an average employment constraint. Average employment is the simplest target to deal with and seems to reflect U.S. social norms rather accurately. For practical purposes, in the case study below, norms that heavily weight variation in employment are irrelevant anyway, since the variation is virtually identical under all types of import control. The constraint on employment formally is

$$E[L(Y(Q(s), s), s)] = E[l(Q(s), s)] \geqslant \bar{L},$$ (2)

where $Y(Q(s), s) = R_H(H(Q(s), S), S)$ is the domestic output reduced form function, with the influence of P^* and r subsumed in s, and $L(Y, s)$ is the labor demand function. $l(\cdot)$ is the reduced form labor demand function. If l is concave in $Q(s)$, the feasible set formed by (2) is convex, and the problem has a unique global maximum.

In the Pelzman-Martin model of the textile industry used below, $P(\cdot)$, $Y(\cdot)$, and $L(\cdot)$ are all loglinear functions, as is typical of empirical work on commercial policy evaluation. In this case l is convex in Q, and it is possible in principle for that convexity to exceed in curvature the concavity of the objective function. Then the interior first-order condition defines a minimum and the optimum involves boundary values of Q. In practice, the work reported on in section 6.3 did not encounter this problem.

With no restrictions on trade instruments, the maximization of (1) subject to (2) implies the optimal set of state contingent quotas $Q^*(s)$, or equivalent state contingent taxes. These must satisfy, for an interior optimum,

$$P(Q(s), s) - P^*(s) = -\mu l_Q(Q(s), s) \qquad \text{for all } s,$$ (3)

where μ is the Lagrange multiplier on the constraint.

The implications of (3) are easy to see. The left-hand side is the benefit from more trade; the right-hand side is the damage to employment of more imports. The optimum involves marginal benefit equal to marginal cost in each state. For a linear reduced form labor demand function, (3) implies that the optimal policy is a noncontingent specific tariff. In other cases, the optimal policy involves a varying tax. The height of the tax will vary directly with the absolute slope of labor demand, which measures the rate of damage to the constraint.

More insight into the structure of the optimal policy can be gained by examining the set of "comparative static derivatives" dQ^*/ds, obtained from differentiating (3):

$$dQ^*/ds = -\frac{[(P_s - P_s^*)/(P - P^*)] - (l_{Qs}/l_Q)}{[P_Q/(P - P^*)] - (l_{QQ}/l_Q)}. \tag{4}$$

The denominator is negative, since I assume an interior optimum. The terms in $P - P^*$ represent the influence of arbitrage: if the margin on imports rises (e.g., $P_s - P_s^* > 0$, s rises), then the optimal response is to increase imports (since $P_Q < 0$). The terms in l represent possible offsetting influences, due to the linkage of employment demand with imports and with the state of the world.

6.2.3 Ranking Tariffs versus Quotas

This leads naturally to examining the properties of restricted trade instruments, such as fixed tariffs and quotas. A fixed quota has $dQ/ds = 0$, if the quota always binds. This convenient assumption can be relaxed at the cost of somewhat complicating intuition, and the proofs of the propositions below. (see appendix 6.A). A fixed specific tariff, t, has

$$dQ^t/ds = -(P_s - P_s^*)/P_Q.$$

A fixed *ad valorem* tariff, τ has

$$dQ^\tau/ds = -(P_s - (1 + \tau)P_s^*)/P_Q.$$

Intuitively, if arbitrage effects dominate in (4), either form of the tariff appears to mimic the optimal policy better than a quota.

A rearrangement of (4) reveals a bit more useful structure. The specific tariff and optimal import schedules are related by

$$dQ^*/ds = (dQ^t/ds)\left\{\frac{1 - [(l_{Qs}/l_Q)/[(P_s - P_s^*)/(P - P^*)]]}{1 - [(l_{QQ}/l_Q)/(P_Q/(P - P^*))]}\right\}. \tag{4'}$$

The denominator of (4') must be positive, by the second-order condition. The numerator of the curly bracket expression can have either sign. Intuitively, the tariff should dominate so long as the response rate of imports under the tax is bounded between zero and the optimal value [the curly bracket expression in (4′) is > 1]. Again, for linear labor demand, the specific tax is optimal.

The alternative possibility of quota dominance occurs if the curly bracket expression is negative, since tariffs cause the import quantity to move in the wrong direction. This happens when l_{Qs} differs in sign from $P_s - P_s^*$ (i.e., the labor demand slope and the import premium are negatively correlated for given Q) and the former dominates. Approximately, this means the covariance of the import premium and the labor demand slope is negative and exceeds in absolute value the variance of the import premium. These conjectures are verified in the following propositions:

PROPOSITION 1   If

$$\frac{l_{QQ}/l_Q}{P_Q/(P - P^*)} > \frac{l_{Qs}/l_Q}{(P_s - P_s^*)/(P - P^*)},$$

the tariff dominates.

Proof   See appendix 6.A.

The condition in proposition 1, using the second-order condition

$$1 > \frac{l_{QQ}/l_Q}{P_Q/(P - P^*)},$$

implies $dQ^*/ds > dQ^t/ds > 0$. Note that these conditions are sufficient to bound the specific tariff import derivative between the optimal derivative and zero. They are not necessary for tariff dominance.

PROPOSITION 2   If the optimal policy $Q^*(s)$ has dQ^*/ds opposite in sign to dQ^t/ds, or

$$1 < \frac{l_{Qs}/l_Q}{(P_s - P_s^*)/(P - P^*)},$$

the quota dominates the specific tariff.

Proof   See appendix 6.A.

The expressions of the two propositions are rather abstract. Their application to the loglinear case used below is instructive. Let θ be the reduced form (absolute) elasticity of employment with respect to Q and let α be the import demand (absolute) price elasticity. Then $1/\alpha$ is the inverse elasticity. Let v be the multiplicative disturbance term for the inverse import demand function and ω be the multiplicative disturbance term for the reduced form labor function. Solving for the special case and substituting into the propositions gives

PROPOSITION 1'   The specific tariff dominates if

$$\frac{1 + \theta}{1/\alpha} > \frac{\omega_s/\omega}{(v_s/v) - [(P^* - P_s^*)/(P - P^*)]}.$$

PROPOSITION 2'   The quota dominates if

$$1 < \frac{\omega_s/\omega}{(P/P - P^*)(v_s/v) - [P^*/(P - P^*)](P_s^*/P^*)}.$$

On the right-hand side of the inequalities the random terms v, ω, and P^* are regarded as functions of the state s. One random variable can arbitrarily be made monotonic in s, but save for the case of perfect correlation (positive or negative) the others are necessarily nonmonotonic in s. Nevertheless, it is useful to use the derivatives and their implied contribution to covariation to develop intuition.

Nonpositive correlation of the import premium with labor demand means the RHS (right-hand side) of proposition 1' is predominantly nonpositive, hence the tariff dominance condition should be met. For positive correlation, the condition is still likely to be met if the variation of the import premium is large relative to the variation of labor demand. Quota dominance occurs when this is reversed, with positive correlation and large relative variation of labor demand.

These results at first seem counterintuitive. Negative correlation would seem to favor quotas over tariffs, as high premia, indicating greater imports under a tariff, tend to coincide with low states of labor demand. The apparent paradox is resolved by noting that the variation of labor demand is not directly relevant, but enters instead via its influence on the labor demand slope. For the loglinear case, a low state of labor demand implies a low state of $-l_Q$ in (3). With negative correlation, this coincides with a high value of $P - P^*$. The tariff instrument raises Q, and by the second-order condition, decreases the gap between the left- and right-hand sides of (3). The quota cannot do as well. With positive correlation the low state of labor demand, hence low $(-\mu l_Q)$, coincides with low $P - P^*$. With the tariff instrument, it is possible for the lower Q to increase the gap between the left- and right-hand sides of (3); this will occur as the slope change in response to s is greater than the premium change. Then the quota dominates the tariff.

Propositions 1 and 2 are about as far as theory can go to illuminate the possibilities. There is perhaps a presumption for tariff dominance based on the usual assumed dominance of first derivatives over second derivatives, which validates the use of linear approximation. This can be a dangerous presumption. As always, it should be buttressed with empirical work. In any case, the magnitude of the difference in efficiency of the instruments is an important issue.

6.3 The Simulation Model

A convenient industry on which to measure the relative efficiency of instruments is the textile industry. It is a significant employer (.7 to .8 million workers in the '70s) that has enjoyed special quota treatment since the '50s, subject to periodic multilateral negotiation under USTR auspices.

This section first discusses the econometric model used in the simulation. Then it describes how the estimated model and sample data are used to generate the random environment facing the policymaker, i.e., the dependence on s of section 6.2.

6.3.1 Pelzman-Martin's Textile Model

Pelzman and Martin (1981) have estimated an econometric model of the aggregate textile industry SIC 22 for the United States for the time period 1964–1977, and used it to simulate the effect of tariff changes on welfare and employment in the standard long run certainty equivalent framework. Its use for present purposes has two advantages. First, its loglinear form is typical of the models and methods used in evaluation of commercial policy save for a more elaborate econometric treatment of the link between employment demand and imports. (Even logquadratic models often find insignificant higher order terms.) Second, their model seems to be the reference model for textiles. I have taken the same model and data, taking seriously the presence of randomness, and used it to simulate the welfare effects of tariffs and aggregate quotas required to meet average employment increases of 10% and 25%.

It would be very desirable to use a disaggregated model that could incorporate the actual quotas in effect. There is ample reason to believe that the cost of quotas relative to tariffs rises sharply as disaggregation is performed (see Anderson (1985a, chapter 3). Unfortunately, the highly detailed set of quota restrictions cannot be concorded with detailed industry classifications, so that a disaggregated model of the actual behavior of quotas is apparently unattainable (see Pelzman and Martin, 1981).

All exercises with the aggregate model must be regarded as simulations disciplined by a serious effort to fit the data.

The model was fitted to time series data; hence it has a considerable amount of structure devoted to modeling adjustment over time. In principle, welfare analysis could proceed satisfactorily with a dynamic version of the theoretical model of section 6.2. It is better to start with simple cases first, however. Also, comparative static exercises fit better into the tradition of commercial policy evaluation, rendering the present chapter more readily comparable with the previous literature.[4]

Since the dynamic structure of Pelzman-Martin is irrelevant to the comparative static exercises that are my concern, their model is here compressed into its long run version. One side effect of this is that movements in labor and imports that the econometric model treats as explained by lagged adjustment are here made exogenous shocks. This increases the variance used to characterize the uncertainty of the environment. The alternative was to use the error variances of the short run econometric study, which would be appropriate only if the welfare analysis were also short run and dynamical. An offsetting effect is that the exogenous variables are effectively treated as known with certainty, whereas forecast errors in them certainly form part of the randomness facing the policymaker.

In the Pelzman-Martin model import demand is a loglinear function of the price of imports relative to the price of the domestic substitute and a domestic activity term. Home output is a loglinear reduced form function of the relative price, factor prices, disposable income, and imports. Implicitly, the market clearing equation for domestic goods has been solved for the reduced form domestic price as a function of exogenous variables in demand and supply. The resulting function is then substituted back into the supply function. The term relating output to imports is justified in Pelzman-Martin by appeal to an imperfect competition story. Another rationale is that errors in variables so contaminate the unit value used as the import price that the import quantity is a better proxy for the behavior of the unmeasured true price of imports. This interpretation is buttressed by the finding (see Pelzman and Martin, (1981) that the relative price has no statistical or economic significance in the output equation. The final equation is a loglinear labor demand function (in its short run version a part of a Nadiri-Rosen dynamic factor demand system). The arguments are output and factor prices.

Formally, the model used in this chapter may be written as three loglinear equations. The effect of terms other than import price, imports, or output is collapsed into the "constant" terms or disturbance terms, as will be explained. The import demand function is

$$\log Q = a' + \alpha' \log(P/H) + u', \tag{5}$$

where u' is a normal zero mean disturbance term, P is the domestic price of imports, and H is the price of domestic textiles. a' is a constant term and α' is the price elasticity. The inverse elasticity used below is the inverse of it. The output reduced form supply function is

$$\log Y = k' + \delta \log Q + e', \tag{6}$$

where k' is a constant term and e' is a normal zero mean disturbance term. The labor demand function is

$$\log L = b' + \gamma \log Y + v', \tag{7}$$

where v' is a normal zero mean disturbance term.

6.3.2 The Random Environment

The development of the constant and error terms used below is now readily described. The new constants a', k', and b' are calculated to yield the mean value of the LHS (left-hand side) variable when the RHS variable is set at its mean in (5)–(7). The new constant thus includes the effect of all other variables set at their mean value (in logs). The sample data are used to calculate "residuals" from the long run model, which is (5)–(7) expanded to include the other terms that are buried at their mean values under the constant terms. For example,

$$e' = \log Y + .26 \log Q - \beta \log z - k',$$

where $.26 = -\delta$, β is the vector of estimated long run coefficients, and $\log z$ is the vector of deviations from means of other variables in the long run output supply equation. Thus e' does not include sample variation in $\log z$. In effect, the policymaker is assumed to be able to forecast $\log z$ perfectly when evaluating trade instruments.[5]

The variance of e', v', and u' so generated is calculated. So is the variance of the foreign price P^*, needed in welfare and tax calculations. Covariances are also calculated. Correlation coefficients are low, however, and the t-statistics for testing the null hypothesis lie well below 2. Thus a "population" covariance matrix structure that is diagonal is used below, with the calculated variances on the diagonal.[6]

The structure of the simulation study faces a practical constraint that forces a choice of methods in dealing with randomness. Large sample methods (allowing for parameter and disturbance uncertainty) can in principle be used to compare the welfare effects of specific and *ad valorem* tariffs and fixed quotas subject to (2). On the other hand, it is infeasible to calculate the large sample state contingent instrument settings and their welfare effect (the number of first order conditions equals the number of "observations" plus one). Since comparison with the optimal instrument is very interesting, I chose to use small sample methods.

Repeated samples on disturbances of size 30 (selected arbitrarily as the sample size at which the *t*-distribution converges on the normal) are used. This also represents 7.5 years of the quarterly data, which may be an appropriate policy horizon. Draws for u', v', e', and P^* are generated by selections from the standard normal distribution. Use of repeated sampling gives an opportunity to examine the variability of the relative inefficiency measure as the sample shifts. (Large sample methods in principle could yield conclusions on this, but the problem of deriving variances appears intractable.) The results of section 6.4 indeed show substantial variation, but the qualitative results are preserved.

Besides e', v', u', and P^*, the other source of uncertainty facing the policymaker is in the elasticity parameters (the effect of constant term uncertainty is subsumed in the disturbance terms). Econometric modeling routinely yields a covariance structure for parameter estimates. The long run version of the model is nonlinear in the parameters of the short run model; hence its asymptotic elasticity covariance structure does not have a closed form solution in the covariance structure of the short run model parameters. This is awkward, but not impossible to handle with Taylor's series approximation. Its small sample distribution is, however, unknown. My crude alternative approach was to do a sensitivity analysis on the elasticity parameters. Standard errors provide convenient increments for the conduct of sensitivity analysis. The welfare effects of the various instruments are calculated for high and low values of the elasticities based on + or − one standard deviation for a representative sample. The ranking results turn out to be robust to parameter variation.

6.4 The Relative Inefficiency of Quotas: The Textile Case

The textile industry study reveals that in the base case of elasticities at their point estimates, quotas cost on average 30% more of base import expenditure than tariffs to achieve the same 10% increase in employment. The *ad valorem* tariff almost always is around 1–2% worse than the specific tariff, while the specific tariff is less than 5% worse than the (infeasible) state-contingent tariff or quota system. The conclusion is that the specific tariff is the preferred instrument, and is close enough to the optimal instrument so that further refinements are unnecessary.

A further feature of the comparison is that an accounting was made of the differences in variability of employment under the various instruments. These turned out to be trivial, swamped by a factor of thousands by the consumer's surplus effects, so they are not reported.[7]

The results are based on given parameters for the model (5)–(7) and drawings of random variables, u', e', P^*, and v'. Pelzman-Martin report point estimates of α, γ, and δ together with standard errors (of the short run elasticities, which are used here to calculate standard errors of the long run elasticities as if there were no error in estimation of the adjustment structure). $\alpha = -.33$ with a "standard error" of .212. $\gamma = .8$ with a "standard error" of .08. $\delta = -.26$ with "standard error" of .09. As they discuss, a low price elasticity of import demand is reasonable a priori for textiles. The low substitutability of imports for domestic production $(-.26)$ is also a priori reasonable in light of their generic difference: imports are predominantly natural fibers and domestic production is predominantly man-made fibers.

Welfare is given by substituting the inverse of (5) into (1):

$$w = E_s \left[\int_0^{Q(s)} ax^{1/\alpha} u(s)\, dx - P^*(s) Q(s) \right], \tag{8}$$

where $(1/\alpha)\log a = a'$, $(1/\alpha)\log u = u'$.

This is written

$$w = \begin{cases} \dfrac{\alpha}{1+\alpha} a E_s[u(s)Q(s)^{(1+\alpha)/\alpha}] - E[P^*(s)Q(s)] & \text{for } \alpha < -1 \\[2ex] N + \dfrac{\alpha}{1+\alpha} a E_s[u(s)Q(s)^{(1+\alpha)/\alpha}] - E[P^*(s)Q(s)] & \text{for } \alpha > -1, \end{cases} \tag{8'}$$

where N is a large positive number.

All trade instruments must meet the average employment constraint. For the quota case this is

$$E_s[bv(s)\,Y(s)^\gamma] = E_s[bv(s)\{ke(s)Q(s)^\delta\}^\gamma] = \bar{L}_0, \tag{9}$$

where $\log b = b'$, $\log k = k'$, $\log v = v'$, $\log e = e'$, and $\bar{Q}(s)$ is the lesser of $\bar{Q}$ and the import quantity implied by $P = P^*$. For the certainty equivalent fixed quota, (9) is solved assuming that the quota always binds. The minimum cost quota is the largest possible quota satisfying (9), which can be obtained with numerical methods.

For the optimal tariff/quota case, the first-order conditions are

$$aQ(s)^{1/\alpha}u(s) - P^*(s) = \mu(\delta\gamma bk^\gamma)v(s)e(s)^\gamma Q(s)^{\delta(\gamma-1)}, \tag{10}$$

and the constraint. (9) and (10) suffice with computational methods to determine the optimal $\{Q(s)\}$ and μ, the shadow price on the constraint.

For the tariff instrument, we have a specific and an *ad valorem* tax solution to the constraint. In the *ad valorem* case, the solution is obtained from

$$\underset{s}{E}[bv(s)\{ke(s)\{P^*(s)(1 + \tau)\}^{\alpha\delta}\{au(s)\}^{-\alpha\delta}\}^\gamma] = \overline{L}. \tag{9'}$$

This has a closed form solution in τ. The specific tax is obtained from

$$\underset{s}{E}[bv(s)\{ke(s)\{P^*(s) + t\}^{\alpha\delta}\{au(s)\}^{-\alpha\delta}\}^\gamma] = \overline{L}. \tag{9''}$$

This is readily evaluated with numerical methods. Welfare is evaluated in the tariff cases by substituting for $Q(s)$ in (8′) the appropriate import demand function of tax-inclusive price.

In all the cases where the numerical methods were used they were very well behaved in this study. In other simulations with made-up numbers, trouble is encountered occasionally with the optimal state-contingent calculations, but the other calculations were well behaved. This is encouraging, since nonlinear evaluation can be tricky.

Table 6.1 presents the results for the base case of elasticities at their point estimate values. A 10% increases in average (i.e., sample mean) employment is required via various import control instruments. The resulting consumer's surplus (net of taxes or rent) averages are calculated. The numbers in the table are percentages equal to the change in expected surplus over the unconstrained ("free trade") value as a proportion of "free trade" expenditure on imports.

The high percentages are due to the low substitutability of domestic and foreign textiles combined with the inelasticity of import demand. Protection is a very expensive method of raising employment in this case. The top left-hand number is the average of such numbers across the nine samples drawn, for the case of the certainty equivalent quota, CEQUO. The minimum cost quota, MCQUO, potentially differs from it when account is taken of the possibility that quotas do not always bind. In this study they were almost always the same. ADVALT is the *ad valorem* tariff label, SPECT is the specific tariff label, and OPTT is the optimal state

Table 6.1
Welfare losses as a fraction of expenditure

Variable name	Mean	Standard deviation	Variance	Minimum	Maximum
CEQUO	0.49122	0.44860E-01	0.20124E-02	0.42600	0.55700
MCQUO	0.49056	0.44032E-01	0.19388E-02	0.42600	0.55700
ADVALT	0.38292	0.35978E-03	0.12944E-06	0.38200	0.38330
SPECT	0.37867	0.24495E-02	0.60000E-05	0.37600	0.38400
OPTT	0.36700	0.51962E-02	0.27000E-04	0.35800	0.37200
RELCTQ	0.29733	0.11978	0.14348E-01	0.13298	0.48138
RELCTO	0.31929E-01	0.12455E-01	0.15512E-03	0.13477E-01	0.53073E-0

Table 6.2
Sensitivity of relative inefficiency to import price elasticity[a]

	$\alpha = -.5$	$\alpha = -.33$	$\alpha = -.125$
CEQUO	.265	.504	6.665
MCQUO	.265	.504	6.661
ADVALT	.214	.383	3.021
SPECT	.212	.379	2.993
OPTT	.208	.368	2.936

a. $\gamma = .8$, $\delta = -.26$, $\Delta L/L = .10$.

contingent tariff or quota label. The basic result of this study is that quotas do worse than tariffs, about 11% of base expenditure on imports worth (CEQUO or MCQUO minus SPECT or ADVALT). This is a very significant disadvantage. Another revealing way to scale the results is to find the ratio of the added inefficiency to the unavoidable loss due to the employment constraint. The results for RELCTQ show that on average the specific tariff is about 30% more efficient than the quota (the percent of base expenditure given up to protect employment is about 30% bigger with the quota). Across the nine samples these numbers range from 13 to 48%. In contrast, the *ad valorem* tariff is very close to the specific tariff on average, although it costs more in all but one of the nine draws. Both tariffs come within around 5% of the optimum, on average and in each case in the nine. RELCTO gives the inefficiency of the specific tariff relative to the optimal state contingent tariff schedule.

Tables 6.2, 6.3, and 6.4 present results on the sensitivity to changes in the elasticity values. The numbers reflect the same concept as in table 6.1: the change in expected surplus as a proportion of unconstrained expenditure on imports. They are calculated for one drawing of the nine, chosen because its results are closest to the overall mean for the base case. The import price elasticity is varied by one standard deviation upward and downward in table 6.2, with the other two elasticities at their point estimates. In table 6.3, the labor elasticity is varied. Here I varied it by more than two standard deviations to obtain sufficient variation to stress the model. Finally, in table 6.4 the output elasticity with respect to imports is varied one standard deviation upward and downward with the other elasticities at their point estimates.

The results show that the qualitative results are robust to the parameter variation. The qualitative results also hold for the implausible but interesting case of price elasticity greater than one, save that the *ad valorem* tariff is

Table 6.3
Sensitivity of relative inefficiency to elasticity of labor demand with respect to output[a]

	$\gamma = .6$	$\gamma = .8$	$\gamma = 1$
CEQUO	.907	.504	.333
MCQUO	.907	.504	.332
ADVALT	.740	.383	.234
SPECT	.733	.379	.232
OPTT	.715	.368	.2246

a. $\alpha = -.33$, $\delta = -.26$, $\Delta L/L = .10$.

Table 6.4
Sensitivity of relative inefficiency to elasticity of output with respect to imports[a]

	$\delta = -.17$	$\delta = -.26$	$\delta = -.35$
CEQUO	1.225	.504	.294
MCQUO	1.225	.504	.292
ADVALT	1.027	.383	.199
SPECT	1.019	.379	.197
OPTT	.996	.368	.190

a. $\alpha = -.33$, $\gamma = .8$, $\Delta L/L = .10$.

now slightly better than the specific. An exception to the relative inefficiency of the quota in principle could occur when the import demand
function becomes highly price inelastic. It appears from diagrammatic
reasoning that as $-\alpha$ goes to infinity, tariffs and quotas should eventually
converge in cost (at very large value). Also, in terms of the formulas for
dQ/ds in section 6.1, all policies converge on $dQ/ds = 0$ as the absolute
value of P_Q grows large. In table 6.2, instead, the quota becomes markedly
more inefficient. This property continues to hold in still more inelastic
ranges, but eventually the numerical welfare measures blow up. More
refinement in the evaluation programs would be needed to examine the
asymptotic behavior. A further factor to consider is that low absolute price
elasticities should be associated with larger absolute elasticities of output
with respect to imports. Common sense leads to this conclusion, buttressed
by the obvious identification problem with this elasticity noted previously.
The latter factor will substantially soften the tendency of cost to blow up.

    Save for the case of highly inelastic import demand, the relative in-
efficiency quantitative results are not very sensitive to the parameter
variation. In the lower range of α and in tables 6.3 and 6.4, the quota is

Table 6.5
The effect of higher labor targets and export restraints[a]

	Export mode, $\Delta L/L = .10$	Import mode, $\Delta L/L = .25$
CEQUO	2.633	3.548
MCQUO	2.633	3.548
ADVALT	2.251	3.116
SPECT	2.233	3.094
OPTT	2.172	3.023

a. $\alpha = -.33, \gamma = .8, \delta = -.26$.

20–50% more inefficient than the tariff, which is similar to the sample variation range. In tables 6.3 and 6.4, the welfare cost of employment increases falls as the sensitivity of employment to imports rises, as expected. The relative inefficiency of quotas rises as this sensitivity rises, which is not a result I fully expected. Some insight into the reason this happens is given by considering the optimal policy. The effect of δ and γ enters through the terms in l in equation (4). For the functional forms chosen, l is convex in Q and increasingly so as the parameters γ and δ increase in absolute value. This reduces the absolute value of the denominator of (4) (but fortunately never reverses its sign in the region of evaluation). For the functional form chosen, the numerator term in l is unaffected by changes in γ and δ. Thus the optimal policy increases in absolute slope. It may approach the fixed specific tariff policy, assuming it lies below it initially. The bottom two lines of tables 6.3 and 6.4 show this. So long as the tariff and the optimal policy have the same sign, the steeper slope of the optimal policy increases the advantage of the tariff over the quota, since the latter lies farther from the optimal policy. The discussion also makes clear that there is no reason to expect this property always to hold: with the optimal policy steeper than the tariff policy, increases in convexity of l in Q drive the optimum away from both fixed tariffs and fixed quotas.

Table 6.5 shows the results, for the same draw as tables 6.2–6.4, of increasing the required increases in average employment to 25% in the base case, and of switching to a "voluntary export control" mode. The relative inefficiency of quotas is reduced due to the very large inefficiency of all the interventions in table 6.5. Nevertheless, the inefficiency of quotas is still significant: the use of a VER rather than a voluntary export tax wastes a further 40% of base expenditure in the base case (table 6.5).

6.5 Conclusion

The results show that the relative efficiency of specific tariffs over quotas is quite robust for the textile industry. The welfare loss due to the use of quotas is too persistently large to dismiss as an irrelevant refinement. This is especially so because there is good reason to believe that the high level of aggregation of the study very seriously understates the relative inefficiency of quotas. The type of arbitrage efficiency that tariffs enjoy over quotas extends to dimensions of product type and country of origin (see Anderson, 1985a). In the present case these other arbitrage inefficiency sources will interact with the inefficient allocation of imports over states, an interaction that compounds the inefficiency of quotas.

The information requirements for the type of analysis done here are no greater than for the commercial policy evaluation studies already routinely done by the U.S. government. Therefore the method developed here should be widely, even routinely, emulated whenever there is an employment motive for protection. I shall provide the programs to interested parties. I expect that as more cases are studied, an overwhelming case for the relative inefficiency of quotas will develop.

Advocates of VERs claim that they have an advantage in transferring rent to foreign producers, providing compensation for the loss of markets. If this is truly compelling, it still would be significantly better to switch to "voluntary" export taxes. Foreign producers can presumably be compensated out of the tax revenues.

Future work should refine the method used here in two ways. First, most simply, the functional forms used should be further relaxed, especially to accommodate multiple commodities. Second, a serious attempt to deal with short run dynamics should be made along lines sketched in the notes to section 6.2. The usual unemployment argument for protection has validity only in the short run, and policy certainly has to deal with predictable short run dynamics. A treatment of time and uncertainty in a model of quotas also involves the further complication of license pricing. See Anderson (1985b) for an exploration of quota licenses priced as options.

Appendix 6.A: Proof of Propositions 1 and 2

Proof of Proposition 1   Form the Lagrangean function for maximization of (1) subject to (2),

$$\mathscr{L}(\{Q\}, \mu) \equiv \underset{s}{E} \int_0^{Q(s)} [P(v, s) - P^*(s)] \, dv - \mu \left[\bar{L} - \underset{s}{E} \int_0^{Q(s)} l_Q(v, s) \, dv \right]. \qquad (A.1)$$

Assume that the constraint binds for all admissible $\{Q\}$. Differences in μ do not then affect values of $\mathscr{L}$, and it can be set at a convenient value. Then the difference in welfare between a specific tariff respecting the constraint (with imports $\{Q^{\iota}(s)\}$) and the quota $\bar{Q}$ is

$$\Delta\mathscr{L} = E_s \int_{\bar{Q}}^{Q^{\iota}(s)} [P(v,s) - P^*(s) + \mu(v)l_Q(v,s)]\,dv$$

(A.2)

$$\geqslant E_s\{[P(Q^{\iota}(s),s) - P^*(s) + \mu^{\iota}l_Q(Q^{\iota}(s),s)][Q^{\iota}(s) - \bar{Q}]\}$$

using the second mean value theorem for a concave function, and $\mu^{\iota} =$ marginal cost of employment at the optimal specific tariff.

Then the RHS of (A.2) can be expanded to

$$\Delta\mathscr{L} \geqslant E[P - P^* + \mu^{\iota}l_Q E](Q^{\iota} - \bar{Q}) + \text{cov}(P - P^* + \mu^{\iota}l_Q, Q^{\iota}).$$ (A.3)

At the optimal specific tariff respecting the constraint, the first term of the RHS of (A.3) is zero. The covariance term is between two functions of s, and has the sign of the product of their first derivatives, if these are one-signed. Thus

$$\text{sign(cov)} = \text{sign}\left\{\left[P_s - P_s^* + \mu^{\iota}l_{Qs} + (P_Q + \mu^{\iota}l_{QQ})\frac{(-(P_s - P_s^*))}{P_Q}\right]\frac{(-(P_s - P_s^*))}{P_Q}\right\}$$

$$= \text{sign}\left\{\left(\frac{l_{Qs}}{P_s - P_s^*} - \frac{l_{QQ}}{P_Q}\right)\left(\mu^{\iota}\frac{(P_s - P_s^*)^2}{-P_Q}\right)\right\}.$$

The covariance is positive if

$$\frac{l_{Qs}}{P_s - P_s^*} - \frac{l_{QQ}}{P_Q} > 0.$$

Multiply through by $1/l_Q < 0$, and the condition is

$$\frac{l_{Qs}/l_Q}{P_s - P_s^*} - \frac{l_{QQ}/l_Q}{P_Q} < 0$$

on $\Delta\mathscr{L} \geqslant 0$ if

$$\frac{l_{QQ}/l_Q}{P_Q/(P - P^*)} > \frac{l_{Qs}/l_Q}{(P_s - P_s^*)/(P - P^*)}. \qquad \text{QED}$$

Proof of Proposition 2   From (A.1), the Lagrangean is $\mathscr{L} = E_s[h(Q(s), \mu, s)]$ and $h(\cdot)$ is concave in $Q(s)$. Welfare under the tariff minus welfare under the quota is the difference in $\mathscr{L}$ under the two regimes, $\{Q(s)\}$, and $\bar{Q}$ and is, by the second mean value theorem,

$$\Delta\mathscr{L} \leqslant E_s[h_Q(\bar{Q},s)[Q^{\iota}(s) - \bar{Q}]] = \text{cov}(h_Q, Q^{\iota} - \bar{Q}) + E[h_Q]E[Q^{\iota} - \bar{Q}].$$ (A.4)

Evaluating h_Q at $\bar{Q}$, note that the optimal setting for a fixed Q and μ for the fixed quota involves $E[h_Q] = 0$. (This is the first-order condition for a fixed quota.)

$dQ^*(s)/ds$ has the sign of $h_{Qs}(\bar{Q}, s)$; if this differs from the sign of $dQ^!/ds$, the covariance is negative. Then $\Delta\mathscr{L} \leqslant 0$.   QED

The Effect of a Nonbinding Quota

If the quota sometimes does not bind, then imports in a quota regime are $\bar{Q}(s) \leqslant \bar{Q}$, where $\bar{Q}(s) < \bar{Q}$ implies $P(\bar{Q}(s), s) = P^*(s)$. The proof of proposition 2 goes through simply substituting $\bar{Q}(s)$ for $\bar{Q}$, understanding that the optimal fixed quota $\bar{Q}$ induces a schedule $\bar{Q}(s)$.

The proof of proposition 1 proceeds with the same substitution through (A.2). The covariance term may be broken into conditional covariances based on a binding and a nonbinding regime. For the former, the analysis is as before, and the conditional covariance is positive under the same condition. For the latter, covariance is signed (under monotonicity) by

$$\left(\frac{l_{Qs}}{P_s - P_s^*} - \frac{l_{QQ}}{P_Q}\right)(P_s - P_s^*)(Q_s^! - \bar{Q}_s).$$

Evidently,

$$\bar{Q}_s = -\frac{P_s - P_s^*}{P_Q}$$

when the quota does not bind. For linear inverse demand, $Q_s^! - \bar{Q}_s = 0$. The evaluation of $Q_s^! - \bar{Q}_s$ is rather messy in general, so added sufficiency conditions are not offered. Based on the above, the influence of the nonbinding regime covariance should ordinarily be negligible. Then the unconditional covariance is positive and the rest of the proof goes through as before.

Appendix 6.B: Accounting for Employment Risk Aversion

The accounting is done using standard risk premium theory. Suppose that the wage is constant. Income is wL, and the variance of income facing workers is $w^2 \, \mathrm{var}(L)$. The percentage reduction in a certain income which equates it in utility to the uncertain income wL is given by

$$RP = 2\rho w^2 \, \mathrm{var}(L)/(wE(L))^2 = \rho \, \mathrm{var}(L)/2E(L)^2,$$

where ρ is the coefficient of relative risk aversion (see any standard treatment of risk premium theory). The equation can be used to evaluate changes in riskiness of labor income as a result of switches in policy. The percent of labor income implied can be compared to the percentage change in import expenditure as in comparisons below. The two can be made comparable by finding the ratio of labor income to import expenditure.

In the evaluation, a risk coefficient of 3 was used, based on Blume and Friend's finding for financial markets. The percent of labor income required to compensate workers for the riskier employment under the tariffs was always thousands of times smaller than the changes in surplus relative to import base expenditure.

In future work, a refinement of this accounting may be worthwhile. A full treatment of changes in the variation of labor income can be rigorously developed on the lines of section 6.1. Suppose that the constraint is to attain a target expected utility of labor income, where utility is a concave function of income, $U = [1/(1 - \rho)](wL)^{1-\rho}$. The coefficient of relative risk aversion, ρ, is a parameter. The optimal policy is defined by

$$P - P^* = -\lambda l_Q l^{-\rho}.$$

The optimal policy is characterized as in (4) by the comparative static derivative:

$$\frac{dQ^*}{ds} = -\frac{[(P_s - P_s^*)/(P - P^*)] - (l_{Qs}/l_Q) + \rho(l_s/l)}{[P_Q/(P - P^*)] - (l_{QQ}/l_Q) + \rho(l_Q/l)}. \tag{4'}$$

The empirical results assure that a refined accounting for the variation of labor income is unnecessary for the textile case, but obviously this need not always hold. (4') and proposition 2 reveal that quota dominance occurs when (i) the import margin and labor demand are negatively correlated and (ii) risk averse workers experience large relative variation of employment.

Research support from the Bureau of International Labor Affairs, U.S. Department of Labor, is gratefully acknowledged.

Notes

1. Anderson (1985a, chapter 3) has developed the closely related logic for the case where the dimension of heterogeneity is quality. An efficient tariff on cheese is calculated to be 31% less inefficient than a quota yielding the same aggregate quantity of cheese.

2. Let $\bar{w}$ = the fixed money wage. The competitive production structure of the economy implicitly solves

$$\max_{Y,L,Z} \{HY - \bar{w}L + r' \cdot Z \,|\, (Y, L, Z) \in T(Y, L, Z, K)\} = R(H, \bar{w}, r'),$$

with $R_H = Y(H, \bar{w}, r')$. Evidently, $R_{\bar{w}} = -L(H, \bar{w}, r')$.

3. That is, in comparing any two instruments such as $Q'(s)$, the quantity implied by a fixed tariff in state of nature s, and Q^0, a fixed quota, the average employment change $E[\Delta L]$ is identical due to the constraint. The change in expected welfare using $Q'(s)$ for all s less the change in welfare using Q^0 will be

$$\Delta w = \text{tariff welfare change} - \text{quota welfare change}$$

$$= E\left[\int_0^{Q'(s)} (P(x, s) - P^*(s)\,dx\right] - E\left[\int_0^{Q^0} (P(x, s) - P^*(s)\,dx\right]$$

$$+ \mu E[\Delta L] - \mu E[\Delta L],$$

where the second line equals zero. Thus employment changes are irrelevant for the choice of instrument. This assumes for simplicity that μ is constant over states, so that μ comes outside the expectations operator. A special Keynesian case is where all employment changes are evaluated with μ set at the fixed money wage rate; the opportunity cost of labor is always zero. More generally, μ could vary over states, and the quota and tariff would behave differently in arbitraging such differences. This is an unnecessary refinement to the present analysis.

4. A full treatment of dynamics and short run adjustment is an important topic for future research. It is crucial for sensible welfare evaluation to identify fully the lagged adjustment parameters in terms of a deeper underlying cost function. Most econometric work with time series models is sloppy in this regard (the Pelzman-Martin model is no exception). Until models are available in which the adjustment costs can be taken seriously, comparative statics may be the best method.

5. The alternative procedure would be to treat $\log z$ as random, to develop forecasting equations for these variables, and to use only the "unexplained" deviation from mean of $\log z$ in generating e', the composite error term. This is a superior procedure when the model is used to predict out-of-sample costs of trade policies. It is an unnecessary refinement for present purposes: evaluation of alternatives within sample, where the settings of $\log z$ are given, as in the classical econometrics model.

Future users of the techniques of this chapter will want to evaluate out of sample, and thus undoubtedly adopt the alternative procedure. It should be noted then that a further division of instruments can be made: those inflexible with respect to all changes and those inflexible only with respect to unpredictable changes. The latter will permit the analysis of policies that evolve as functions or forecast variables in a steady-state growth model, for example. New rankings are possible. Does a nonevolving tariff do better than a quota that evolves?

6. An alternative simulation with the point estimate covariance structure was done to see what difference it made. All qualitative results were the same. The relative inefficiency of quotas was somewhat greater.

7. See appendix 6.B.

References

Anderson, J. E. (1985a), "The Relative Inefficiency of Quotas: The Cheese Case," *American Economic Review*, 75, 178–190.

Anderson, J. E. (1985b), "Quotas as Options: Optimality and Quota License Pricing under Uncertainty," delivered to the 5th World Congress of the Econometric Society, Cambridge, August 1985.

Anderson, J. E., and L. Young (1982), "The Optimality of Tariff Quotas," *Journal of International Economics*, 13, 337–352.

Bhagwati, J. N., and T. N. Srinivasan (1983), *Lectures on International Trade*, Cambridge, MA: MIT Press.

Pelzman, J., and R. C. Martin (1981), "Direct Employment Effects of Increased Imports: A Case Study of the Textile Industry," *Southern Economic Journal*, 412–426.

Young, L., and J. E. Anderson (1980), "The Optimal Instruments for Restricting Trade under Uncertainty," *Review of Economic Studies*, 46, 927–932.

Young, L., and J. E. Anderson (1982), "Risk Aversion and Optimal Trade Restrictions under Uncertainty," *Review of Economic Studies*, 48, 291–305.

7

The Optimality of Tariff Quotas under Uncertainty

7.1 Introduction

Recently, Young and Anderson (1980, chapter 4) have examined the optimal policies for restricting trade under uncertainty. They obtained conditions under which the most common forms—the specific tariff and the *ad valorem* tariff—are optimal. However, trade restrictions often also take the form of tariff *schedules* in which the tariff rate depends on the quantity imported. A particularly common form is the *tariff quota* in which the tariff rate steps upward (perhaps from zero) when imports exceed a certain amount or value.[1,2] There are a number of rationales for this form of trade restriction. For example, the rights to export at the lower tariff rate can be allocated to developing countries to foster their industries.[3] Alternatively, such rights can be allocated to maintain customary trade flows for a time after the formation of a customs union, thereby easing the adjustment process.[4] In this chapter, however, we are concerned with the desirable properties of *unallocated* tariff quotas in the face of uncertainty about domestic demand and supply and about foreign supply conditions.

In section 7.2 we show that a specific tariff quota is the policy maximizing domestic expected surplus when the policymaker wishes to restrict not only the average level of imports but also the average amount by which imports exceed some critical level. This pair of constraints is a useful way of representing the policymaker's trade-off between the interests of producers and those of consumers and foreign exporters. Our analysis identifies the ways in which the tariff quota could be superior to both a fixed tariff and a fixed quota whenever such trade-offs are required.

Section 7.3 discusses the optimality of an *ad valorem* tariff quota in

Reprinted, with changes, by permission from *Journal of International Economics* (1982), 13, 337–351. © 1982 North-Holland Publishing Company.

similar terms. Section 7.4 extends the argument to the case of a large country and points out that if the representative domestic consumer is risk averse, then there is an additional role for tariff quotas in helping to buffer the domestic economy against exogenous income shocks.

7.2 Specific Tariff Quotas

In this section we suppose that the importing country is small and faces a world price $P^*(\theta)$ for the good in question. This price depends on θ, the random variable representing the state of the world. The domestic inverse excess demand function $P(Q, \theta)$ is assumed to be decreasing function of imports Q and also depends on θ. In state θ, domestic surplus from imports $Q(\theta)$ is

$$\int_0^{Q(\theta)} \{P(v, \theta) - P^*(\theta)\} \, dv.$$

We shall suppose that the objective function is domestic expected surplus, i.e., that the marginal utility of income of the representative consumer is constant. The implications of a nonconstant marginal utility of income will be discussed in section 7.4.

Any policy restricting trade is equivalent to a rule $Q(\theta)$ for determining the equilibrium quantity of imports in state θ. Young and Anderson (1980, chapter 4) showed that a fixed specific tariff is the policy maximizing domestic expected surplus subject to a ceiling q_1 on the average level of imports, i.e.,

$$E[Q(\theta)] \leq q_1. \tag{1}$$

Such a "noneconomic" constraint[5] is a way of representing the political concessions by the government to domestic producers who are damaged by imports. However, it is often reasonable to suppose that the *rate* of damage is low when imports are low but rises as imports increase. The interests of consumers and foreign exporters might then be better accommodated by permitting more imports on average but restricting the probability weight at the upper tail of the import distribution.

A simple way of representing this balance of interests is to suppose that the ceiling q_1 on average imports is set relatively high, but that a low ceiling q_2 is imposed on the average amount by which imports exceed the critical level Q_1 (at which domestic producers begin to "hurt"). Thus, we suppose that the government also imposes the constraint

$$E[\{Q(\theta) - Q_1\}^+] \leqslant q_2, \tag{2}$$

where $z^+ \equiv \max(z, 0)$. The importance of this apparently ad hoc representation is that the optimal trade restriction is then the commonly used specific tariff quota, i.e., a schedule of specific tariffs contingent upon the import level Q:

$$s(Q) = \begin{cases} s_1 & \text{if} \quad Q \leqslant Q_1 \\ s_2 & \text{if} \quad Q > Q_1, \end{cases} \tag{3}$$

where s_1 and s_2 are nonnegative constants.

THEOREM 1   The policy maximizing domestic expected surplus subject to constraints (1) and (2) is a specific tariff quota of the form (3) where $s_1 \leqslant s_2$.

Proof   The problem is to

$$\max_{\{Q(\theta)\}} E\left[\int_0^{Q(\theta)} \{P(v, \theta) - P^*(\theta)\}\, dv\right]$$

subject to

$$E[Q(\theta)] \leqslant q_1 \qquad \text{and} \qquad E[\{Q(\theta) - Q_1\}^+] \leqslant q_2.$$

The Lagrangean for this problem is

$$E\left[\int_0^{Q(\theta)} \{P(v, \theta) - P^*(\theta)\}\, dv - \lambda Q(\theta) - \mu\{Q(\theta) - Q_1\}^+\right] + \lambda q_1 + \mu q_2,$$

where λ and μ are the Lagrange multipliers corresponding to constraints (1) and (2), respectively. λ and μ satisfy the usual complementary slackness conditions:

$$\lambda(E[Q(\theta)] - q_1) = 0 = \mu(E[\{Q(\theta) - Q_1\}^+ - q_2). \tag{4}$$

We have

$$\frac{\partial}{\partial Q(\theta)} \int_0^{Q(\theta)} \{P(v, \theta) - P^*(\theta)\}\, dv = P(Q(\theta), \theta) - P^*(\theta),$$

$$\frac{\partial Q(\theta)}{\partial Q(\theta)} = 1,$$

and[6]

$$\frac{\partial \{Q(\theta) - Q_1\}^+}{\partial Q(\theta)} = \begin{cases} 0 & \text{if} \quad Q(\theta) \leqslant Q_1 \\ 1 & \text{if} \quad Q(\theta) > Q_1. \end{cases}$$

Therefore, the first-order conditions for the constrained maximization problem are

$$P(Q(\theta), \theta) - P^*(\theta) = \begin{cases} \lambda & \text{if} \quad Q(\theta) \leqslant Q_1 \\ \lambda + \mu & \text{if} \quad Q(\theta) > Q_1. \end{cases} \tag{5}$$

Suppose that the following schedule of specific tariffs is imposed:

$$s(Q) = \begin{cases} \lambda & \text{if} \quad Q \leqslant Q_1 \\ \lambda + \mu & \text{if} \quad Q > Q_1. \end{cases} \tag{6}$$

Then imports $Q(\theta)$ in state θ satisfy

$$P(Q(\theta), \theta) - P^*(\theta) = s(Q(\theta)). \tag{7}$$

Hence, the tariff schedule (6) ensures that $Q(\theta)$ always satisfies the first-order conditions (5).

Since the domestic excess demand function is downward-sloping, domestic surplus is a concave function of imports. Moreover, the constraint functions in (1) and (2) are convex functions of imports. Hence, the first-order conditions (5) are sufficient for a maximum.[7]   QED

By (4), if constraint (2) is not binding, then $\mu = 0$ and the optimal policy is a fixed specific tariff. On the other hand, if constraint (1) is not binding, then $\lambda = 0$. Thus, if the government is concerned not with average imports at all but only with average imports beyond the critical level Q_1, then a positive tariff should be imposed only beyond Q_1. This form of tariff quota is quite common.

An alternative interpretation of theorem 1 is possible in the case where

$$Q_1 = q_1.$$

If constraint (1) is binding, then constraint (2) can be written as

$$E[\{Q(\theta) - E[Q(\theta)]\}^+] \leqslant q_2.$$

Denoting the absolute value of z by $|z|$, we have

$$E[|Q(\theta) - E[Q(\theta)]|] = 2E[\{Q(\theta) - E[Q(\theta)]\}^+].$$

Hence, (2) is equivalent to the constraint

$$E[|Q(\theta) - E[Q(\theta)]|] \leqslant 2q_2, \tag{8}$$

i.e., to a ceiling on the mean absolute deviation of imports from their mean. Thus, theorem 1 shows that a specific tariff quota is optimal, given ceilings on the mean and on the mean absolute deviation of imports. Obviously, it is also optimal if a ceiling were placed on some weighted combination of the mean and the mean absolute deviation, with the weights preselected by the policymaker.

To bring out the intuition underlying theorem 1, let us suppose that any imports of the good require a license (called "type 1") and that any imports above the level Q_1 require an additional license (called "type 2"). Any policy $Q(\theta)$ satisfying constraints (1) and (2) is equivalent to an allocation of q_1 state-contingent type-1 licenses and q_2 state-contingent type-2 licenses. A specific tariff quota ensures that the rents on type-1 licenses are equal in all states where imports are less than Q_1 and that the sum of rents paid for the two types of licenses are equal in all states where imports exceed Q_1. Moreover, the two tariff levels in the schedule can be chosen so that the implicit rents on the two types of licenses reflect their marginal social value (λ and μ, respectively). Hence, a tariff quota can ensure optimal arbitrage of the licenses across states.

By contrast, under a fixed specific tariff, the sum of the rents paid for the relevant licenses are equal in all states, whether or not imports exceed Q_1. This would be optimal if only constraint (1) were binding. However, if constraint (2) were also binding, then the required specific tariff would lie between λ and $\lambda + \mu$. Hence, if imports are less than Q_1, the implicit rent on type-1 licenses would exceed their marginal social value, while if exports exceed Q_1, the implicit rents paid on the two licenses would be *less* than their marginal social value. It follows that, under a specific tariff, the average level of imports would be too low and there would not be sufficient incentive to restrict additional imports in states where imports tend to be high.

A fixed quota may actually be superior to a fixed specific tariff in achieving constraints (1) and (2). Young and Anderson (1980) show that for the same average restrictiveness the tariff dominates, but (2) could be satisfied by a fixed quota without restricting imports by as much on average. However, under a quota, a fixed number of the licenses are assigned to each state and their rents are determined by market equilibrium in that state alone. Hence, there remain welfare-improving arbitrage opportunities across states—opportunities that are exploited under a tariff quota.

The above discussion shows why the tariff quota is an attractive instrument even when the policymaker's objectives cannot be represented satisfactorily by constraints (1) and (2). Compared to a fixed tariff, it restricts more sharply the high import levels that are especially damaging to import-competing producers—without an excessive restriction of imports overall. Compared to a fixed quota, it encourages a shift of imports from states where their social value is low to states where it is high.

We can also derive the optimal form of trade restriction under alternative formulations of the government's concessions to import-competing producers. Constraint (2) implies that marginal increases of imports are regarded as equally damaging in all states, so long as the base level exceeds Q_1. To model a situation where the rate of damage rises continuously with the import level, we could replace (2) by a ceiling v on the variance of imports:

$$E[(Q(\theta) - E[Q(\theta)])^2 \leqslant v. \tag{9}$$

THEOREM 2   The policy that maximizes domestic expected surplus subject to constraints (1) and (9) is a schedule of specific tariffs that increases linearly with the level of imports. Thus

$$S(Q) = \lambda + 2\mu(Q - q_1). \tag{10}$$

Proof   See appendix 7.B.

Although there is no difficulty, in principle, in operating the optimal policy of theorem 2, administrative considerations might lead the government to approximate its effects using a tariff quota.

7.3 *Ad Valorem* Tariff Quotas

Young and Anderson (1980, chapter 4) showed that an *ad valorem* tariff is the policy maximizing domestic expected surplus subject to a ceiling on foreign exchange expenditure on the good:

$$E[P^*(\theta)Q(\theta)] \leqslant e_1. \tag{11}$$

Such a "noneconomic restraint" might be imposed when political considerations prevent adjustment of the exchange rate in face of a persistent payments deficit. However, if the real concern is with unusually large losses of foreign exchange, then the government might wish to restrict the probability weight at the upper tail of the expenditure distribution without tight restrictions on its mean. The former objective can be represented by a ceiling e_2 on the average amount by which expenditure exceeds the critical level E_1; i.e.,

$$E[\{P^*(\theta)Q(\theta) - E_1\}^+] = e_2. \tag{12}$$

Again, the interest of this representation is that the resulting optimal policy is the commonly observed *ad valorem* tariff quota.

THEOREM 3 The policy maximizing domestic expected surplus subject to constraints (11) and (12) is a schedule of *ad valorem* tariffs:

$$a(Q(\theta)) = \begin{cases} a_1 & \text{if} \quad P^*(\theta)Q(\theta) \leqslant E_1 \\ a_2 & \text{if} \quad P^*(\theta)Q(\theta) > E_1, \end{cases} \tag{13}$$

where a_1 and a_2 are nonnegative constants and $a_1 \leqslant a_2$.

Proof See appendix 7.B.

Schedule (3) is a first approximation to the case where increasing weight is placed on larger deviations from E_1 due to rising borrowing costs. The latter would call for more steps in the tariff schedule. Almost trivially, (12) could be replaced by an expenditure variance constraint analogous to (9), implying a linear *ad valorem* tariff schedule as a function of expenditure.

Each item in the discussion on theorem 1 has an analogue here: if constraint (12) is not binding, then the optimal policy is a fixed *ad valorem* tariff; if constraint (11) is not binding, then there should be a positive *ad valorem* tariff only when foreign exchange expenditure exceeds E_1; if $e_1 = E_1$, then constraint (12) can be replaced by a ceiling on the mean absolute deviation of expenditure from its mean; there is an obvious analogue of theorem 2 concerning the optimal policy given constraints on the mean and the variance of the expenditure distribution; finally, the optimal policy in theorem 3 can be interpreted as ensuring optimal arbitrage of the two types of state-contingent *foreign exchange* licenses corresponding to the two constraints. This last interpretation brings out the similarity between the optimal policy here and some multiple exchange rate schemes.

The optimal policy in theorem 3 involves a higher *ad valorem* tariff rate when import expenditure exceeds a certain *value*. Such "qualitative" *ad valorem* tariff quotas exist but often the higher tariff rate is applied when imports exceed a specified *quantity*, i.e. the *ad valorem* tariff schedule has the form

$$a(Q) = \begin{cases} a_1 & \text{if} \quad Q \leqslant Q_1 \\ a_2 & \text{if} \quad Q > Q_1, \end{cases} \tag{14}$$

where Q_1, a_1, and a_2 are nonnegative constants. We shall identify some important cases where the optimal policy in theorem 3 reduces to this form.

THEOREM 4   Suppose that either (a) there is uncertainty only about domestic demand or (b) there is uncertainty only about the world price and the demand elasticity always exceeds 1. Then the policy maximizing domestic expected surplus subject to constraints (11) and (12) is an *ad valorem* tariff quota of the form (14) with $a_1 \leqslant a_2$.

Proof   See appendix 7.B.

The intuition behind theorem 4(b) is that if demand is elastic, then, under an optimal policy, high import expenditure is associated with low domestic and world prices and hence with high imports. In order to prevent excessive weight at the upper tail of the expenditure distribution it is then necessary to raise the *ad valorem* tariff rate when imports are high. However, if demand is *inelastic*, then, under an optimal policy, high import expenditure is associated with *high* domestic and world prices and hence with *low* imports. We therefore have the unexpected result that the higher tariff rate should be imposed when imports are low.

THEOREM 5   Suppose that there is uncertainty only about the world price and that the demand elasticity is always less than 1. Then the policy maximizing domestic expected surplus to constraints (11) and (12) is an *ad valorem* tariff quota:

$$a(Q) = \begin{cases} a_1 & \text{if} \quad Q < Q_1 \\ a_2 & \text{if} \quad Q \geqslant Q_1. \end{cases} \tag{15}$$

where Q_1, a_1, and a_2 are nonnegative constants and $a_1 \geqslant a_2$.

Proof   See appendix 7.B.

If the domestic demand elasticity exceeds unity over one range of imports and is less than unity over another range (as with a linear demand function), then, under an optimal policy, the set of imports whose foreign exchange cost is less than E_1 need not comprise a connected interval. The optimal policy could involve a low *ad valorem* tariff rate when imports are very low or very high but a high tariff rate for intermediate levels of imports.

The above analysis also shows that if there is uncertainty in both demand and supply, then a tariff quota in which the tariff rate depends on the *quantity* of imports would generally fail to ensure that the first-order conditions behind theorem 3 are satisfied [see equations (B.2a) and (B.2b) in appendix B, which yield (15)]. It would be necessary to set the tariff rate according to the *value* of imports.

7.4 Extensions

The above analysis can readily be extended to the case where the importing country is large and the world price of the good depends on the quantity imported as well as on θ:

$$P^* = P^*(Q, \theta).$$

We shall only sketch the results: the proofs are an obvious amalgam of the arguments above and those in Young and Anderson (1980, chapter 4) and Young (1980). Theorems 1 and 2 remain valid for a large country if we take the objective function to be world expected surplus:

$$E\left[\int_0^{Q(\theta)} \{P(v, \theta) - P^*(v, \theta)\} \, dv\right].$$

However, theorems 3, 4, and 5 would be valid for this objective function only if the inverse supply function has constant elasticity with respect to imports. If the desired objective function is *domestic* expected surplus,

$$E\left[\int_0^{Q(\theta)} \{P(v, \theta) - P^*(Q(\theta), \theta)\} \, dv\right],$$

then the optimal policies are tariff schedules that are essentially those derived above plus an Edgeworth-Bickerdike "optimal tariff" designed to exploit the importing country's monopoly power.[8]

To examine the implications of a nonconstant marginal utility of income, let the objective function be the expected value of the representative consumer's indirect utility function $V(P, I)$, where P is the price of the imported good in terms of the exportable and I is total production revenue plus tariff revenue. It can be shown[9] that the first-order condition for a maximum of $E[V(P, I)]$ subject to constraints (1) and (2) is

$$\{P(Q(\theta), \theta) - P^*(\theta)\} \frac{\partial V}{\partial I} = \begin{cases} \lambda & \text{if} \quad Q(\theta) \leqslant Q_1 \\ \lambda + \mu & \text{if} \quad Q(\theta) > Q_1. \end{cases}$$

Hence, optimal arbitrage of the two types of import licenses must now take account of the variation in the marginal utility of income $\partial V/\partial I$. In effect, the optimal trade restriction must be modified to buffer the domestic economy against the income changes resulting from random domestic and foreign shocks. This consideration implies that, although a tariff quota will no longer be optimal, it can be superior to both a pure tariff and a pure quota, even in the absence of a constraint like (2).

For example, if the world price fluctuates, then it would be desirable to lower the tariff rate when imports are low in order to augment the country's "gains from trade" in states where it is being impoverished by a rise in the world price. On the other hand, if domestic production suffers random shocks (such as weather) then it would be desirable to lower the tariff rate when imports are *high* in order to augment the country's "gains from trade" in states where it is being impoverished by a reduction in domestic production. A detailed analysis of these questions is beyond the scope of this chapter, but the above discussion at least indicates how the additional degree of freedom available in tariff quotas can be exploited to meet a number of policy objectives.

Appendix 7.A

We shall show that the first-order conditions (3) and the complementary slackness conditions (4) are sufficient for a constrained maximum in theorem 1. The Kuhn–Tucker theorem cannot be invoked because the constraint function $\{Q(\theta) - Q_1\}^+$ is not differentiable everywhere and because there could be an infinity of states θ and hence an infinity of decision variables $Q(\theta)$.

In state θ, let $Q^0(\theta)$ be imports under the policy defined by (3) and (4) and let $Q(\theta)$ be imports under any other policy which satisfies constraints (1) and (2). Domestic surplus under $Q^0(\theta)$ exceeds that under $Q(\theta)$ by

$$\Delta(\theta) \equiv \int_{Q(\theta)}^{Q^0(\theta)} \{P(v, \theta) - P^*(\theta)\}\, dv.$$

Since $P(Q, \theta)$ is decreasing in Q, the second mean value theorem implies that

$$\Delta(\theta) \geqslant \{P(Q^0(\theta), \theta) - P^*(\theta)\}\{Q^0(\theta) - Q(\theta)\}.$$

By (3),

$$\Delta(\theta) \geqslant \begin{cases} \lambda\{Q^0(\theta) - Q(\theta)\} & \text{if} \quad Q(\theta) \leqslant Q_1 \\ (\lambda + \mu)\{Q^0(\theta) - Q(\theta)\} & \text{if} \quad Q(\theta) > Q_1. \end{cases} \tag{A.1}$$

But

$$Q^0(\theta) > Q_1 \quad \text{implies} \quad Q^0(\theta) - Q(\theta)$$
$$\geqslant \{Q^0(\theta) - Q_1\}^+ - \{Q(\theta) - Q_1\}^+. \tag{A.2}$$

This obviously holds if $Q(\theta) \geqslant Q_1$, while if $Q(\theta) < Q_1$, then

$$\{Q(\theta) - Q_1\}^+ > Q(\theta) - Q_1,$$

so again (A.2) holds. Moreover,

$$E[\{Q^0(\theta) - Q(\theta)\}^+ | Q^0(\theta) > Q_1] - E[\{Q(\theta) - Q_1\}^+ | Q^0(\theta) > Q_1]$$
$$\geqslant E[\{Q^0(\theta) - Q_1\}^+] - E[\{Q(\theta) - Q_1\}^+]. \tag{A.3}$$

By (A.1), (A.2), and (A.3),

$$E[\Delta(\theta)] \geqslant \lambda E[Q^0(\theta) - Q(\theta)] + \mu(E[\{Q^0(\theta) - Q_1\}^+]$$
$$- E[\{Q(\theta) - Q_1\}^+]).$$

Since $Q^0(\theta)$ satisfies the complementary slackness conditions (4),

$$E[\Delta(\theta)] \geqslant \lambda(q_1 - E[Q(\theta)]) + \mu(q_2 - E[\{Q(\theta) - Q_1\}^+]).$$

Since $Q(\theta)$ satisfies the constraints (1) and (2),

$$E[\Delta(\theta)] \geqslant 0.$$

Hence, $Q^0(\theta)$ is indeed the optimal policy. For all the other theorems, the proof that the first-order conditions and the complementary slackness conditions are sufficient for optimality is similar.

Appendix 7.B

Proof of Theorem 2   The Lagrangean of the constrained maximization problem of theorem 2 is

$$E\left[\int_0^{Q(\theta)} \{P(v, \theta) - P^*(\theta)\}\, dv - \lambda Q(\theta) - \mu\{Q(\theta) - E[Q(\theta)]\}^2 \right] + \lambda q_1 + \mu v,$$

where λ and μ are the Lagrange multipliers corresponding to constraints (1) and (9). Hence, the first-order condition is

$$P(Q(\theta), \theta) - P^*(\theta) = \lambda + 2\mu\{Q(\theta) - E[Q(\theta)]\}. \tag{B.1}$$

This condition is satisfied if the following linear schedule of specific tariffs is imposed:

$$s(Q) = \lambda + 2\mu(Q - q_1).$$

The first-order condition is sufficient for a maximum because the objective function is concave and the constraint functions are convex in Q.   QED

Proof of Theorem 3   An argument like that in theorem 1 shows that the first-order conditions of the constrained maximization problem are

$$P(Q(\theta), \theta) - P^*(\theta) = \begin{cases} \lambda P^*(\theta) & \text{if } P^*(\theta)Q(\theta) \leqslant E_1 & \text{(B.2a)} \\ (\lambda + \mu)P^*(\theta) & \text{if } P^*(\theta)Q(\theta) > E_1, & \text{(B.2b)} \end{cases}$$

where λ and μ are the Lagrange multipliers associated with constraints (11) and (12), respectively. These first-order conditions will be satisfied if the schedule (13) of *ad valorem* tariffs is imposed with $a_1 = \lambda$ and $a_2 = \lambda + \mu$. The first-order conditions are sufficient for a maximum since the objective function is concave and the constraint functions are convex in Q.   QED

Proof of Theorem 4   In case (a) the world price is fixed at some level P^* and the conclusion follows from theorem 3 with

$$Q_1 = E_1/P^*.$$

In case (b) let $Q^0(\theta)$ be the optimal level of imports in state θ, let θ_1 be defined implicitly by

$$P^*(\theta_1)Q^0(\theta_1) = E_1, \tag{B.3}$$

and let

$$Q_1 \equiv Q^0(\theta_1). \tag{B.4}$$

We shall show that

$$Q^0(\theta) \gtreqless \qquad \text{implies} \quad P^*(\theta)Q^0(\theta) \gtreqless E_1. \tag{B.5}$$

Since $\lambda \geqslant 0$, (B.3) and (B.4) imply that

$$P^*(\theta)Q^0(\theta) \leqslant E_1 \qquad \text{implies} \quad (1 + \lambda)P^*(\theta)Q^0(\theta)$$
$$\leqslant (1 + \lambda)P^*(\theta_1)Q_1. \tag{B.6}$$

Combining this with the first-order condition (B.2a) yields

$$P^*(\theta)Q^0(\theta) \leqslant E_1 \qquad \text{implies} \quad P(Q^0(\theta), \theta)Q^0(\theta)$$
$$\leqslant P(Q_1, \theta_1)Q_1. \tag{B.7}$$

We assumed that $P(Q, \theta)$ is independent of θ and that the demand elasticity always exceeds 1, so

$$P(Q^0(\theta), \theta)Q^0(\theta) \leqslant P(Q_1, \theta_1)Q_1 \qquad \text{implies} \quad Q^0(\theta) \leqslant Q_1. \tag{B.8}$$

By (B.7) and (B.8),

$$P^*(\theta)Q^0(\theta) \leqslant E_1 \qquad \text{implies} \quad Q^0(\theta) \leqslant Q_1. \tag{B.9}$$

Therefore

$$Q^0(\theta) > Q_1 \qquad \text{implies} \quad P^*(\theta)Q^0(\theta) > E_1. \tag{B.10}$$

Since $\lambda \geqslant 0$ and $\mu \geqslant 0$, (B.3) and (B.4) imply that

$$P^*(\theta)Q^0(\theta) > E_1 \qquad \text{implies} \quad (1 + \lambda + \mu)P^*(\theta)Q(\theta)$$
$$> (1 + \lambda)P^*(\theta_1)Q_1. \tag{B.11}$$

Combining this with the first-order conditions (B.2a) and (B.2b) yields

$$P^*(\theta)Q^0(\theta) > E_1 \qquad \text{implies} \quad P(Q^0(\theta), \theta)Q^0(\theta)$$
$$> P(Q_1, \theta_1)Q_1. \tag{B.12}$$

We assumed that $P(Q, \theta)$ is independent of θ and that the demand elasticity is always greater than 1, so

$$P(Q^0(\theta), \theta)Q^0(\theta) > P(Q_1, \theta_1)Q_1 \qquad \text{implies} \quad Q^0(\theta) > Q_1. \qquad (B.13)$$

By (B.12) and (B.13)

$$P^*(\theta)Q^0(\theta) > E_1 \qquad \text{implies} \quad Q^0(\theta) > Q_1. \qquad (B.14)$$

Therefore

$$Q^0(\theta) \leqslant Q_1 \qquad \text{implies} \quad P^*(\theta)Q^0(\theta) \leqslant E_1. \qquad (B.15)$$

(B.10) and (B.15) imply that the first-order conditions (B.2a) and (B.2b) are equivalent to the conditions

$$P(Q(\theta), \theta) - P^*(\theta) = \begin{cases} \lambda P^*(\theta) & \text{if} \quad Q(\theta) \leqslant Q_1 \\ (\lambda + \mu)P^*(\theta) & \text{if} \quad Q(\theta) > Q_1. \end{cases}$$

These conditions will be satisfied if the *ad valorem* tariff quota (14) is imposed with $a_1 = \lambda$ and $a_2 = \lambda + \mu$.   QED

Proof of Theorem 5   Define Q_1 as in (B.4). If the import demand function is deterministic and always has elasticity less than 1, then

$$P(Q^0(\theta), \theta)Q^0(\theta) \lessgtr P(Q_1, \theta)Q_1 \qquad \text{implies} \quad Q^0(\theta) \gtrless Q_1. \qquad (B.16)$$

This means that the inequalities in the conclusions on (B.9) and (B.13) must be reversed and that instead of (B.10) and (B.14) we have

$$Q^0(\theta) < Q_1 \qquad \text{implies} \quad P^*(\theta)Q^0(\theta) > E_1, \qquad (B.17)$$

$$Q^0(\theta) \geqslant Q_1 \qquad \text{implies} \quad P^*(\theta)Q^0(\theta) \leqslant E_1. \qquad (B.18)$$

(B.17) and (B.18) imply that the first-order conditions (B.2a) and (B.2b) are equivalent to the conditions

$$P(Q(\theta), \theta) - P^*(\theta) = \begin{cases} \lambda P^*(\theta) & \text{if} \quad Q(\theta) \geqslant Q_1 \\ (\lambda + \mu)P^*(\theta) & \text{if} \quad Q(\theta) < Q_1. \end{cases}$$

These conditions will be satisfied if the *ad valorem* tariff quota (15) is imposed with $a_1 = \lambda + \mu$ and $a_2 = \lambda$.   QED

Notes

1. These are sufficiently common to warrant a book-length treatment by Rom (1979), from whom the subsequent examples are taken. In his analytical section (chapter 6) Rom does not treat the questions raised here but concentrates on comparing specific tariff quotas, *ad valorem* tariff quotas, fixed tariffs, and quotas on quantity and on value in terms of their effects on prices and on quantities imported.

2. The higher tariff rate is sometimes levied when imports exceed a certain percentage of domestic production, e.g., the former U.S. tariff quota on woollen and worsted products (Rom, 1979, pp. 107–114). Our analysis can easily be modified to derive the conditions under which this form of tariff quota is optimal.

3. E.g., the tariff quota granted by Australia to developing countries (Rom, 1979, pp. 178–186).

4. E.g., in the Benelux customs union (Rom, 1979, p. 7). Other rationales are listed in Rom (1979, pp. 5–11).

5. Bhagwati and Srinivasan (1969).

6. Appendix 7.A confirms that the correct first-order conditions are obtained if the derivative of $\{Q(\theta) - Q_1\}^+$ at $Q(\theta) = Q_1$ is interpreted as the left derivative.

7. The formal proof is given in appendix 7.A.

8. Young (1980, p. 429) shows that if there is multiplicative uncertainty in the foreign supply function, then this "optimal tariff" is a deterministic schedule of tariffs depending only on the world price. If the supply function is linear or constant elastic, then this schedule is a mixture of specific and *ad valorem* tariffs.

9. The proof is similar to that in Young and Anderson (1981, chapter 9).

References

Bhagwati, J. N. and T. N. Srinivasan (1969), "Optimal Intervention to Achieve Non-Economic Objectives," *Review of Economic Studies*, 36, 27–38.

Rom, M. (1979), *The Role of Tariff Quotas in Commercial Policy*, London: Macmillan.

Young, L. (1980), "Optimal Revenue-Raising Trade Restrictions under Uncertainty," *Journal of International Economics*, 10, 425–440.

Young, L., and J. E. Anderson (1980), "The Optimal Policies for Restricting Trade under Uncertainty," *Review of Economic Studies*, 46, 927–932.

Young, L., and J. E. Anderson (1981), "Risk Aversion and Optimal Trade Restrictions," University of Canterbury, mimeo.

8

Optimal Commercial Policy with Price Supports

It is common for agricultural product markets to have price floors. The floor is maintained by government purchases when necessary, possibly balanced by sales in above-limit periods. An important adjunct of support policies is an accompanying commercial policy designed to avoid excessive purchases that would in effect maintain the price floor for foreign farmers.

A combination of import quotas or taxes and export subsidies is used, depending on circumstances. The EC (European Community) has variable levies on imports (a tax that equates the tax inclusive price of imports with the support price), and export subsidies. The United States has imposed occasional import quotas on meat, occasional export subsidies (e.g., on dairy products shipped to New Zealand in 1981), and cheese import quotas with a "price break": foreign cheese selling below the support price is restricted. The effect of these measures is to reduce the positive correlation normally expected between prices in traded goods markets. Indeed, the use of some of these measures could even induce negative correlation.

This chapter attempts to gain insight into the structure of such policies by considering the optimal trade and buffer policy in a simple model. It abstracts from some potentially significant features of price stabilization that have received attention in the recent literature, but it will be argued that the qualitative results are robust with respect to this simplification.

It will also abstract from the foreign repercussions of such policies by imposing the small country assumption. For a large country the omitted interaction effects can be very important, as the recent U.S.-EC confrontation over wine and cheese versus grain illustrates. Consideration of strategic trade policy in conjunction with stabilization motives is best deferred to a later paper.

Optimality requires a buffer policy targeted to the goal of stabilization. Commercial policy is a pleasingly simple and feasible combination of fixed specific and *ad valorem* components designed to respect optimally the constraints on the buffer agency. Remarkably, it requires that foreign and domestic prices become perfectly negatively correlated. It can involve either import or export taxation or subsidization, or switches in regime, depending on the state of domestic or foreign conditions. The optimal policy thus helps make sense of the confusing variety of real-world policies, while suggesting modifications that would improve efficiency. Also, the bizarre implications of the optimal policy indicate the great cost of raising farm income via a price floor. Furthermore, it is shown below that a rise in the floor need not improve farmers' average income.

A closely related set of policies is encountered in Eastern European economies that maintain ceiling prices for basic foodstuffs and combine storage and trade instruments. The study of optimal policies is again instructive. Formally, the only difference in the problem facing planners is the direction of the inequality constraint on domestic price. The "Soviet" case adds an average self-sufficiency constraint. The model below is easily reinterpreted to cover this case.

The structure of optimal commercial policy in the presence of buffering is of some theoretical interest apart from its application to agriculture. In the absence of storage costs, buffering and trade appear at first sight to be perfect substitutes (see Pelcovits, 1979, for example). If so, a proper commercial policy could completely evade the real-world cost of storage. It would thus dominate present mixed policies. This chapter will show that trade policy and buffer policy are not perfect substitutes in the absence of storage costs. They are perfect substitutes in meeting the price floor constraint, of course, but not in the objective function or other constraints. Pelcovits's (1979) result follows from the assumption that the price floor is also a price ceiling, so that complete stabilization is required. More generally, buffer policy can arbitrage across states (for the set of states where the price floor does not bind). Thus in a model of costless storage there is a natural dominance of buffer policy for stabilization purposes. In models with costly storage and a more complex set of dynamic feasibility constraints, this advantage can disappear (see Newbery and Stiglitz, 1981).

It is also interesting to see whether buffering and trade are substitutes in the weaker sense of correlation. It turns out that the two policies may or may not be substitutes in the sense of correlation: optimal stock sales and imports need not be negatively correlated. In one important special case they can be shown to be perfectly negatively correlated.

Section 8.1 sets out the basic model. Section 8.2 develops the optimal commercial-cum-buffer policy and its properties. Section 8.3 considers some "third-best" commercial policies such as fixed quotas and tariffs, and variable levies. Rankings are usually possible. Theorem 5 gives plausible circumstances in which quotas can dominate tariffs, which is significant because recent work has suggested the practical dominance of tariffs. Section 8.4 goes behind the price floor constraint to consider the relation of producer welfare to the floor. Conditions are presented in which producers could lose from rises in the floor. Section 8.5 provides some concluding comments and suggestions for further work, particularly in policy analysis.

8.1 The Model

The analysis is based on a partial equilibrium competitive model of a small economy. Welfare is based on a representative consumer, in keeping with the standard base case of commercial policy analysis. All activities of the government other than buffer and trade policy in the supported good occur offstage, including any tax-and-transfer policies necessary to validate the representative consumer structure. This is the usual simplification, with well-known dangers.

Buffering and the accompanying commercial policy are inherently dynamic activities. Nevertheless, with no private decisions made in advance of knowing the state, the dynamic aspects of the problem are inessential and all qualitative results may be developed in a simpler static model (see appendix 8.B for a proof). That is the strategy of this chapter.

In what follows, the reader can always interpret the government planner's problem as one of selecting the present level of trade and buffer purchases given the present state of nature, incorporating the expected future impact of these decisions on the constraints.

The potentially most troublesome assumption is that production choice is made after the state is known, abstracting from the ex ante commitment problem of farmers. This makes no difference to the qualitative results so long as production choice is optimally made. Nonoptimal choice introduces new elements but the factors isolated in this chapter continue to play a part (see section 8.2). Thus it makes sense to focus on them initially.

The welfare measure is expected surplus, which may be justified by assuming that securities markets exist that permit smoothing real income over states to occur in the background. Thus the marginal utility of income is maintained offstage (see Young and Anderson, 1982, chapter 9, for the effect of relaxing this assumption). For a single agricultural product in a diversified developed economy, such an assumption is reasonably innocuous.

A single homogeneous product is supplied from trade, Q (positive for import and negative for export), production, Y, and sales from stock, $-B$ (where B has either sign, positive for purchases and negative for sales). All activities potentially occur in each state of nature s; where necessary for clarity the state is specified as in $Q(s)$. Buffering activity is assumed to have a fixed cost sufficient to deter private action, but zero marginal cost. This is a simplifying assumption with some realism: private buffering is quite limited.

Under these assumptions, appendix 8.A shows that the objective function may be reduced to the expectation over s of

$$w(s) = K(s) + \int_0^{Q(s)-B(s)} p(v, s)\, dv - P^*(s)Q(s). \tag{5}$$

In (5), $p(Q(s) - B(s), s)$ is the inverse excess demand function. $P = p(\cdot)$ is the domestic price. $P^*(s)$ is the foreign price. $K(s)$ is a constant with respect to Q and B. The separate influence of Y has disappeared in (5) via the constraint that marginal production cost = domestic price.

The main constraint is a price floor:

$$p(Q(s) - B(s), s) \geqslant \overline{P}. \tag{6}$$

These are common in agriculture. Section 8.4 considers whether it is in producers' interests.

The model is completed by two more constraints on the buffer agency. The buffer agency must first of all meet a basic feasibility constraint: it cannot sell what it does not hold. This leads to inessential complications in a dynamic model. To make this simple in a static framework, assume that feasibility is guaranteed by

$$E[B(s)] \geqslant 0; \tag{7}$$

the average of purchases is nonnegative. The constraint maintains the expected value of an assumed initial stock. If it is large enough, this will ensure feasibility over some considerable time. The dynamic structure of the buffer stock, as is well known, follows a random walk. A large enough initial stock will guarantee that the policies satisfying (7) will not be infeasible save in highly discounted low probability states and times. Thus the analyst can reasonably neglect them in studying commercial policy. With only constraint (7), the optimal policy is to stabilize world price at the minimum foreign price by buying up an infinite amount at that price and reselling it at an (incipiently) higher price. Free trade is the accompanying commercial policy.

The second constraint imposed on the buffer agency is more ad hoc. Realistically, some restraint is placed on the size of support purchases. On the other hand, governments do appear to tolerate large fluctuations in such budgets, stabilization being indeed one of the objectives of support policy. In a dynamic model, this might be expressed as a limit on the amount by which buffering reduces the net worth (capitalization) of the fund, while permitting it to borrow subject to the constraint. This can then be compressed into a static version as a constraint on average expenditures on support:

$$E[PB] \leqslant G. \tag{8}$$

The problems with the expenditure constraint (8) deserve discussion. First, it imposes no constraint on trade revenue, $E[(P - P^*)Q]$. This appears realistic for many countries, and reflects the fact that agricultural export subsidies do not break budgets like support payments, while import tax revenues are a trivial fraction of total revenue. Nevertheless, there is an asymmetry with (8). It is a routine matter to extend the model to include a constraint on trade revenue.

Second, constraint (8) coexists uncomfortably with the assumed off-stage nature of other tax-and-transfer government activities. It can be rationalized as an imperfect recognition of the costs of raising government revenue, while at the same time the agricultural product in question is too small to alter these costs in a systematic fashion. A full analysis involves Ramsey pricing of a type both familiar to theorists and remote from the way agricultural policy is ever likely to be set.

Finally, consider the structure of the programming problem. In what follows, the expectation over s of $w(s)$ will be maximized with respect to the set of control variable settings $Q(s)$ and $B(s)$. Note that in (5), w is concave in Q and B and $p_Q < 0$. So long as the feasible set [defined by (6)–(8)] to which they are constrained is convex, a unique global optimum is assured. The constraints are in fact such that this need not always be so, but the analysis of the chapter is based only on finding a local maximum. This is usually possible, in the sense that the second-order conditions at an interior solution do not appear inconsistent with any of the other requirements of the optimum. In what follows, the second-order conditions are assumed.

8.2 Optimal Policy

This section develops the optimal commercial and buffer stock policies to maximize the expectation of (5) subject to the price floor (6) and the constraints (7) and (8) on the operation of the buffer policy. The optimal structure turns out to have an appealing specialization of function: buffer policy is dedicated to arbitrage over states and to meeting the price floor, and commercial policy is dedicated to optimizing the constraints on the buffer agency. Surprisingly, this leads to a tariff schedule with a fixed specific and fixed *ad valorem* component. It is thus feasible in the sense that it could be set in advance of knowing the state.

The planner's solution to the program is a set of contingent quotas $Q(s)$ and a set of contingent buffer stock purchases $B(s)$, the latter at contingent price $p(Q(s) - B(s), s)$. The first-order conditions characterize the optimum under the assumed second-order conditions. Then optimal policy satisfies

$$P - P^* + \tilde{\lambda}(s)p_Q - \mu p_Q B = 0 \qquad (Q(s)), \tag{9}$$

$$-P - \tilde{\lambda}(s)p_Q + \mu p_Q B - \mu P + \beta = 0 \qquad (B(s)), \tag{10}$$

where $\tilde{\lambda}(s) = \lambda(s)/\text{prob}(s)$, $\text{prob}(s) = $ probability of state s, $\lambda(s)$ is the Lagrange multiplier on the price floor constraint in state s, β is the Lagrange multiplier on the expected stock-out constraint (7), and μ is the Lagrange multiplier on the expenditure constraint (8). The Lagrange multipliers are nonnegative, and their product times the constraints equals 0.

Before proceeding with the implications of these conditions, it is important to note that (9) and (10) remain the first-order conditions with ex ante commitment by producers provided the production choice is socially optimal. In this case the objective function (4′) (see appendix 8.A), which is closely related to (5), has its expectation simultaneously optimized over $Q(s)$, $B(s)$, and the output activity commitment $\bar{Y}$. (9) and (10) retain their form because at the optimal setting for $\bar{Y}$ there is no welfare consequence of the induced effect of changes in the $Q(s)$ and $B(s)$ schedule upon $\bar{Y}$ (see appendix 8.A for further details). This justifies neglecting such effects in the remainder of the chapter.

8.2.1 Implications of Optimal Policy

First we note a handy property of the stock-out constraint. It is easy to see that it never pays to have $E[B] > 0$. If this were so the government could sell from stock while canceling the effect on P by reducing imports (increasing exports). All constraints would still be met and welfare would change at the rate of P^* per unit reduction in imports (increase in exports). The other constraints may or may not bind.

The first order conditions (9)–(10) imply

THEOREM 1   The optimal interior commercial policy is a specific import tax (export subsidy) schedule that is a combination of a fixed specific tax (subsidy) and a fixed *ad valorem* subsidy (tax):

$$P - P^* = t(Q(s) - B(s), s) = (\beta/\mu) - ((1 + \mu)/\mu)P^*, \tag{11}$$

where $\beta > 0, \mu > 0$.

Proof   At an interior maximum, (9) and (10) hold with equality. Substituting (9) into (10) and solving for P, $P = (\beta - P^*)/\mu$. Subtract P^* from both sides to obtain (11).   QED

(11) has real-world counterparts in step functions that control cheap imports but allow free trade in imports above a limit price. For example, the United States has "price-break quotas" in certain cheeses, which control imports selling below the support price for American-type cheese and allow free trade in cheese above the support price. Another counterpart is in "tariff-quotas," in which the specific tax rate steps upward with the volume of imports, save that in the present case the tariff should decrease with volume (this being associated with a rise in P^*, *ceteris paribus*).

Note that (11) also implies $P = (\beta/\mu) - (1/\mu)P^*$. In other words, the optimal setting of instruments requires that domestic and foreign price be perfectly negatively correlated, so long as there is any variation in foreign price. This is a drastic antimarket forces policy. It makes sense in terms of the constraints on the buffer agency, however, and appears to rationalize the host of odd-looking real-world agricultural commercial policies, which may tend to raise domestic price as world price falls.

Assuming that $P - P^* > 0$ for the moment, (11) implies that the optimal policy is dedicated to discouraging imports, and accumulation of stock if imports and support purchases move together (see theorem 4). This is perhaps the normal case reflected in real world U.S. policies. Note that it can, however, be optimal to subsidize imports or tax exports to increase accumulation: at the optimal $P < P^*$.

Figure 8.1 illustrates this. The price floor requires $P \geqslant \bar{P}$. $P = P^*$ is drawn for reference. The optimal price schedule may or may not intersect $P = P^*$ in the feasible region—if it does there is a range of high foreign

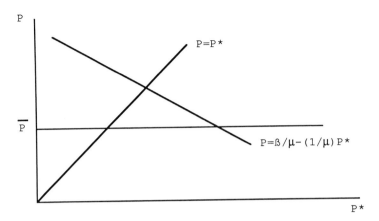

Figure 8.1

prices for which imports (exports) must be subsidized (taxed) in the interests of domestic stabilization.

Interestingly, it is difficult to establish in general whether the average $P - P^*$ is positive. For one important special case, it can be shown:

COROLLARY   For linear demand and supply at the interior solution, the average tax on imports (subsidy on exports), $E[P - P^*]$, is positive.

Proof   From (9),

$$E[P - P^*] = -E[\lambda p_Q] + \mu E[p_Q B]$$

$$= -\text{cov}(\lambda, p_Q) + \mu \text{cov}(B, p_Q)$$

$$- E[\lambda]E[p_Q] + \mu E[B]E[p_Q].$$

The assumption implies that p_Q is a constant. Then the covariance terms are zero. It is never optimal for $E[B]$ to be positive; hence the last term is zero. The third term is positive provided that the price floor binds in at least one state.   QED

It is apparently possible for the covariance terms to be negative, given the right sort of curvature. I have not found useful general conditions to order the possibilities.

The optimal buffer policy has a similarly pleasing structure:

THEOREM 2   The optimal stock policy is to purchase more the greater is λ, the shadow price of the price floor, and the less is $P - P^*$, the import tax (export subsidy).

Proof From (9),

$$\mu B = (P - P^*)/p_Q + \tilde{\lambda}. \quad \text{QED} \tag{12}$$

The intuition behind (12) is straightforward. The first term represents the desirability of arbitrage over states: buy low, sell high. The second term offsets the first when the price floor is reached.

More insight into the structure of the optimal policy is given by considering the shape of the optimal trade and purchase schedule as a function of the state of nature. The set of first-order conditions define an optimal set of B and Q values, $B^*(s)$, $Q^*(s)$. Assume a continuous distribution of states. (This is not necessary, but eases understanding.) It is simplest to think of the state changing causing a small shift in the foreign price ($P_s^* > 0$) or domestic marginal benefit schedule ($p_s > 0$), where the subscript denotes partial differentiation. Then the set of first-order conditions (11) and (12) can be differentiated with respect to s to form the comparative static derivatives dQ^*/ds and dB^*/ds.

THEOREM 3 The optimal consumption response to domestic (foreign) uncertainty is pro- (anti-) arbitrage:

$$d(Q - B)^*/ds = (\mu p_s + P_s^*)/(-p_Q\mu) > 0. \tag{13}$$

Proof Totally differentiate (11) and solve. QED

The intuition of theorem 3 is that cheaper imports require smaller consumption in the domestic market in order to maintain the optimal setting of domestic price at $P = (\beta - P^*)/\mu$. An increase in domestic marginal value, on the other hand, induces higher consumption to reduce the price to its optimal setting, the usual arbitrage response.

An important issue in this chapter is the substitutability of Q and B policy. (9) and (10) show that both are useful, so that they are not perfect substitutes. An alternative weaker definition of substitutability is in terms of correlation. Optimal Q (imports) and $-B$ (stock sales) can be either positively or negatively correlated in general. An important special case neatly captures the major factors.

THEOREM 4 In the linear case, optimal imports and buffer sales have correlation coefficient $= -1(0)$ as foreign (domestic) uncertainty dominates.

Proof Totally differentiate (11) and (12) using the linearity assumption, and solve using (13).[1] Then

$$\mu dB^*/ds = -P_s^*(1 + \mu)/\mu p_Q,$$

$$\mu dQ^*/ds = -[\mu^2 p_s + (2 + \mu)P_s^*]/\mu p_Q. \tag{14}$$

The standard algebra of correlation shows that under (14), with $p_s = 0$, $-B^*$ and Q^* are perfectly negatively correlated.[2] For $P_s^* = 0$ the correlation is obviously zero.   QED

If foreign prices alone are uncertain, Q and $-B$ are perfectly negatively correlated, but $d(Q - B)/ds = -P_s^*/\mu p_Q$. Thus (14) implies a weak version of the perfect substitution response. It is also interesting to consider "complementarity." (14) implies that in the linear case, a necessary condition for optimal $-B$ and Q to be positively correlated is that p_s and P_s^* differ in sign (there is negative correlation of foreign and domestic price shocks).

Finally, consider the "Soviet" case. "Soviet" agricultural policy is characterized by not only price ceilings and buffering, but also a self-sufficiency constraint that plausibly has the form $E[Q] \leq 0$. Without the latter, the first-order conditions above are simply reinterpreted with the sign of λ reversed. With it, the optimal specific tax schedule picks up an additional positive term. It is interpreted exactly as in Young and Anderson (1980, chapter 4). No additional complications ensue.

8.3 "Third"-Best Commercial Policy

Suppose that the optimal commercial policy and buffer policy are not followed. The optimal policy is $B^*(s)$, $Q^*(s)$ and we define an alternative that satisfies the constraints as $\hat{B}(s)$, $\hat{Q}(s)$. When can two such alternatives be ranked? In general, this can be done only with simulation. But some revealing special cases can be analytically ranked.

The real world has a variety of commercial policies in agriculture, with support schemes that appear more similar across both crops and countries. Thus, the most relevant cases are probably those comparisons where the B policy is identical and the commercial policy is a fixed tariff or quota, or a variable levy. In this case the B policy is uninteresting and it is convenient to suppress it altogether. Then, trivially, with the Q policy alone, complementary slackness in combination with equation (9) defines a variable levy:

$$P = \overline{P} \quad \text{for} \quad P^* \leq \overline{P} \qquad \text{and} \qquad P = P^* \quad \text{for} \quad P^* > \overline{P}.$$

The appropriate variable levy is obviously superior to other commercial policy instruments.

A ranking of a fixed import quota and a fixed specific tariff is considered below (i.e., a choice that must be made in advance of knowing the state of nature), but other comparisons can be made on similar lines. The result is that an import quota dominates a specific tariff when the source of uncertainty is foreign, and is dominated when the uncertainty is domestic. For the mixed case, the specific tax dominates, provided it implies higher average imports. The reason for these rankings is intuitive: for foreign (domestic) uncertainty the specific tax moves Q in the wrong (right) direction, based on the shape of the optimal schedule. The quota does not move it at all.

To develop these points let $Q^t(s)$ be the specific tax regime import in state s, and $\bar{Q}$ be the quota regime import in state s. The expression for the difference in welfare with the quota and with the specific tax is

$$\Delta w = \mathop{E}_s \int_{Q^t(s)}^{\bar{Q}(s)} p(v, s)\, dv - P^*(s)[\bar{Q}(s) - Q^t(s)], \tag{15}$$

where

$$\bar{Q}(s) = \begin{cases} \bar{Q} & \text{for} \quad \bar{P} \geqslant P^* \\ \{\bar{Q}(s) \mid p(\bar{Q}(s), s) = P^*\} & \text{for} \quad P^* > \bar{P}. \end{cases}$$

$Q^t(s)$ is the specific tax regime import such that $p(Q^t(s), s) = P^*(s) + t$. In writing (15), $B = 0$ is imposed, in comparison with (5). A slightly more convenient form of (15) is

$$\Delta w = \mathop{E}_s \int_{Q^t(s)}^{\bar{Q}(s)} [p(v, s) - P^*(s)]\, dv. \tag{16}$$

The quota and tariff must both satisfy the price floor constraint. With the convention that p_s and P_s^* are both positive, the minimum P^* is associated with minimum s. For simplicity, assume that $p(0, s_{min}) > \bar{P}$; the constraint does not require subsidized exports. The quota satisfies

$$p(\bar{Q}, s_{min}) = \bar{P}, \qquad \bar{P} \geqslant P^*,$$

$$p(\bar{Q}(s), s) = P^*, \qquad \bar{P} \leqslant P^*.$$

The tariff satisfies

$$P^*(s_{min}) + t = \bar{P} = p(Q^t(s_{min}), s_{min}).$$

Evidently, $Q(s_{min}) = \bar{Q}.$

THEOREM 5   The quota (tariff) dominates if the source of uncertainty is purely foreign (domestic).

Proof   the derivative of the import quantity with respect to the state is

$$dQ^t/ds = (p_s - P_s^*)/-p_Q.$$

The quota import quantity derivative is either zero or has the same form when the quota does not bind. With pure foreign uncertainty, the volume of imports with the quota is (weakly) higher in every state. With pure domestic uncertainty the volume of imports is (weakly) lower in every state. Since $P > P^*$ in all states with import control alone, Δw depends only on the sign, for each s, of the change in Q.   QED

The same proof suffices to show that the tariff is superior (inferior) if domestic (foreign) uncertainty predominates in the sense that $p_s - P_s^*$ has one sign. What if this is not so? The mean value theorem for a concave function such as Δw implies that

$$\Delta w \leqslant E[\{P - P^*\}\{\bar{Q}(s) - \bar{Q}^t(s)\}] = tE[\{\bar{Q}(s) - \bar{Q}^t(s)\} \mid P \geqslant P^*].$$

For $E[Q^t(s)] > E[\bar{Q}(s)]$, $\Delta w < 0$; if average imports are higher under the tariff, the tariff predominates.

Step functions, such as tariff quotas or price-break quotas, offer an ability to combine the features of the two simple instruments. Intuitively, it would seem that this is likely to be especially useful when $p_s - P_s^*$ is not one-signed. Such conjectures can be shown to hold up in simple cases.

8.4 Producers' Welfare and Price Floors

The analysis has thus far shoved producer interests far into the background, save as they create a price floor constraint for policy. It is now useful to inquire whether such constraints make sense for producers to pursue in the context of this model. It turns out that it may well not be advisable for producers to push for increases in the price floor.

The cost of a rise in the floor is that high range prices may be reduced, reducing the variability of prices and possibly the mean price. *Ceteris paribus*, risk neutral producers prefer mean-preserving increases in price dispersion. The desirability of price floor increases is on this account more likely the less that high range prices fall. But the argument is incomplete because profits may also vary due to domestic supply shocks, with covariation effects on price. Thus a further investigation is provided. (Risk

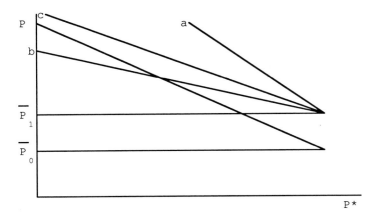

Figure 8.2

aversion further modifies the conclusion by making desirable a mean-preserving reduction in variance of price.[3])

The effect of the rising floor on the optimal price schedule is that (1) in the linear case the higher price floor does indeed reduce high range prices, but (2) nevertheless the mean price is raised. General results do not seem possible.

Turning to the effect on profits, there are two results. First, expected profits fall if a rise in the price floor lowers mean price and if foreign and domestic supply shocks are negatively correlated. Second, expected profits rise in the linear case, if foreign and domestic shocks are positively correlated, and if output is sufficiently insensitive to price (which reduces the *ceteris paribus* desirability of price variation).

8.4.1 The Shift in the Optimal Price Schedule

The issue of the behavior of the optimal price schedule as $\bar{P}$ rises has a fairly simple resolution in principle. If a rise in the floor price causes an effective slackening of the expenditure constraint on buffering, $\partial \mu / \partial \bar{P} < 0$, then domestic prices rise in all states. This case is illustrated by schedule (a) in figure 8.2. Intuitively it seems implausible, but I have not been able to rule it out in general.

Now consider the shift in the intercept β / μ. Note that

$$\beta / \mu = (\partial E(W)/\partial S)/(\partial E(W)/\partial G),$$

where S is the expected stock maintenance level, set at zero previously.

This is equal to the additional average government expenditure induced by a one-unit rise in the stock maintenance requirement, in order to maintain expected welfare:

$$\beta/\mu = \frac{dG}{dS}\bigg|_{E(W)}.$$

Intuitively, this seems likely to fall with a rise in $\bar{P}$. If a rise in the price floor causes a fall (rise) in β/μ, the compensated expected revenue cost of a unit of stock, then the domestic price schedule falls at high levels and rises at low levels (rises at all levels). These possibilities are illustrated by case (b) [case (c) or case (a)] in figure 8.2. The two sets of optimal price schedules are related as shown since $P \geqslant \bar{P}$ is required, and the form of optimal P is $P = (\beta - P^*)/\mu.$ $\partial\mu/\partial\bar{P} < 0$ ensures that the new price schedule looks like (a), with higher price for every P^*. A fall in β/μ produces a new price schedule like (b); a rise causes a price line that lies everywhere above the old one [case (a) or (c)].

The effect of a rise in $\bar{P}$ on the Lagrange multiplier μ and β/μ is determined by the comparative static derivatives of the complete system of first-order conditions. These turn out to allow either sign in rather complex and unintuitive fashion in general. The intuitive case might appear to be $\partial\mu/\partial\bar{P} > 0$ and $\partial(\beta/\mu)/\partial\bar{P} < 0$—a rise in the floor increases the pressure on support funds and reduces the expected revenue cost of a unit of stock (because more purchase at the floor is required), creating case (b). Some tedious algebra establishes that this indeed holds true for the linear case (see appendix 8.C), provided $E(P)$ is not too far below $E(P^*)$. $E(P) \geqslant E(P^*)$ is of course the normal case of protected agriculture.

Obviously, producers benefit with a dominant price schedule [case (a) or (c)]. Thus the only interesting case is when β/μ falls. For the linear case, despite β/μ falling, $E(P)$ rises (see appendix 8.B).

8.4.2 The Shift in Expected Profits

Do producers ever lose expected profits with a rise in $\bar{P}$? Let $Z(P,s)$ be the restricted profit function for the producer. By the envelope theorem, $Z_P = Y$, and $Z_{PP} = Y_P \geqslant 0$ with a convex technology. It is convenient to substitute into $Z(P,s)$ the optimal price schedule $P(s) = (\beta/\mu) - (1/\mu)P^*(s)$. The problem is now to sign

$$E[\partial Z/\partial\bar{P}] = \mathop{E}_{s}\left[Y(P(s),s)\frac{\partial P(s)}{\partial\bar{P}}\right]. \tag{17}$$

The sign of (17) is generally a rather complex matter. To lead into it gently, first consider the case of no randomness in domestic output apart from that induced by price. The sign of the expected profit change turns solely on the behavior of the new price schedule relative to the old. Because of the form of the optimal price schedule, a lower mean price must be accompanied by less variation in P. By the convexity of profits in P, a mean-preserving reduction in variance lowers expected profits—a fortiori for lower mean price. The same consideration shows that expected profits may fall even with a rise in mean price.

The second case modifies the first insight by allowing for domestic output shocks. Lower correlation of the optimal price with the supply shock will lower expected profits. If raising the price floor lowers (raises) this correlation, then on this account it lowers (raises) expected profits. Putting these effects together, I shall show that (1) expected profits fall if expected price falls and foreign and domestic output shocks are negatively correlated, and (2) expected profits rise.

Proceeding more formally, manipulate (17) to form

$$E[\partial Z/\partial \overline{P}] = \underset{s}{E}[Y(P(s),s)]E\left[\frac{\partial P(s)}{\partial \overline{P}}\right] + \text{cov}\left(Y(P(s),s),\frac{\partial P(s)}{\partial \overline{P}}\right). \qquad (18)$$

THEOREM 6   If $E[P]$ falls with a rise in the price floor, and if supply shocks and foreign price shocks are negatively correlated, then expected profits fall with a rise in the price floor.

Proof   By assumption the left term of (18) must be negative. The second term has the sign of the product of the implicit derivatives of the two arguments in s, provided these are one-signed (see Anderson and Riley, 1976, for a proof). With $E(P)$ lower, the optimal price schedule in this case has lower absolute slope. Thus

$$\partial P(s)/\partial \overline{P} = \frac{\partial \beta/\mu}{\partial \overline{P}} + \frac{P(s)}{\mu^2}\frac{\partial \mu}{\partial \overline{P}}$$

has positive slope in $P(s)$; hence it does with respect to s with the convention $P_s^* > 0$. The implicit derivative of Y with respect to s is $Y_P[-(1/\mu)P_s^*] + Y_s$. Thus

$$\text{sign}\{\text{cov}\} = \text{sign}\left\{\frac{P^*}{\mu^2}\frac{\partial \mu}{\partial \overline{P}}\left(Y_s - \frac{1}{\mu}Y_P P_s^*\right)\right\} \leqslant 0$$

under the assumptions.   QED

Note from the proof of theorem 6 that it is possible for $E[P]$ to rise and yet have expected profits fall, so long as β/μ falls. This reflects the reduced variation in P acting through the convexity of the profit function in P. An implication of the structure behind theorem 6 is

COROLLARY   In the linear case, with foreign and domestic supply shocks positively correlated, expected profits will rise so long as Y is sufficiently inelastic with respect to P.

Now consider risk attitudes of producers. Consideration of producer risk aversion is not properly part of an analysis using expected surplus as a criterion. Its introduction can be defended by claiming that the rest of the economy is risk neutral, and that the price floor is an instrument to constrain producer welfare. Producer risk aversion can help rationalize producer lobbying to raise price floors even if expected profits will fall. If risk aversion is sufficiently strong to make utility of profits concave in price,[4] then producers could gain even if the expected price falls. Intuitively, lower mean and lower variance trade off. In the limit of infinite risk aversion the maximin criterion holds, and welfare of producers depends only on the worst outcome, the floor price.

8.5 Conclusion

This chapter has shown that the optimal commercial and buffer policies under price support systems have a rich and intuitively appealing structure that in some degree approximates real-world policies. The latter are not based on formal optimization, however, which suggests that their groping efforts can be improved upon. While derived in a very simple model, the qualitative structure should be robust with respect to a fair amount of generalization.

An important caveat concerns the unrealistic simplification of ex post production choice. A realistic model of production requires commitment to planting before harvest and price uncertainty are resolved. Qualitatively, optimal commercial and buffer policy can be shown to be the same,[5] but the quantitative implementation of the model is another matter. Another use of an ex ante model worth exploring is the analysis of imperfect production controls, such as acreage controls.

Such ex ante decisions must be studied in a dynamic model. This would also allow a more realistic account of the feasibility constraints on the buffering agency, and of the time structure of commercial policies (for example, the licensing period of the quota; see chapter 10 for a start in treatment of the latter). In such a context, it might also be interesting to allow private buffering and study its interaction with public buffering and commercial policy.

Appendix 8.A: The Welfare Measure

The main task of this appendix is to lay out the basic welfare model and show how the domestic production can be subsumed into a convenient reduced form with trade and stock changes as decision variables, and domestic and foreign shocks as the state variables. The area under the inverse demand curve in state s is

$$CS(s) = \int_0^{Y(s)+Q(s)-B(s)} c(v, s)\, dv, \tag{1}$$

where c is the consumer's marginal benefit (inverse demand) function. Domestic resource cost of production for sale to consumers is

$$R(s) = \int_0^{Y(s)-B(s)} r(v, s)\, dv, \tag{2}$$

where r is the marginal cost function.

By assumption domestic taxes or subsidies are ruled out as instruments. Then at equilibrium, $r(Y, s) = c(Y + Q - B, s) = P$. P is the domestic price for both consumers and producers. Trade and buffer policy affect the producers' price, by first shifting the consumer's price and then by imposing the equilibrium condition $r = c$. Thus domestic price is functionally written $P = P(Y + Q - B, s)$, read off the inverse demand curve, with the understanding that Y satisfies $r(Y, s) = P$.

The remaining elements of the welfare measures may now be assembled. P^* is the foreign price. Trade tax revenue (of either sign) is $(P - P^*)Q$, the cost of imports to consumers is PQ (export sales for $Q < 0$), and support payments are PB. Rent earned on production to stock is

$$T(s) = -\int_{Y(s)-B(s)}^{Y(s)} r(v, s)\, dv + P(Y(s) + Q(s) - B(s), s)B(s). \tag{3}$$

Welfare in state s is consumer benefit (1) less cost of production for consumption (2) less cost of imports P^*Q (or plus export earnings) less support payments PB (or plus earnings from stock sales) plus rent earned on production to stock (3) plus government trade revenue $(P - P^*)Q$. This simplifies to

$$W(s) = \int_0^{Y(s)+Q(s)-B(s)} c(v, s)\, dv$$
$$- P^*(s)Q(s) - \int_0^{Y(s)} r(v, s)\, dv. \tag{4}$$

Welfare measure (4) can be reduced further under the restriction that equilibrium $r(Y, s) = c(Y + Q - B, s)$. Note that $dW/dY = 0$ under the restriction. Further, the restriction implies, with increasing marginal cost and decreasing marginal benefit (downward-sloping demand), that Y is a decreasing function of $Q - B$: $Y = f(Q(s) - B(s), s)$. Let

$$p(Q(s) - B(s), s) = c(f(Q(s) - B(s)) + Q(s) - B(s), s),$$

be the reduced form domestic price function. It is the inverse excess demand function. Then welfare becomes

$$W(s) = K(s) + \int_0^{Q(s) - B(s)} p(v, s)\, dv - P^*(s)Q(s), \tag{5}$$

where

$$K(s) = \int_0^{f(sQ(s) - B(s), s)} [c(v, s) - r(v, s)]\, dv.$$

$K(s)$ is invariant to Q and B under the restriction $r = c$ that defines $F(\cdot)$. Thus $K(s)$ may be suppressed for analytical simplicity in what follows.

Now consider the welfare measure under ex ante commitment: $Y(s) = h(\overline{Y}, s)$. Substitute this into (4) and simplify to obtain

$$W'(s) = K'(\overline{Y}, s) + \int_0^{Q(s) - B(s)} P'(v, s) - P^*(s)Q(s), \tag{4'}$$

where $P'(Q(s) - B(s)), s) \equiv c(h(\overline{Y}, s) + Q(s) - B(s), s)$,

$$K'(\overline{Y}, s) \equiv \int_0^{h(\overline{Y}, s)} [c(v, s) - r(v, s)]\, dv.$$

If $\overline{Y}$ is invariant to $Q(s)$, $B(s)$, or more plausibly if $\overline{Y}$ is chosen to optimize the expectation of (4') for any $Q(s)$, $B(s)$ schedule, then (4') differs only inessentially from (5).

An added property of welfare measures of (4)–(5) is significant. If the constraint $r = c$ at equilibrium is removed, from (4) it will obviously be most efficient to attain a target producer price via production control or an equivalent subsidy on production. That is, if in each state the constraint is

$$r(Y(s), s) \geq \overline{r}, \tag{6'}$$

the optimal selection of Y requires $c - r$ negative and proportional to r_Y. The optimum in Q (free trade) and B (consumer price = "storage cost"—see section 8.2) is not affected by the constraint. The infeasibility of direct contingent production controls or the dual equivalent, contingent production subsidies is what necessitates the commercial and buffer policies studied in this chapter. These are inherently second-best policies.

Finally, as a further aid to understanding, consider in figure 8.A1 a diagram of welfare measure (4). Welfare in state s is given by the vertically shaded area plus the horizontally shaded area, minus the diagonally shaded area. In forming (4), the additions to stock are socially billed at external price P^* forming the latter area, since in effect they are supplied from imports. B is purchased at price P, but

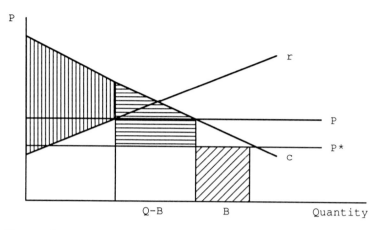

Figure 8.A1

$(P - P^*)B$ is a pure transfer from consumers (via lump sum taxes) to the government. Similarly, for the case of stock sales in figure 8.A2, their social value is based on external price P^*, the social cost of the imports displaced. Welfare is the vertically shaded area plus the horizontally shaded area plus the diagonally shaded area.

Appendix 8.B: Equivalence of Static and Simple Dynamic Models

A dynamic model in the absence of ex ante commitment adds nothing essential to the analysis. This claim is worth documenting.

Suppose that the stock-out and government expenditure constraints are defined over 2 periods (with discount factor δ for the latter). Then in period 2 the program given state s_2 is

$$\max_{Q_2(s_2), B_2(s_2)} \int_0^{Q_2(s_2) - B_2(s_2)} p_1(v, s_2)\, dv - P_2^*(s_2) Q_2(s_2) + K_2(s_2)$$

such that

$$B_2(s_2) + B_1 + B_0 \geqslant 0 \qquad [\beta(s)],$$

$$p_2(Q_2(s_2) - B_2(s_2), s_2) \geqslant \overline{P} \qquad [\lambda_2(s_2)],$$

$$p_2(\cdot)B_2(s_2) + p_1(Q_1(s_1) - B_1(s_1), s_1)B_1 \delta \leqslant G/\delta \qquad [\mu(s_2)].$$

The values of the optimum can be substituted into the objective function to form $V(Q_1, B_1, s_2)$. Then the stage 1 problem is for state s_1,

$$\max_{Q_1(s_1), B_1(s_1)} \int_0^{Q_1(s_1) - B_1(s_1)} p_1(v_1, s_1)\, dv - P_1^*(s_1) Q_1(s_1) + K_1(s_1)$$

$$+ \delta E_{s_2} V(Q_1, B_1, s_2)$$

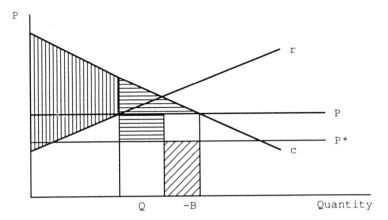

Figure 8.A2

such that

$$p_1(Q_1(s_1) - B_1(s_1), s_1) \geqslant \bar{P}.$$

Using the structure of the stage 2 problem, the solution to the first stage problem is

$$P_1 - P_1^* + \lambda_1(s_1)p_Q(s_1) + \delta E_{s_2} V_{Q_1}(B_1, Q_1, s_1) = 0,$$

$$-P_1 - \lambda_1(s_1)p_Q(s_1) + \delta E_{s_2} V_{B_1}(B_1, Q_1, s_1) = 0.$$

Note that

$$V_{Q_1} = -\mu B_1 P_1 / \delta,$$

$$V_{B_1} = \beta - \mu P_1 / \delta + \mu B_1 P_Q / \delta.$$

The optimal rules are based on

$$P_1 = \frac{E(\beta) - P_1^*}{E(\mu)},$$

$$B_1 = \frac{P_1 - P_1^*}{E(\mu)P_Q} + \frac{\lambda_1}{E(\mu)},$$

the same essentially as in the 1 period case.

Appendix 8.C: The Effect of a Price Floor Shift

In the linear case (a constant p_Q), a rise in $\bar{P}$ will (A.1) raise $E(P)$; (A.2) raise μ, hence lower the slope of the price schedule, if $E(P) \geqslant E(P^*)$, and (A.3) lower β/μ.

Proof of (A.1)

$$\partial E(P)/\partial \bar{P} = p_Q E \frac{\partial (Q - B)}{\partial \bar{P}}$$

in the linear case. This is positive if $E[\partial(Q - B)/\partial\bar{P}] < 0$. Taking expectations in (12),

$$\mu E(B) = \frac{E(P - P^*)}{p_Q} + E(\tilde{\lambda}). \tag{19}$$

Optimality requires $E(B) = 0$. Taking the derivative of the right-hand side with respect to $\bar{P}$, using constancy of p_Q and $E(B) = 0$,

$$E\left(\frac{\partial(Q - B)}{\partial\bar{P}}\right) + E\left(\frac{\partial\tilde{\lambda}}{\partial\bar{P}}\right) = 0. \tag{20}$$

At an interior maximum, $\partial\tilde{\lambda}/\partial\bar{P} > 0$, hence $E[\partial(Q - B)/\partial\bar{P}] < 0$.   QED

Proof of (A.2)   First, note that the optimal price schedule implies $\beta = \mu\bar{P} + P^*_{max}$. Substituting the optimal price schedule $P = \bar{P} + (P^*_{max} - P^*)/\mu$ into (19) and using $E(B) = 0$,

$$\mu = -\frac{P^*_{max} - E(P^*)}{\bar{P} - E(P^*) + E(\tilde{\lambda})p_Q}. \tag{21}$$

Differentiate (21) using linearity to form

$$\frac{d\mu}{d\bar{P}} = \frac{\mu^2}{P^*_{max} - E(P^*)}\left[1 + p_Q\frac{dE(\tilde{\lambda})}{d\bar{P}}\right]. \tag{22}$$

Next, use $E(PB) = G$ to develop another restriction on the relation of $d\mu/d\bar{P}$ to $dE(\lambda)/d\bar{P}$. First,

$$G = Prob(P^*_{max})\bar{P}\left[\frac{\bar{P} - P^*_{max}}{\mu p_Q} + \frac{\tilde{\lambda}}{\mu}\right] \tag{23}$$

$$+ Prob(P^* < P^*_{max})E\left[\frac{P(P - P^*)}{\mu p_Q}\middle| P^* < P^*_{max}\right].$$

Recalling that $\tilde{\lambda} = \lambda/Prob(P^*_{max})$, (23) can be solved for λ:

$$p_Q\lambda = -\left\{Prob(P^*_{max})(P - \bar{P}^*_{max})\right.$$

$$\left. + Prob(P^* < P^*_{max})E\left[\frac{P(P - P^*)}{\bar{P}}\right]\middle| P^* < P^*_{max}\right\} + \frac{\mu G p_Q}{\bar{P}}. \tag{24}$$

Differentiating with respect to $\bar{P}$,

$$p_Q \frac{d\lambda}{d\overline{P}} = -\text{Prob}(P_{\max}^*) - \frac{p_Q}{\overline{P}^2} \mu G$$

$$+ \frac{\text{Prob}(P^* < P_{\max}^*)}{\overline{P}^2} E[P(P - P^*) \mid P^* < P_{\max}^*] \qquad (25)$$

$$+ \frac{G p_Q}{\overline{P}} \frac{d\mu}{d\overline{P}} + \frac{\text{Prob}(P^* < P_{\max}^*)}{\overline{P}} \frac{\partial E(P(P - P^*) \mid P^* < P_{\max}^*)}{\partial \overline{P}}.$$

Evaluating the rightmost term of (25),

$$P(P - P^*) = \left(\overline{P} + \frac{P_{\max}^* - P^*}{\mu} \right)\left(\overline{P} + \frac{P_{\max}^* - P^*}{\mu} \right) - P^*.$$

Hence

$$\frac{\partial E[P(P - P^*) \mid P^* < P_{\max}^*]}{\partial \overline{P}}$$

$$= E[2P - P^* \mid P^* < P_{\max}^*] \qquad (26)$$

$$+ E[(P^* - P_{\max}^*)(2P - P^*) \mid P^* < P_{\max}^*] \frac{1}{\mu^2} \frac{d\mu}{d\overline{P}}.$$

Substituting (26) into (25), and (25) into (22), the solution for $(d\mu/d\overline{P})(1/\mu^2)$ is

$$\frac{1}{\mu^2} \frac{d\mu}{d\overline{P}} = \frac{1}{P_{\max}^* - E(P^*) + \alpha} \left\{ 1 - \text{Prob}(P_{\max}^*) - \frac{p_Q \mu G}{\overline{P}^2} \right.$$

$$\qquad (27)$$

$$\left. + \frac{\text{Prob}(P^* < P_{\max}^*)}{\overline{P}} E[q \mid P^* < P_{\max}^*] \right.$$

where $q \equiv P(P - P^*)/\overline{P} + 2P - P^*$,

$$\alpha \equiv 1 - \frac{G p_Q}{\overline{P}} \mu^2 + \frac{\text{Prob}(P^* < P_{\max}^*)}{\overline{P}} E[(P_{\max}^* - P^*)(2P - P^*) \mid P^* < P_{\max}^*].$$

If $E(q) \geq 0$ and if the rightmost term of $\alpha \geq 0$, then $\partial \mu / \partial \overline{P} > 0$. Both properties hold in the linear case, provided the "natural region" of operation is attained, $\tilde{E}(P - P^*) \geq 0$, where the tilde denotes conditional on $P^* < P_{\max}^*$:

$$E[q \mid P^* < P_{\max}^*]$$

$$= \frac{1}{\overline{P}} E[P(P - P^*) \mid P^* < P_{\max}^*] + E[(2P - P^*) \mid P^* < P_{\max}^*] \qquad (28)$$

$$= \frac{\tilde{E}(P)}{\overline{P}} \tilde{E}(P - P^*) + \frac{\widetilde{\text{cov}}(P, P - P^*)}{\overline{P}} + 2\tilde{E}(P) - \tilde{E}(P^*).$$

Using the optimal price function $P = (\beta - P^*)/\mu$, the covariance in (28) is positive. The other two terms are positive if $E(P - P^*) \geq 0$.

Turning to the evaluation of

$$\tilde{E}[(P^*_{max} - P^*)(2P - P^*)]$$

$$= \tilde{E}(P^*_{max} - P^*)\tilde{E}(2P - P^*) + \widetilde{cov}\left(P^*_{max} - P^*, 2\frac{\beta}{\mu} - \frac{2}{\mu}P^* - P^*\right),$$

the covariance is >0 and the first term is positive if $E(P - P^*) \geqslant 0$.   QED

Proof of (A.3)   Previously it was noted that $\beta = P^*_{max} + \mu\overline{P}$, hence

$$\frac{d\beta}{\beta} = \frac{\mu\overline{P}}{\beta}\frac{d\overline{P}}{\overline{P}} + \frac{\mu\overline{P}}{\beta}\frac{d\mu}{\mu}.$$

Let the circumflex denote proportional change. Then

$$\widehat{\beta/\mu} = \frac{\mu\overline{P}}{\beta}\hat{\overline{P}} - \left(1 - \frac{\mu\overline{P}}{\beta}\right)\hat{\mu} \tag{29}$$

and

$$\frac{\widehat{\beta/\mu}}{\hat{\overline{P}}} = \frac{\mu\overline{P}}{\beta} - \frac{P^*_{max}}{\beta}\frac{\hat{\mu}}{\hat{\overline{P}}}. \tag{30}$$

This is negative iff

$$\frac{\hat{\mu}}{\hat{\overline{P}}} > \frac{\mu\overline{P}}{P^*_{max}}. \tag{31}$$

From (27),

$$\frac{\hat{\mu}}{\hat{\overline{P}}} = \frac{\mu\overline{P}}{P^*_{max} - E(P^*) + \alpha}\left\{1 - \text{Prob}(P^*_{max}) - \frac{p_Q\mu G}{\overline{P}^2} - \frac{\text{Prob}(P^* < P^*_{max})}{\overline{P}}\tilde{E}(q)\right\}$$

$$= \frac{\mu\overline{P}}{P^*_{max}}\frac{P^*_{max}}{P^*_{max} - E(P^*) + \alpha}\{\ \}$$

$$= \frac{\mu\overline{P}}{P^*_{max}}\frac{1}{1 - [E(P^*)/P^*_{max}] + (\alpha/P^*_{max})}\{\ \}.$$

Evaluating the key elements,

$$\frac{\alpha}{P^*_{max}} = \frac{1}{P^*_{max}} - \frac{G p_Q\mu}{\overline{P}^2}\frac{\mu\overline{P}}{P^*_{max}} + \frac{\text{Prob}(P^* < P^*_{max})}{\overline{P}}\left(\tilde{E}(2P - P^*) - \tilde{E}\frac{P^*(2P - P^*)}{P^*_{max}}\right),$$

$$\{\ \} = 1 - \text{Prob}(P^*_{max}) - \frac{G p_Q\mu}{\overline{P}^2} + \frac{\text{Prob}(P^* < P^*_{max})}{\overline{P}}\left(\frac{\tilde{E}(2P - P^*)}{\overline{P}} + \frac{\tilde{E}(P(P - P^*))}{\overline{P}}\right).$$

For convenience scale prices P^* so that $\overline{P} = 1$. From $\beta = \mu\overline{P} + P^*_{max}$, $\mu\overline{P}/P^*_{max} < 1$. Then $1 < \alpha/P^*_{max} < \{\ \}$. Therefore (30) indeed is negative.   QED

Notes

1. One complication in forming the derivatives is that the price floor may or may not bind, depending on the state. For pure foreign price uncertainty, (11) assures that the constraint binds in at most one state. Then the influence of change in $\tilde{\lambda}$ over states may be neglected in forming the derivatives. With domestic uncertainty this is no longer true. For states where the price floor binds, the three equation system of (11), (12), and $P = \bar{P}$ is now used to obtain a solution for B, Q, and λ. The first and third equations are linearly dependent, implying indeterminacy. Thus for states where the constraint binds, the convention is imposed that $\tilde{\lambda}$ is a constant. Then the derivative of $\tilde{\lambda}$ with respect to s is zero everywhere that it is defined. In all cases, where the comparative static derivatives are defined, they are not dependent on $\tilde{\lambda}$.

2. The correlation coefficient in this case is defined to be

$$\rho = \operatorname{cov}(Q^*(s), -B^*(s))/\sqrt{\operatorname{var}(B^*(s))\operatorname{var}(Q^*(s))}.$$

Let $Q^*(s) = q_0 + q_1 s$, and $-B^*(s) = -b_0 - b_1 s$ under the linearity assumption. q_1 and b_1 are both positive. The covariance is

$$\operatorname{cov}(Q^*(s), -B^*(s))$$

$$= E[(Q^*(s) - E[Q^*(s)])(-B^*(s) + E[B^*(s)])]$$

$$= E[q_1(s - E[s])b_1(s - E[s])]$$

$$= -q_1 b_1 \operatorname{var}(s),$$

where $\operatorname{var}(s) = E[(s - E(s))^2]$, the variance of s. The two variances, $\operatorname{var}(B^*(s))$ and $\operatorname{var}(Q^*(s))$, are similarly $b_1^2 \operatorname{var}(s)$ and $q_1^2 \operatorname{var}(s)$. Substituting, we find $\rho = -1$.

3. The consideration of producer welfare under buffering is well explored in the literature. The question often considered is the value of mean price stabilization versus laissez-faire. See Young (1981), who motivates floor-ceiling stabilization as optimal in terms of a fixed cost of buffer transactions. The convexity of profits in price implies, by Jensen's inequality, that producers focused on expected profits prefer uncertainty to mean price stabilization (Oi's theorem). Risk aversion modifies this conclusion. The differences from Young in this case are that (1) the buffer agency is subject to an expenditure constraint, (2) trade at externally given random price is being optimally controlled, and (3) we consider movements in an arbitrary price floor.

4. Let $I = $ profits, and $U(I)$ be utility of profits. Then

$$U_{PP} = U_I I_{PP} + U_{PP}(I_P)^2 = U_I \left[Y_P + \frac{U_{II} Y^2}{U_I} \right]$$

$$= \frac{U_I Y}{P} \left[\varepsilon - \rho \frac{PY}{I} \right],$$

where

$$\varepsilon = \frac{P}{Y} Y_P, \qquad \rho = -\frac{U_{II}}{U_I} I.$$

5. Newbery and Stiglitz (1981) emphasize that ex ante resource commitment by producers is critical to a proper assessment of buffer policies—it is more realistic and fundamentally changes the analysis. It can be shown that the present analysis survives the introduction of ex ante production choice qualitatively unscathed, so long as the ex ante choice is optimally made. This requires (noncontingent) production taxation to offset the effect of a price floor on resource allocation. In the absence of such corrective taxation, optimal trade and buffer policy has added complex "second-best" elements. So long as the distortion cost is small, or the response of production is small, the qualitative results of the text predominate.

The preceding discussion assumes credible commitment by the government. In its absence, time inconsistency rears its head, and policy must be studied in the context of a game between private agents and the government.

References

Anderson, J. E. (1986), "Quotas as Options: Optimality and Quota License Pricing under Uncertainty," mimeo. Delivered to the World Congress of the Econometric Society, Cambridge, August 1985.

Anderson, J. E., and J. G. Riley (1976), "International Trade with Fluctuating Prices," *International Economic Review*, 17, 76–97.

Bhagwati, J. and T. N. Srinivasan (1969), "Optimal Intervention to Achieve Noneconomic Objectives," *Review of Economic Studies*, 36, 27–38.

Newbery, D. M. G., and J. Stiglitz (1981), *The Theory of Commodity Price Stabilization*, Oxford: Oxford University Press.

Pelcovits, M. (1979), "The Equivalence of Quotas and Buffer Stocks as Alternative Stabilization Policies," *Journal of International Economics*, 9, 303–307.

Young, L. (1981), "Optimal Buffer Stock Policies and the Welfare Economics of Floor-Ceiling Price Stabilization," mimeo.

Young, L., and J. E. Anderson (1980), "The Optimal Policies for Restricting Trade under Uncertainty," *Review of Economic Studies*, 46, 927–932.

Young, L., and J. E. Anderson, (1982), "Risk Aversion and Optimal Trade Restrictions," *Review of Economic Studies*, 49, 291–305.

9

Risk Aversion
and Optimal Trade
Restrictions

9.1 Introduction

Economists have long recognized the equivalence of price and quantity controls under certainty. The comparison of these control modes and the characterization of the optimal form of control under uncertainty has been undertaken by two groups of authors. Weitzman (1974, 1978) considered a planning authority that faces uncertainty about the costs and benefits of producing a good. He showed that the ranking of price and quantity controls depends on the curvature of the cost and benefit functions and that an optimal policy can be considered as a mixture of price and quantity controls. His work was developed by Laffont (1977), Ireland (1977), Malcomson (1978), and Yohe (1978). In the context of international trade, the comparison of tariffs and quotas under uncertainty has been undertaken by Fishelson and Flatters (1975), Pelcovits (1976), Dasgupta and Stiglitz (1977), Young (1979, 1980a, b), and Helpman and Razin (1980).[1] Recently, Young and Anderson (1980, chapter 4) showed that the policy maximizing expected consumer's surplus given a constraint on expected imports (expected import expenditure) is a specific tariff (an *ad valorem* tariff). In contrast to Weitzman's planning model, the price instrument is superior to the quantity instrument—whatever the curvature of the benefits function.[2]

The conclusion of Young and Anderson appears to provide a strong argument against using quantity instruments to restrict trade. However, the expected surplus criterion is a valid welfare measure only if the marginal utility of income is constant. In this chapter we characterize the optimal form of trade restriction if the representative consumer of the importing country exhibits risk aversion toward income fluctuations. The

Reprinted, with changes, by permission from *Review of Economic Studies* (1982), XLIX, 291–305. © 1982 The Society for Economic Analysis Limited.

optimal policy can have surprising properties—properties that, with high risk aversion, are better approximated by a quota rather than a tariff. Hence the "second-best" justification for using quantity controls to restrict trade turns out to depend on the curvature of utility as a function of income rather than its curvature as a function of consumption of the imported good.[3]

Section 9.2 motivates our model and presents an intuitive discussion. Section 9.3 sets out the general equilibrium model of a trading country facing a random world price for imports. Section 9.4 characterizes the optimal trade restriction given a ceiling on expected imports. Section 9.5 gives conditions under which a quota is superior to a tariff and conditions under which the reverse is true. Section 9.6 considers the case where the source of uncertainty is in domestic production. Quotas are then always inferior to tariffs but the optimal policy could involve a schedule of tariffs whose level *falls* as imports increase. Conclusions and possible extensions are presented in section 9.7.

9.2 Motivation and Intuitive Discussion

Most textbook comparisons of tariffs and quotas (e.g., Caves and Jones, 1977, p. 226; Richardson 1980, p. 357) argue that tariffs are superior because they permit imports to respond "appropriately" to changes in world prices and in domestic demand and supply conditions. We evaluate this argument for a small country, assuming ex post choices in production and consumption.[4] In these circumstances, free trade is optimal and the motivation for the trade restriction (and the basis for comparing tariffs and quotas) must be sought in some "noneconomic" constraint[5] imposed on the government by subgroups threatened by imports. Political expediency is likely to lead such a subgroup to advance claims, not directly in terms of its own welfare level, but indirectly by focusing on the highly visible and emotive issue of the level of foreign imports.

If the noneconomic constraint were on the level of imports per period and world supply conditions were uncertain, then this could be achieved *only* by a quota. In practice, such rigidity in the face of random shocks is rare. For example, in 1973 and again in 1974, U.S. dairy product quotas were substantially increased by the Nixon administration to dampen rises in food prices. The balance of political forces that creates import restrictions appears to allow—or even to require—some averaging across periods. Clearly, the argument that tariffs permit a desirable flexibility in imports assumes that the noneconomic constraint permits such flexibility.

We shall therefore assume that the noneconomic constraint is on the average level of imports. While the government might also be concerned with fluctuations in the level of imports, an argument that "rigid" quotas can be superior to "flexible" tariffs would have particular force if it applies even when the government is neutral toward import fluctuations.[6]

Consider first the case where the country faces fluctuations in world prices. The fact that tariffs encourage (restrict) imports when the world price is low (high) means that it leads to "arbitrage" of imports across states of the world. Hence expected import expenditure is lower under a tariff. However, this arbitrage also implies that real income fluctuations are greater under the tariff because the country's "gains from trade" become further restricted just when it is being impoverished by the income effects of a rise in world price.

Under a quota, the reduction in real income from high world prices is *not* accompanied by further restriction of trade. With sufficiently high risk aversion, this greater income stability under a quota can outweigh the "arbitrage" benefits of tariffs. These considerations also imply that, as the world price rises, the optimal trade restriction could involve an increase in imports and a fall in the domestic price.

The above argument is incomplete. It ignores for example, income effects on demand and the effects of changes in domestic prices on domestic production and on the marginal utility of income. We now set out a general equilibrium model of a trading country that captures such effects.[7]

9.3 The Model

We assume that there are two goods and take the exportable as numeraire. As in Dixit and Norman (1980) and Woodland (1980), domestic production possibilities are represented by a revenue function $R(P)$, where P is the domestic price of the importable. The domestic supply function of the importable is then

$$Y(P) = R_P(P). \tag{1}$$

(A subscript denotes partial differentiation with respect to the corresponding variable.) The preferences of the representative consumer are embodied in the indirect utility function $V(P, I)$ where I is income. The domestic demand function for the importable, $X(P, I)$, satisfies Roy's formula:

$$V_P(P, I) = -D(P, I)V_I(P, I). \tag{2}$$

The country is small and faces a random world price P^* for the importable. When imports are Q and the domestic price of the importable is P, consumer income is

$$I(P, P^*, Q) \equiv R(P) + (P - P^*)Q,$$

i.e., production revenue (profits plus factor payments) plus tariff revenue. Domestic excess supply of the importable is then

$$S(P, P^*, Q) \equiv Y(P) - D(P, I(P, P^*, Q)).$$

Let $\tilde{P}(Q, P^*)$ be the equilibrium domestic price when imports are Q and the world price is P^*. Then $\tilde{P}$ is the solution to

$$Q + S(P, P^*, Q) = 0. \tag{3}$$

The slope of the general equilibrium excess supply function for the importable is

$$S_P = Y_P - D_P - YD_I - QD_I \qquad \text{by (1)}$$

$$= Y_P - D_P - DD_I \qquad \text{when } P = \tilde{P}(Q, P^*).$$

The supply function has slope $Y_P > 0$ and the compensated demand function has slope $D_P + DD_I < 0$, so

$$S_P > 0. \tag{4}$$

Our arguments use the "indirect utility function over imports":

$$\tilde{V}(Q, P^*) \equiv V(\tilde{P}(Q, P^*), I(\tilde{P}(Q, P^*), P^*, Q)). \tag{5}$$

This equals domestic utility in equilibrium when imports are Q and the world price is P^*. Differentiating (5) and substituting from (1) yields

$$\tilde{V}_Q(Q, P^*) = \tilde{P}_Q V_P + \tilde{P}_Q (Y + Q) V_I + (\tilde{P} - P^*) V_I.$$

(3) and (2) then imply that

$$\tilde{V}_Q(Q, P^*) = (\tilde{P} - P^*) V_I(\tilde{P}, I(\tilde{P}, P^*, Q)). \tag{6}$$

Thus, the marginal utility of imports in state P^* equals the rent $(\tilde{P} - P^*)$ on a quota license for imports in that state, multiplied by the marginal utility of income in that state. The analysis of the behavior of these two terms permits us to express precisely the trade-off between the arbitrage and the income stabilizing (or destabilizing) effects of trade restrictions that was discussed in section 9.2.

We frequently refer to the effect of a rise in the domestic price P on the marginal utility of income. We have

$$dV_I(P, I(P, P^*, Q))/dP = V_{PI} + (Y + Q)V_{II}$$

$$= V_{PI} + DV_{II} \qquad \text{when } P = \tilde{P}.$$

Differentiating (2) with respect to I,

$$V_{PI} = -D_I V_I - DV_{II}. \tag{7}$$

Therefore

$$dV_I(P, I(P, P^*, Q))/dP = -D_I V_I \qquad \text{when } P = \tilde{P}(Q, P^*); \tag{8}$$

i.e., a rise in the domestic price of a noninferior good always lowers the marginal utility of income when the effects on domestic production and tariff revenue are taken into account.

We shall assume that

$$V_{II}(P, I) \leqslant 0 \qquad \text{for all } P, I; \tag{9}$$

i.e., the representative consumer is always risk averse or risk neutral. A simple calculation (see the appendix) then shows that

$$\tilde{V}_{QQ}(Q, P^*) < 0; \tag{10}$$

i.e., the utility function over imports Q is concave in Q for a given world price.

9.4 The Optimal Trade Restriction

As discussed in section 9.2, we suppose that the government wishes to maximize domestic expected utility subject to a ceiling $\bar{Q}$ on expected imports. If only the world price P^* of the importable is uncertain, then any policy restricting trade is equivalent to a rule $Q(P^*)$ for determining the quantity to be imported in each state P^*. [Note that $Q(P^*)$ is *actual* imports rather than a ceiling on imports in state P^*.] The optimal policy ex ante is the solution, $Q^0(P^*)$, to the problem

$$\max_{Q(P^*)} E[\tilde{V}(Q(P^*), P^*)] \qquad \text{subject to} \quad E[Q(P^*)] \leqslant \bar{Q}. \tag{11}$$

The first-order condition is

$$\tilde{V}_Q(Q, P^*) = \lambda, \tag{12}$$

where λ is the Kuhn-Tucker multiplier corresponding to the constraint on expected imports. By (10), $\tilde{V}_{QQ}(Q, P^*) < 0$ so the solution to (12) is unique and the first-order condition indeed defines an optimum.[8] The optimal domestic price in state P^* is

$$P^0(P^*) \equiv \tilde{P}(Q^0(P^*), P^*).$$

To characterize the optimal policy we define

$$\rho \equiv -IV_{II}/V_I$$

the Arrow-Pratt coefficient of relative risk aversion;

$$\eta \equiv ID_I/D,$$

the income elasticity of demand for the importable;

$$T \equiv (P - P^*)Q/I,$$

the share of tariff revenue in national income; and

$$M = 1 - (P - P^*)D_I.$$

Note that $M = 1 - PD_I t/(1 + t)$, where t is the implicit *ad valorem* tariff rate. If neither good is inferior, then $0 < PD_I < 1$ and $0 < M < 1$. Given any P^*, we say that the above parameters are "evaluated at $Q(P^*)$" when $Q = Q(P^*)$, $P = \tilde{P}(Q(P^*), P^*)$, and $I = I(\tilde{P}(Q(P^*), P^*), P^*, Q(P^*))$. Only the parameter ρ involves cardinal properties of the utility function. Hence, at any $Q(P^*)$, we can make assumptions about the value of ρ independently of assumptions about the other parameters. The following result shows that, for sufficiently high values of ρ, the perverse features of the optimal policy mentioned in section 9.2 indeed occur.

THEOREM 1   Suppose that $\lambda > 0$, i.e., expected utility would be increased if the constraint on expected imports were relaxed. Then

(A) $\rho \gtreqless (1 + QMD_I/S_P)/T$ implies $Q^0_{P^*} \gtreqless 0,$

(B) $\rho \gtreqless M/T$ implies $0 \gtreqless P^0_{P^*},$

(C) $\rho \gtreqless \eta DM/\{Q + (\tilde{P} - P^*)S_P\}$ implies $1 \gtreqless P^0_{P^*}.$

[All functions are evaluated at $Q = Q^0(P^*)$.]

Proof   If $\lambda > 0$, then (12) and (6) imply that, in all states P^*, $(\tilde{P} - P^*)V_I > 0$. It follows that, for all states P^*

$$\tilde{P}(Q^0(P^*), P^*) - P^* > 0, \qquad Q^0(P^*) > 0, \qquad \text{and} \qquad T > 0;$$

i.e., we have positive denominators in the first inequalities in (A), (B), and (C) above.

Applying the implicit function theorem to (12),

$$Q^0_{P^*}(P^*) = -\tilde{V}_{QP^*}/\tilde{V}_{QQ}. \tag{13}$$

Differentiating (6) and substituting from (8),

$$\tilde{V}_{QP^*} = (\tilde{P}_{P^*} - 1)V_I + (\tilde{P} - P^*)(-\tilde{P}_{P^*} \cdot D_I V_I - QV_{II}). \tag{14}$$

Applying the implicit function theorem to (3),

$$\tilde{P}_{P^*}(Q, P^*) = -D_I Q/S_P. \tag{15}$$

Therefore

$$\tilde{V}_{QP^*} = (\rho T - 1 - QD_I M/S_P)V_I. \tag{16}$$

(A) follows from (13), (10), and (16). Moreover,

$$P^0_{P^*}(P^*) = \tilde{P}_{P^*}(Q^0, P^*) + \tilde{P}_Q(Q^0, P^*)Q^0_{P^*}. \tag{17}$$

(B) and (C) then follow by substituting from (15) and (13) and simplifying (see the appendix).   QED

To see the underlying intuition, note that by (6) the first-order condition (12) can be written as

$$\{\tilde{P}(Q, P^*) - P^*\}V_I(\tilde{P}(Q, P^*), I(\tilde{P}(Q, P^*), P^*, Q)) = \lambda; \tag{18}$$

i.e., the contingent quotas $Q(P^*)$ should be allocated so that the rent on a quota license times the marginal utility of income is the same in all states P^*. If the marginal utility of income is constant, i.e., expected consumer's surplus is a valid welfare measure, then (18) implies that the rents $\tilde{P} - P^*$ on quota licenses should be the same in all states. As Young and Anderson (1980, chapter 4) have noted, this condition can be met by setting a specific tariff equal to the common value of these rents. Under this policy, imports decrease (increase) as P^* rises (falls).

To see how risk aversion affects the optimal response of imports to changes in P^*, consider the effect of P^* on the marginal utility of imports, $\tilde{V}_Q(Q, P^*)$, when Q is fixed. A rise in P^* lowers the rent on the quota Q (unless the importable is very inferior). However, it also lowers the country's real income and, given risk aversion, this tends to raise the marginal utility of income V_I. Moreover, for fixed Q and a noninferior importable, the income effect of the increase in P^* lowers the domestic price P and this increases V_I also [see (8)]. If the last two effects are sufficiently strong, then the increase in P^* will increase $\tilde{V}_Q(Q, P^*)$. Optimal imports $Q^0(P^*)$ would then increase with the increase in P^*. Theorem 1A shows that this becomes more likely with higher values of T, the share of tariff revenue in national income; ρ, the coefficient of relative risk aversion; and S_p, the slope of the domestic excess supply function. This is in line with the discussion in section 9.2, since T is associated with the impact of the world price on national income, ρ with the aversion to variations in income, and S_p with the additional "gains from trade" from an increase in imports. Theorems 1B and 1C shows that this increase in optimal imports can lead the optimal domestic price to *fall*—or, at least, to increase more slowly than P^*.[9]

The optimal policy, characterized in theorem 1, could be achieved by imposing a schedule of specific tariffs $P^0(P^*) - P^*$ depending on the world price P^*. Such a tariff schedule is operational, in principle, since P^* is readily monitored. However, the cost of collecting the information required to calculate the schedule could be prohibitive. We therefore consider second-best comparisons between simpler forms of trade restriction. Our analysis of the optimal ex ante policy illuminates this issue also.

9.5 Second-Best Comparisons

Theorem 1A showed that if there is a constraint on expected imports and the representative consumer is highly risk averse, then it is optimal to restrict imports when the world price is low. In these circumstances, we would expect a fixed quota to be superior to a tariff—which leads to an *increase* in imports when the world price is low. In fact, condition (19) which ensures that the quota is superior, is essentially the condition in theorem 1A that ensures that $Q^0_{P^*}(P^*) \geqslant 0$. The only difference is that it is evaluated at the quota level $\bar{Q}$ rather than at $Q^0(P^*)$.

THEOREM 2   Suppose that the quota $\bar{Q}$ on imports is binding in all states P^* and that

$$\rho \geqslant (1 + QD_I M/S_P)/T \qquad \text{for all} \quad P^* \qquad \text{when } Q = \bar{Q}. \tag{19}$$

Then the quota $\bar{Q}$ yields higher expected utility than any other policy $Q(P^*)$ such that

$$E[Q(P^*)] = \bar{Q} \qquad \text{and} \qquad Q_{P^*}(P^*) \leqslant 0. \tag{20}$$

Proof by (10), $\tilde{V}_{QQ}(Q, P^*) < 0$, so the second mean value theorem implies that

$$\tilde{V}(\bar{Q}, P^*) - \tilde{V}(Q(P^*), P^*) \geqslant \tilde{V}_Q(\bar{Q}, P^*)\{\bar{Q} - Q(P^*)\}.$$

The inequality will be strict on a set of positive measure if the policy $Q(P^*)$

differs from the quota $\bar{Q}$. Therefore

$$E[\tilde{V}(\bar{Q}, P^*) - \tilde{V}(Q(P^*), P^*)] > E[\tilde{V}_Q(\bar{Q}, P^*)\{\bar{Q} - Q(P^*)\}].\qquad(21)$$

If (19) holds, then by (16)

$$\tilde{V}_{QP^*}(\bar{Q}, P^*) \geqslant 0.$$

Therefore, if $Q_{P^*}(P^*) \leqslant 0$, then $\tilde{V}_Q(\bar{Q}, P^*)$ and $\bar{Q} - Q(P^*)$ are nonnegatively correlated as P^* varies and

$$E[\tilde{V}_Q(\bar{Q}, P^*)\{\bar{Q} - Q(P^*)\}] \geqslant E[\tilde{V}_Q(\bar{Q}, P^*)]E[\bar{Q} - Q(P^*)]$$

$$= 0 \qquad \text{by hypothesis (20).}\qquad(22)$$

The theorem then follows from (21).   QED

The intuition is similar to that given for theorem 1A. A high P^* lowers the rent associated with the fixed quota $\bar{Q}$. However, it also raises the marginal utility of income V_I—both through the direct effect of P^* in lowering real income and through its indirect effect in lowering the domestic price. If the latter effects are sufficiently strong, then a rise in P^* raises the marginal utility of imports $\tilde{V}_Q(\bar{Q}, P^*)$. Hence, the quota will be superior to any policy that *reduces* imports as P^* rises. It is readily shown that the latter occurs under a specific or an *ad valorem* tariff or under a foreign exchange quota.

We next give conditions under which a tariff is superior to the mean-equivalent quota. We consider a *specific* tariff because this is the optimal trade restriction given constant marginal utility of income. (An *ad valorem* tariff can be inferior to a quota—even with risk neutrality; see Pelcovits, 1976.)

Let $Q^s(P^*)$ be imports in state P^* under a specific tariff of s dollars. Condition (23) for the specific tariff to dominate the mean-equivalent quota is essentially the condition in theorem 1C that ensures that $P^0_{P^*} \geqslant 1$. The only difference is that it is evaluated at $Q^s(P^*)$ rather than at $Q^0(P^*)$.

THEOREM 3   Suppose that neither good is inferior, $Q^s(P^*) > 0$ for all P^* and

$$\rho \leqslant \eta DM/(Q + sS_P) \qquad \text{for all} \quad P^* \qquad \text{when } Q = Q^s(P^*).\qquad(23)$$

Then the specific tariff s yields higher expected utility than any policy $Q(P^*)$ such that

$$E[Q(P^*)] = E[Q^s(P^*)] \qquad \text{and} \qquad Q_{P^*}(P^*) \geqslant 0.\qquad(24)$$

Proof   We first show that the hypotheses imply that $Q_{P^*}^s(P^*) - Q_{P^*}(P^*)$
< 0. $Q_{P^*}^s(P^*)$ satisfies

$$Q + S(P^* + s, P^*Q) = 0.$$

By the implicit function theorem,

$$Q_{P^*}^s(P^*) = -(S_P + QD_I)/(1 - sD_I). \tag{25}$$

If neither good is inferior, then $1 - (P^* + s)D_I > 0$ and $D_I > 0$, so

$$M \equiv 1 - sD_I > 0 \tag{26}$$

(25), (4), (26), and hypothesis (24) then imply that

$$Q_{P^*}^s(P^*) - Q_{P^*}(P^*) < 0. \tag{27}$$

By (10) $\tilde{V}_{QQ}(Q, P^*) < 0$, so by the second mean value theorem

$$\tilde{V}(Q^s(P^*)P^*) - \tilde{V}(Q(P^*), P^*) \geqslant \tilde{V}_Q(Q^s(P^*), P^*)\{Q^s(P^*) - Q(P^*)\}.$$

(27) implies that this inequality is strict on a set of positive measure, so

$$E[\tilde{V}(Q^s(P^*), P^*) - \tilde{V}(Q(P^*), P^*)]$$
$$> E[\tilde{V}_Q(Q^s(P^*), P^*)\{Q^s(P^*) - Q(P^*)\}]. \tag{28}$$

We now consider how $\tilde{V}_Q(Q^s(P^*), P^*)$ changes with P^*. By (16),

$$\tilde{V}_Q(Q^s(P^*), P^*) = sV_I(P^* + s, R(P^* + s) + sQ^s(P^*)).$$

By (1),

$$d\tilde{V}_Q(Q^s(P^*), P^*)/dP^* = s\{V_{IP} + YV_{II} + sQ_{P^*}^s \cdot V_{II}\}.$$

Substituting from (7) and (25),

$$d\tilde{V}(Q^s(P^*), P^*)/dP^* = s[-D_I V_I - V_{II}\{Q + s(S_P + QD_I)/(1 - sD_I)\}]$$
$$= sV_I[-D_I + \rho(Q + sS_P)/I(1 - sD_I)].$$

By (26), $1 - sD_I > 0$, so hypothesis (23) implies that

$$d\tilde{V}_Q(Q^s(P^*), P^*)/sP^* \leqslant 0. \tag{29}$$

(27) and (29) imply that

$$E[\tilde{V}_Q(Q^s(P^*), P^*)\{Q^s(P^*) - Q(P^*)\}] \geqslant E[\tilde{V}_Q(Q^s(P^*), P^*)]E[Q^s(P^*) - Q(P^*)]$$
$$= 0 \qquad \text{by (24)}.$$

The conclusion then follows from (28).   QED

Under a specific tariff, an increase in P^* implies an equal increase in P. The rise in P^* raises V_I by reducing real income but by (8) the rise in P lowers V_I when the importable is not inferior. For sufficiently low ρ, the latter effect dominates so that the marginal utility of imports $\hat{V}_Q = sV_I$ is negatively correlated with P^*. Thus the specific tariff decreases (increases) imports when their marginal utility is low (high)—and is superior to any policy that fails to do this, such as a quota.

9.6 The Model with Domestic Uncertainty

In this section we suppose that the world price of the importable is fixed at some level $\bar{P}^*$ but domestic production possibilities are influenced by a random variable θ. Production decisions are made after θ is known, so θ generally affects the domestic supply function $Y(P, \theta)$ of the importable, the domestic supply function $y(P, \theta)$ of the exportable, and the revenue function $R(P, \theta)$. We shall assume that

$$R_\theta(P, \theta) > 0, \qquad Y_\theta(P, \theta) > 0, \qquad \text{and} \qquad y_\theta(P, \theta) < 0; \tag{30}$$

i.e., an increase in θ increases production revenue and shifts the supply schedule of the importable (exportable) to the right (left). This assumption holds under the following two interpretations of θ:

LEMMA 1   In the neoclassical 2×2 trade model, (30) holds if either

(A) θ is the labor supply and the importable is relatively labor intensive or

(B) θ is a parameter affecting the production function of the importable in a multiplicative (Hicks neutral) fashion.

Proof   See the appendix.

When imports are Q and domestic price is P, consumer income is

$$I(P, Q, \theta) \equiv R(P, \theta) + P - \bar{P}^*)Q \tag{31}$$

and domestic excess supply of the importable is

$$S(P, Q, \theta) = Y(P, \theta) - D(P, I(P, Q, \theta)). \tag{32}$$

Let $\tilde{P}(Q, \theta)$ be domestic equilibrium price in state θ when imports are Q. This is the P satisfying

$$Q + S(P, Q, \theta) = 0. \tag{33}$$

An argument like that yielding (4) shows that

$S_P > 0$ when $P = \tilde{P}(Q, \theta)$. $\qquad\qquad$ (34)

Let $\tilde{V}(Q, \theta)$ be domestic utility in state θ in equilibrium when imports are Q.

Any trade restriction is equivalent to a rule determining the quantity $Q(\theta)$ to be imported in any state θ. Let $Q^0(\theta)$ be the policy maximizing domestic expected utility subject to a constraint on expected imports and let λ be the Lagrange multiplier associated with this constraint.

THEOREM 4   If $\lambda > 0$ and neither good is inferior, then $Q^0_\theta(\theta) < 0$.

Proof   It is readily checked that (6) and (10) remain valid when foreign uncertainty is replaced by domestic uncertainty. Hence $Q^0(\theta)$ is determined by the first-order condition

$$\lambda = \tilde{V}_Q(Q, \theta) = \{\tilde{P}(Q, \theta) - \bar{P}^*\} V_I(\tilde{P}(Q, \theta), I(\tilde{P}(Q, \theta), Q, \theta)). \qquad (35)$$

If $\lambda > 0$, then by (35)

$$\tilde{P}(Q, \theta) - \bar{P}^* > 0. \qquad\qquad (36)$$

Applying the implicit function theorem to (35),

$$Q^0_\theta = -\tilde{V}_{Q\theta}/\tilde{V}_{QQ}. \qquad\qquad (37)$$

Differentiating (6) with respect to θ and substituting from (8),

$$\tilde{V}_{Q\theta} = \tilde{P}_\theta V_I \{1 - (\tilde{P} - \bar{P}^*)D_I\} + (\tilde{P} - \bar{P}^*)V_{II}R_\theta. \qquad (38)$$

Applying the implicit function theorem to (33),

$$\tilde{P}_\theta = -(Y_\theta - D_I R_\theta)/S_P.$$

But

$$R_\theta = y_\theta + PY_\theta, \qquad\qquad (39)$$

so

$$\tilde{P}_\theta = \{y_\theta D_I - Y_\theta(1 - \tilde{P}D_I)\}/S_P. \qquad (40)$$

If neither good is inferior, then $D_I > 0$ and $1 - \tilde{P}D_I > 0$, so by (30) and (34)

$$\tilde{P}_\theta < 0. \qquad\qquad (41)$$

Moreover, if neither good is inferior, then $1 - (\tilde{P} - \bar{P}^*)D_I > 0$, so by (38), (41), (36), and (30)

$$\tilde{V}_{Q\theta} < 0. \qquad\qquad (42)$$

The theorem then follows from (37), (42), and (10).   QED

There is no counterpart to the possibly perverse effect of P^* on optimal imports. A rightward shift in the supply schedule of imports increases the representative consumer's income and hence reduces the marginal utility of income V_I. Moreover, its effect in reducing the rent on a quota license outweighs the rise in V_I due to the fall in P. Hence as θ increases, the marginal utility of imports always decreases, so that optimal imports always decrease also.

In contrast to section 9.4, the optimal policy cannot be effected by a schedule of tariffs depending on the world price P^*, since P^* is now fixed. However, the optimal policy could be effected by a schedule of tariffs depending on the level of imports Q. By theorem 4, if neither good is inferior then, for each Q, there is a unique $\theta = \hat{\theta}(Q)$ such that $Q = Q(\theta)$. The optimal policy is equivalent to levying a specific tariff

$$\hat{s}(Q) = \tilde{P}(Q, \hat{\theta}(Q)) - \bar{P}^*$$

when imports are Q.[10] We now identify an unexpected feature of this optimal tariff schedule.

THEOREM 5   Suppose that $\lambda > 0$, neither good is inferior, the representative consumer is risk averse, and, for all θ, $\tilde{P}(Q^0(\theta), \theta) \leqslant 2\bar{P}^*$. Then $\hat{s}_Q(Q^0(\theta), \theta) < 0$.

Proof   Since $\hat{\theta}(Q)$ is the inverse function of $Q^0(\theta)$,

$$\hat{\theta}_Q(Q) = 1/Q_\theta^0(\hat{\theta}(Q)).$$

Therefore

$$\hat{s}_Q(Q) = \tilde{P}_Q + \tilde{P}_\theta/Q_\theta^0.$$

Noting that $\tilde{P}_Q = -M/S_P$ and substituting from (37) and (40),

$$\hat{s}_Q = -M/S_P + \{Y_\theta(1 - \tilde{P}D_I) - y_\theta D_I\}\tilde{V}_{QQ}/\tilde{V}_{Q\theta}S_P. \tag{43}$$

In the appendix we show that this reduces to

$$\hat{s}_Q = -(\tilde{P} - \bar{P}^*)V_{II}\{(\tilde{P} - \bar{P}^*)D_I y_\theta + \bar{P}^* Y_\theta\}/S_P \tilde{V}_{Q\theta}. \tag{44}$$

We now determine the sign of the term in curly brackets in (44). If $\tilde{P} \leqslant 2\bar{P}^*$ then, $\bar{P}^* \geqslant \tilde{P} - \bar{P}^*$ so

$$(\tilde{P} - \bar{P}^*)D_I y_\theta + \bar{P}^* Y_\theta \geqslant (\tilde{P} - \bar{P}^*)(D_I y_\theta + Y_\theta). \tag{45}$$

By (30), $R_\theta = \tilde{P}Y_\theta + y_\theta > 0$, so

$$(\tilde{P} - \bar{P}^*)(D_I y_\theta + Y_\theta) > (\tilde{P} - \bar{P}^*)y_\theta(\tilde{P}D_I - 1)/\tilde{P}. \tag{46}$$

Since $\lambda > 0$ and the exportable is not inferior,

$$\tilde{P} - \bar{P}^* > 0 \qquad \text{and} \qquad \tilde{P}D_I - 1 < 0. \tag{47}$$

By (30) $y_\theta < 0$, so by (47) the right side of (46) is positive and by (45) and (46) the term in curly brackets in (44) is positive. Since the representative consumer is risk averse, $V_{II} < 0$. Therefore by (44), (47), (34), and (42),

$$\hat{s}_Q < 0. \qquad \text{QED}$$

Theorem 5 shows that if the constraint on expected imports is not so restrictive that the optimal domestic price can be over double the world price, then income stability is again more important than arbitrage considerations. Tariffs should be decreased (increased) when the supply schedule of the importable shifts to the left (right) in order to buffer the domestic economy against the associated shifts in national income.

It may be difficult to administer a tariff schedule that varies continuously with the level of imports. However, the optimal tariff schedule could be approximated by a multiple-block schedule in which the tariff rate steps downward as imports exceed certain critical levels. Multiple-block tariff schedules are, in fact, quite common, but the tariff rate usually steps *upward* as imports increase.[11]

Finally, we compare a quota with a fixed tariff. Since the world price $\bar{P}^*$ is fixed, any fixed tariff is equivalent to some specific tariff s. Let $Q^s(\theta)$ be imports in state θ under this tariff.

THEOREM 6   Suppose that the representative consumer is risk averse, neither good is inferior, $Q^s(\theta) > 0$ for all θ, and

$$\bar{P}^* Y_\theta(\bar{P}^* + s, \theta) + y_\theta(\bar{P}^* + s, \theta) > 0. \tag{48}$$

Then the specific tariff s yields higher expected utility than any trade restriction $Q(\theta)$ such that

$$E[Q(\theta)] = Q(\theta) \qquad \text{and} \qquad Q_\theta(\theta) \geq 0. \tag{49}$$

Proof   To apply the argument of theorem 3, we show that $V_Q(Q^s(\theta), \theta)$ and $Q^s(\theta) - Q(\theta)$ are positively correlated. $Q^s(\theta)$ is the solution to

$$Q + Y(\bar{P}^* + s, \theta) - D(P^* + s, R(\bar{P}^* + s, \theta) + sQ) = 0.$$

By the implicit function theorem,

$$Q_\theta^s(\theta) = -(Y_\theta - D_I R_\theta)/(1 - sD_I).$$

By (39),

$$Q_\theta^s(\theta) = [-Y_\theta\{1 - (\bar{P}^* + s)D_I\} + y_\theta D_I]/(1 - sD_I). \tag{50}$$

Since neither good is inferior, $1 - (\bar{P}^* + s)D_I > 0$ and $1 - sD_I > 0$, so by (30), (50), and hypothesis (49)

$$Q_\theta^s(\theta) - Q_\theta(\theta) < 0. \tag{51}$$

By (6),

$$V_Q(Q^s(\theta), \theta) = sV_I(\bar{P}^* + s, R(\bar{P}^* + s, \theta) + sQ^s(\theta)).$$

Therefore

$$d\tilde{V}_Q(Q^s(\theta), \theta)/d\theta = s\{R_\theta + sQ_\theta^s(\theta)\} V_{II}. \tag{52}$$

By (39) and (50),

$$R_\theta + sQ_\theta^s = y_\theta[1 + sD_I/(1 - sD_I)]$$

$$+ Y_\theta[\bar{P}^* + s - s\{1 - (\bar{P}^* + s)D_I\}/(1 - sD_I)] \tag{53}$$

$$= (y_\theta + \bar{P}^* Y_\theta)/(1 - sD_I).$$

Since the exportable is not inferior, $1 - sD_I > 0$. Therefore, by (53) and hypothesis (48),

$$R_\theta + sQ_\theta^s > 0.$$

(52) then implies that

$$d\tilde{V}_Q(Q^s(\theta), \theta)/d\theta < 0. \tag{54}$$

(54) and (51) imply that $\tilde{V}_Q(Q^s(\theta), \theta)$ and $Q^s(\theta) - Q(\theta)$ are positively correlated. Therefore, the argument of theorem 3 shows that

$$E[\tilde{V}(Q^s(\theta), \theta) - \tilde{V}(Q(\theta), \theta)] > 0. \quad \text{QED}$$

Hypothesis (48) states that the value of domestic production at world prices increases with θ. Since $0 < R_\theta = (\bar{P}^* + s)Y_\theta + y_\theta$, this always holds provided that the tariff s is not too high. In these circumstances, an increase in θ increases domestic income and hence decreases the marginal utility of income. The rightward shift in the domestic supply schedule also lowers the rent on quota licenses. Both these effects lead optimal imports to decrease. Since a tariff indeed decreases imports in these circumstances, it dominates any policy that would fail to decrease imports—such as a quota.

For any quota $\bar{Q}$ we can show that $dV_Q(\bar{Q}, \theta)/d\theta \leqslant 0$. Hence we *cannot* use the argument of theorem 2 to derive circumstances under which a quota is superior to a tariff under domestic uncertainty.

9.7 Conclusions

If the representative consumer of a country is risk averse, then the choice of trade controls must take account of their effects on fluctuations of domestic real income. The source of uncertainty is then critical. If the disturbances arise from abroad then, with high risk aversion, it would be optimal to increase imports and to lower the domestic price as the world price rises. Furthermore, a quota would be superior to a tariff. Under domestic disturbances, not only do we confirm the superiority of a tariff over a quota, but we also conclude that a fixed tariff does not go far enough in encouraging import responses to domestic changes: the optimal domestic price *falls* as imports increase. The intuition for these results was given in section 9.2 and was confirmed by our analysis in terms of the marginal utility of imports. If both domestic and foreign disturbances occur and risk aversion is high, then the ranking of tariffs and quotas would, of course, depend on which source of disturbances is predominant.

It would be a routine matter to extend the above analysis to the case of a large country, or where the "noneconomic constraint" is on expected foreign exchange expenditure or expected tariff revenue or where the policymaker is concerned with higher moments of the distribution of imports. A more challenging problem would be to consider the optimal trade restriction given a constraint on the expected welfare of a "protected" subgroup within the country.

Appendix 9.A

Derivation of (10)   Differentiating (6) and substituting from (8) yields

$$\tilde{V}_{QQ} = \tilde{P}_Q V_I - (\tilde{P} - P^*)\tilde{P}_Q D_I V_I + (\tilde{P} - P^*)^2 V_{II}.$$

Applying the implicit function theorem to (3) yields

$$\tilde{P}_Q = -\{1 - (\tilde{P} - P^*)D_I\}/S_P. \tag{55}$$

Therefore

$$\tilde{V}_{QQ} = -\{1 - (\tilde{P} - P^*)D_I\}^2 V_I/S_P + (\tilde{P} - P^*)^2 V_{II}. \tag{56}$$

By (4) if $V_{II} \leqslant 0$, then $V_{QQ} < 0$.

Proof of Theorems 1B and 1C   In (17), substituting from (15), (55), (13), (16), and (56),

$$P_{P^*}^0 = \frac{-D_I Q}{S_P} + \frac{QD_I M^2 / S_P - (\rho T - 1)M}{M^2 + \rho S_P (\tilde{P} - P^*)^2 / I}$$

$$= \frac{M(1 - \rho T) - QD_I (\tilde{P} - P^*)^2 \rho / I}{M^2 + \rho S_P (\tilde{P} - P^*)^2 / I}$$

$$= \frac{M - \rho T \{ M + (\tilde{P} - P^*) D_I \}}{M^2 + \rho S_P (\tilde{P} - P^*)^2 / I}$$

$$= \frac{M - \rho T}{M^2 + \rho S_P (\tilde{P} - P^*)^2 / I}.$$

Since $S_P > 0$ and $T > 0$, theorem 1B follows immediately. Moreover, the condition $P_{P^*}^0 < 1$ is equivalent to each of the following inequalities:

$$M - \rho T < M^2 + \rho S_P (\tilde{P} - P^*)^2 / I,$$

$$M(1 - M) < \rho \{ T + S_P (\tilde{P} - P^*)^2 / I \},$$

$$M(\tilde{P} - P^*) D_I < \rho \{ (\tilde{P} - P^*) Q / I + S_P (\tilde{P} - P^*) / I \},$$

$$M D_I I < \rho \{ Q + S_P (\tilde{P} - P^*) \}.$$

Since $Q > 0$ and $\tilde{P} - P^* > 0$, theorem 1C now follows.   QED

Proof of Lemma 1   In both cases (A) and (B), an increase in θ leads to an outward shift in the production possibility set of the home country. For any P, this leads to an increase in the maximum value of domestic production at domestic prices, i.e. $R_\theta(P, \theta) > 0$. In case (A) the remaining conclusions in (30) follow from the Rybczynski theorem.

In case (B), let $C^I(w, r, \theta)$ and $C^E(w, r)$ be the minimum unit costs of the importable and exportable in state θ when the wage is w and the rental on capital is r. Let $A^{IL}(w, r, \theta)$, $A^{IK}(w, r, \theta)$ and $A^{EL}(w, r)$, $A^{EK}(w, r)$ be the cost-minimizing inputs of labor and capital required to produce a unit of importable and exportable respectively. If the country has L^0 units of labor and K^0 units of capital and production is not specialized, then, in state θ at price P for the importable, $Y(P, \theta)$ and $y(P, \theta)$ are determined simultaneously with w and r by the equations

$$C^I(w, r, \theta) = P, \qquad C^E(w, r) = 1,$$

$$A^{IL}(w, r, \theta) Y(P, \theta) + A^{EL}(w, r) y(P, \theta) = L^0, \tag{57}$$

$$A^{IK}(w, r, \theta) Y(P, \theta) + A^{EK}(w, r) y(P, \theta) = K^0.$$

Since θ affects the production function of the importable in a multiplicative fashion,

$$C^I(w, r, \theta) = C^I(w, r, 1) / \theta,$$

$$A^{IL}(w, r, \theta) = A^{IL}(w, r, 1) / \theta, \qquad A^{IK}(w, r, \theta) = A^{IK}(w, r, 1) / \theta.$$

Therefore (57) becomes

$$C^I(w, r, 1) = P\theta, \qquad C^E(w, r) = 1,$$

$$A^{IL}(w, r, 1) Y(P, \theta)/\theta + A^{EL}(w, r) y(P, \theta) = L^0, \tag{58}$$

$$A^{IK}(w, r, 1) Y(P, \theta)/\theta + A^{EK}(w, r) y(P, \theta) = K^0.$$

Therefore $Y(P, \theta)/\theta$ and $y(P, \theta)$ satisfy the same equations (58) as those that determine $Y(P\theta, 1)$ and $y(P\theta, 1)$, i.e.,

$$Y(P, \theta) = \theta Y(P\theta, 1) \qquad \text{and} \qquad y(P, \theta) = y(P\theta, 1).$$

Therefore

$$Y_\theta(P, \theta) = Y(P\theta, 1) + \theta P Y_P(P\theta, 1) > 0$$

and

$$y_\theta(P, \theta) = P y_P(P\theta, 1) < 0. \quad \text{QED}$$

Derivation of (44) By (43),

$$-\hat{s}_Q S_P \tilde{V}_{Q\theta} = y_\theta D_I \tilde{V}_{QQ} - Y_\theta(1 - \tilde{P}D_I) \tilde{V}_{QQ} + M \tilde{V}_{Q\theta}.$$

Substituting from (56), (38), and (40) and regrouping,

$$-\hat{s}_Q S_P \tilde{V}_{Q\theta} = y_\theta D_I [-M^2 V_I/S_P + M^2 V_I/S_P + (\tilde{P} - \bar{P}^*)^2 V_{II}]$$
$$+ Y_\theta[-(1 - \tilde{P}D_I)M^2 V_I/S_P + M(\tilde{P} - \bar{P}^*)V_{II}\tilde{P}$$
$$+ (1 - \tilde{P}D_I)M^2 V_I/S_P - (1 - \tilde{P}D_I)(\tilde{P} - \bar{P}^*)^2 V_{II}]$$
$$= y_\theta D_I(\tilde{P} - \bar{P}^*)^2 V_{II} + Y_\theta(\tilde{P} - \bar{P}^*)V_{II}[\tilde{P}\{1 - (\tilde{P} - \bar{P}^*)D_I\}$$
$$- (1 - \tilde{P}D_I)(\tilde{P} - \bar{P}^*)]$$
$$= (\tilde{P} - \bar{P}^*)V_{II}[(\tilde{P} - \bar{P}^*)D_I y_\theta + Y_\theta \bar{P}^*].$$

(44) follows immediately.

The first author acknowledges the hospitality of the Economics Departments at Boston College and MIT while this chapter was being written. We are grateful to a referee for very helpful comments on an earlier version.

Notes

1. Helpman and Razin (1980) focus on uncertainty in production and assume that production decisions are made before the uncertainty is resolved, while consumption decisions are made afterward. The other authors cited assume that both production and consumption decisions are made ex post. The latter assumption is

also made in this chapter. Helpman and Razin assume that intervention is targeted at the levels of inputs allocated to the import-competing sector while the other authors assume constraints on expected imports, import expenditure, or tariff revenue.

2. Provided only that consumer's surplus is a concave function of imports, i.e., the excess demand schedule is downward sloping.

3. This resembles Weitzman's (1977) conclusion that quantity rationing of a good among individuals will be preferable to price rationing if the variance of their marginal utilities of income is large compared to the variance of their marginal utilities from consumption of the good.

4. With ex ante choices in production, the outcome will depend on the opportunities for producers to trade in risk and to enter and exit from the uncertain industry.

5. Bhagwati and Srinivasan (1969).

6. Anderson and Young (1981, chapter 7) consider the optimal policy when the government is also concerned with higher moments of the import distribution.

7. Turnovsky (1975), Anderson and Riley (1976), and Flemming, Turnovsky, and Kemp (1977) use a similar model to determine the effect of exogenous price uncertainty on the optimal ex ante choice of production when only consumption choices are made ex post.

8. This can be proved formally using the second mean value theorem as in Young (1980a, p. 427).

9. Suppose that the implicit tariff rate is 100% $[(P - P^*)/P = 1/2]$, 50% of national income is spent on the importable $[PD/I = 1/2]$, 25% of the importable is domestically produced $[Q/D = 3/4]$, the price elasticity of the general equilibrium excess supply of imports is $2[PS_P/Q = 2]$, and the income elasticity of demand for the importable is 1. Then a simple calculation shows that the breakeven values of ρ in A, B, and C are respectively, $6^2/3$, 4, and 1/2. By comparison, Friend and Blume's (1975) empirical analysis of portfolio choices using the capital asset pricing model suggests values of ρ of about 3 or above.

10. It might appear that an indeterminacy arises because domestic consumers and producers could not make their decisions without knowing the domestic price while the government could not set the tariff level (and hence the domestic price) without knowing final imports. However, the government need only monitor the level of imports and levy $\hat{s}(Q)$ on the marginal unit as it enters. Earlier units might enter under a different tariff but arbitrage would ensure that all units have the same price as the last unit imported. Tariff revenue plus arbitrage gains or losses would equal $Q\hat{s}(Q)$.

11. Richardson (1980, p. 353).

References

Anderson, J. E., and J. G. Riley (1976), "International Trade with Fluctuating Prices," *International Economic Review*, 17, 76–97.

Anderson, J. E., and L. Young (1981, chapter 7), "The Optimality of Tariff Quotas under Uncertainty," University of Canterbury.

Bhagwati, J. N., and T. N. Srinivasan (1969), "Optimal Intervention to Achieve Non-Economic Objectives," *Review of Economic Studies*, 36, 27–38.

Caves, R. E., and R. W. Jones (1977), *World Trade and Payments: An Introduction*, 2nd ed., Boston: Little, Brown.

Dasgupta, P., and J. E. Stiglitz (1977), "Tariffs vs. Quotas as Revenue-Raising Devices under Uncertainty," *American Economic Review*, 67, 975–981.

Dixit, A.K., and V. Norman (1980), *Theory of International Trade*, Welwyn, Herts: Cambridge University Press.

Fishelson, G., and F. Flatters (1975), "The (Non-)Equivalence of Optimal Tariffs and Quotas under Uncertainty," *Journal of International Economics*, 5, 385–393.

Flemming, J. S., S. J. Turnovsky, and M. C. Kemp (1977), "On the Choice of Numeraire and Certainty Price in General Equilibrium Models of Price Uncertainty," *Review of Economic Studies*, 94, 573–584.

Friend, I., and M. E. Blume (1975), "The Demand for Risky Assets," *American Economic Review*, 65, 900–923.

Helpman, E., and A. Razin (1980), "Efficient Protection under Uncertainty," *American Economic Review*, 70, 716–731.

Ireland, N. J. (1977), "Ideal Prices vs Prices vs Quantities," *Review of Economic Studies*, 44, 183–207.

Laffont, J. J. (1977), "More on Prices vs Quantities," *Review of Economic Studies*, 44, 177–182.

Malcomson, J. M. (1978), "Prices vs Quantities: A Critical Note on the Use of Approximations," *Review of Economic Studies*, 45, 203–208.

Pelcovits, M. G. (1976), "Quotas vs. Tariffs," *Journal of International Economics*, 6, 363–370.

Richardson, J. D. (1980), *Understanding International Economics: Theory and Practice*, Boston: Little, Brown.

Turnovsky, S. J. (1975), "Technological and Price Uncertainty in a Neo-Ricardian Model of International Trade," *Review of Economic Studies*, 41, 201–217.

Weitzman, M. L. (1974), "Prices vs Quantities," *Review of Economic Studies*, 41, 50–65.

Weitzman, M. L. (1977), "Is the Price System or Rationing More Effective in Getting a Commodity to Those Who Need it Most?" *Bell Journal of Economics*, 8, 517–524.

Weitzman, M. L. (1978), "Optimal Rewards for Economic Regulation," *American Economic Review*, 68, 683–691.

Woodland, A. D. (1980), "Direct and Indirect Trade Utility Functions," *Review of Economic Studies*, 46, 906–932.

Yohe, G. W. (1978), "Towards a General Comparison of Price Controls and Quantity Controls under Uncertainty," *Review of Economic Studies*, 45, 229–238.

Young, L. (1979), "Ranking the Optimal Tariff and Quota for a Large Country under Uncertainty," *Journal of International Economics*, 9, 249–264.

Young, L. (1980a), "Optimal Revenue-Raising Trade Restrictions under Uncertainty," *Journal of International Economics*, 10, 425–439.

Young, L. (1980b), "Tariffs vs Quotas under Uncertainty: An Extension," *American Economic Review*, 70, 522–527.

Young, L. and J. E. Anderson (1980), "The Optimal Policies for Restricting Trade under Uncertainty," *Review of Economic Studies*, 46, 927–932.

III

Intertemporal Issues

10

Quotas as Options: Optimality and Quota License Pricing under Uncertainty

A puzzling and significant aspect of quota systems is explained in this chapter. Quotas in practice are frequently unfilled, yet the licenses command positive price on organized markets where they exist (for example, textile export quotas in Hong Kong). Even without such markets, non-binding quotas appear to cause international price differences that cannot be explained by transactions and transportation costs. For example, in work reported in Anderson (1985), a study of the U.S. cheese import quota system, I frequently observed such phenomena for some cheese categories.

The explanation is that quota licenses are options. Typically, imports or exports are licensed for one year. The license may be used at any time during the year, making it equivalent to an "American-type" financial option.[1] The result is that licenses have positive price; hence quotas cause protection, even in states of nature when the quota does not bind.

Three further administrative features of quota systems deserve and are given analysis in this light. First, many quota systems have use-it-or-lose-it requirements: a unit license not used this year will not be awarded next year. Second, it is common for governments to issue licenses valid for one year, then impose further constraints on rate of use within the year. Third, while quota licenses are usually given away, there is often effective prohibition of resale of the licenses. All three obviously act to reduce the value of the license, based on the first consideration. They may represent some attempt to mollify consumer interests by reducing import prices in below-limit states.

This chapter is in five sections. Section 10.1 develops two simple, effectively static models of the competitive pricing of quota licenses. The first shows how option valuation creates positive protection on below-limit

Reprinted, with changes, by permission from *Journal of International Economics*, November 1987.

trade; the second shows how use-it-or-lose-it requirements subsidize below-limit trade. These are robust implications that will hold up in more general models.

Recognition that quota licenses are options suggests that an accurate general model of their value should be constructed along the lines of the financial option pricing literature (see, for example, Black and Scholes, 1973). It will require a significant extension of that literature to allow exercise of the option to affect the price of the underlying security.

A number of the administrative regulations regarding quota licenses impair the functioning of the license market. This appears likely to be inefficient. In order to study this in a convenient way, a simple normative model is used in remaining sections of this chapter. The preference of protectionist forces for an annual quota is taken as given. Optimal import control subject to this constraint is studied in section 10.2. Option pricing is, as expected, efficient. This provides a benchmark for evaluating the inefficiency of various regulations in subsequent sections. Such a method is ad hoc, but it conforms to a useful tradition in the literature (see, for example, Bhagwati and Srinivasan, 1983, chap. 24). In the present context, it also illuminates the unnecessary inefficiency of use-it-or-lose-it requirements and resale prohibition by revealing the unconvincing nature of the added noneconomic objectives needed to render these regulations optimal.

Section 10.3 repeats in abbreviated form the analysis of section 10.1 and 10.2 for expenditure (foreign exchange) restrictions. Section 10.4 takes up resale prohibition, mainly to analyze circumstances in which it may be in the interest of the importing country producers or consumers. The effect hinges on ratios analogous to those governing the transfer problem. Thus, such requirements have ambiguous impact on domestic price in general, besides their added inefficiency. Therefore, their use is particularly inadvisable. Sections 10.2 and 10.3 deal with import quotas, but the analysis applies equally to VERs, so in section 10.4 the analysis is illustrated with VERs.

Section 10.5 concludes with a discussion of future research needs and implications for policymakers. The pricing model is very simple as a first step and to suit the focus on commercial policy. It is rich with suggestions for future work.

The focus of this chapter is on trade quotas, but any situation in which an accumulated flow is constrained over some interval of time shares the same characteristics. Some types of pollution controls (e.g., monthly fuel mix constraints on electric power companies), quality controls (e.g., the annual fleet-average mileage constraint on U.S. automakers), and credit controls (e.g., a line-of-credit limit) have this form. In contrast, taxi-cab medallions and tobacco production allotments are entry constraints; ownership has no effect on subsequent rate of use.

10.1 Pricing of Quota Licenses under Uncertainty

A quota license under uncertainty is an option. In the most general formulation of the pricing problem, the license allows exercise (i.e., purchase at world price and resale at domestic price of one unit of imports) at any time during the year (or other time period). In the language of financial markets, this is an "American" option: the exercise date is at the owner's discretion over a specified time interval. The decision to exercise depends on the discounted expected future value versus the rent realized immediately. One important complication is that the ability to obtain free licenses in future periods may depend on proof that licenses have been used in the present period (a property of licenses for both Hong Kong textile exports and U.S. cheese imports). This is the use-it-or-lose-it requirement.

The financial option literature cannot be simply adapted to price quota licenses. That literature assumes that the exercise of the option has no effect on the price of the underlying security, or in this case, on the domestic price of imports. The essence of the quota license valuation problem is precisely the link between exercise and the price of imports. A new model is needed.

For present purposes, the time structure of the general problem is unnecessarily complex, so I simplify to two extreme versions of a static model. These highlight two polar tendencies of actual schemes: (1) to withhold use in the hope of a future gain and (2) to "dump" licenses in the hope of getting another license in the future.

In the first model, Q units of import licenses are extant in each period, with the government issuing only enough new ones to create that total. A license is a perpetual right to import one unit at some date. New licenses are issued at the beginning of each period to randomly chosen licensees (e.g., are dropped out of helicopters). Previous holders of licenses have the same probability of receiving a new one as anyone else. This may be rationalized as a limiting case of real world systems, which often allow limited "carry-forward" of licenses.

Now consider the pricing of licenses. The decision to execute (exercise) in this case depends on the current rent (execution value) versus the expected future rent (reservation value). For simplicity, no discounting is imposed, the distribution is stationary, and the import market is assumed to have a large number of license holders. For states in which the quota does not bind, the equilibrium condition for competitive risk neutral license use is

$$P(Q(s), s) - P^*(s) = E[P(Q(s), s) - P^*(s)], \tag{1}$$

for $Q(s) < Q$. In (1), s is the state of nature, P the domestic price, $Q(s)$ the import quantity in state s, $P(Q(s), s)$ the inverse import demand function, and P^* the exogenous foreign price. For any realization s, licenses are used until $Q(s)$ is just large enough to equate execution with the reservation value of the option. The right-hand side of (1) is of course also the competitive auction price that speculators are willing to pay for a unit quota license. Expectations in (1) may or may not be rational. For $Q(s) = Q$, (1) does not control, and P is obtained from the inverse demand schedule $P(Q, s)$.

Note from (1) that it is not necessary that $Q(s) = Q$ in each state for quota licenses to have value, as in the certainty case. The only requirement for the option to have value is that in some states the license earns rent. This explains why textile licenses command positive price on Hong Kong markets much of the year despite occasional unfilled quotas approaching 50%. Note that (1) also implies that the domestic price of imports will lie above the foreign price if licenses have positive value, even though $Q(s) < Q$. That is, the restrictive effect of quotas is not limited to the states of nature where the quota binds, but will restrict in all states.

To sharpen the focus of the discussion of license pricing, consider the case when (1) holds with rational expectations. Suppose that states of nature in which the quota is exhausted are members of set H: $Q(s) = Q$, $s \in H$. Such states occur when the agents' use of licenses exhausts Q with the left side of (1) greater than or equal to the right side of (1). The other states are members of set L. Let $\alpha(s)$, $\gamma(s)$ be probabilities associated with s for $s \in H$, $s \in L$, respectively. Then the rational expectations equilibrium of license pricing requires

$$E[P] = \sum_{s \in H} P(Q, s)\alpha(s) + \sum_{s \in L} \{P^*(s) - E[P^*] + E[P]\}\gamma(s).$$

This can be solved for

$$E[P] = E[P \mid H] + (\sum \gamma / \sum \alpha)\{E[P^* \mid L] - E[P^*]\},$$

where $E[P \mid H]$ denotes the expectation of P over states in H, $E[P \mid H] = \sum_{s \in H} P(Q, s)\alpha(s) / \sum_{s \in H} \alpha(s)$, and similarly for $E[P^* \mid L]$. Substituting in (1) and noting $\sum \alpha = \mathrm{Prob}(H)$, $\sum \gamma = \mathrm{Prob}(L) = 1 - \mathrm{Prob}(H)$, the solution is

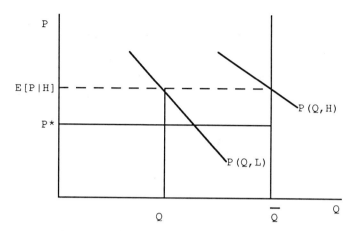

Figure 10.1

$$P - P^* = E[P\,|\,H] - E[P^*\,|\,H]. \tag{1'}$$

(1') states that rational expectations option pricing marks up all non-binding sales to the average markup on binding sales. This makes intuitive sense with no discounting. Evidently, (1') implies premia on licenses (with costs passed through to consumers) even if the probability of a binding quota is low. The only stipulation is that the quota be restrictive when it does bind. The competitive equilibrium is independent of $\mathrm{Prob}(H)$, $\mathrm{Prob}(L)$ so long as they are strictly in the unit interval. With discounting ($\delta \leqslant 1$), (1') holds in the limit (see section 10.2) and thus represents a tendency.

Figure 10.1 illustrates this. There are two states of domestic demand for imports, H and L, with inverse demand $P(Q, H)$ and $P(Q, L)$. Foreign price P^* is fixed at $\bar{P}^*$. Q_L is the equilibrium quantity of imports in state L. $\bar{Q}$ is the quota limit. In state H all licenses are used and rent is earned on each unit equal to $P(\bar{Q}, H) - \bar{P}^*$. In state L, licenses will be used until $P(Q_L, L) - \bar{P}^*$, the realized rent on execution, equals the expected rent from reservation, $E(P\,|\,H) - \bar{P}^*$.

The second model of quota license pricing has similar form but, being built to incorporate a use-it-or-lose-it requirement, it has remarkably different implications. Suppose now that the government requires use in the current period as a condition for obtaining a license in future periods. Q units of licenses, valid only in the current period, are issued at the beginning of each period. They are allocated to eligible previous holders plus any randomly chosen new holders for the "free" portion of the total quota

Q. Again I impose no discounting. In this case the holder of a license has an incentive to use it in the current period, even at a loss, in order to obtain future import licenses with positive expected value. For states of the world where the quota binds, P is obtained from the inverse import demand function $P(Q, s)$. For states where it does not bind, in risk neutral competitive equilibrium, execution is controlled by

$$\{P(Q(s), s) - P^*(s)\} + E[PV] = 0, \tag{2}$$

where PV is the present value of future licenses.

In (2), the left-hand side is the expected return from use, and the right-hand side is the return from no use. (2) implies that the existence of expected future rents from quota license ownership effectively creates a subsidy on current period imports in periods where the quota does not bind. Imposing rational expectations equilibrium, the same steps as above imply[2]

$$-\{P(Q(s), s) - P^*(s)\} = \{\text{Prob}(H)/\text{Prob}(L)\}\{E[P \,|\, H] - E[P^* \,|\, H]\}. \tag{3}$$

In (3), in contrast to (1'), the probability of H or L matters.

The intuition can be illustrated with a 2-point distribution, where $\text{Prob}(H) = \text{Prob}(L) = \frac{1}{2}$. It has the neat property of perfectly complementing (1'): the tax and the subsidy are equal. An agent holding a present license knows that by using it, losing $(P \,|\, L) - (P^* \,|\, L)$ he obtains a future license. This future license gains $E(P \,|\, H) - E(P^* \,|\, H)$ with probability $\frac{1}{2}$, and loses the same stake $(P \,|\, L) - (P^* \,|\, L)$ with probability $\frac{1}{2}$. Over a large number of repetitions, half the time he loses $(P \,|\, L) - (P^* \,|\, L)$ and half the time he wins $E[P \,|\, H] - E[P^* \,|\, H]$; hence his expected profit over a long time is zero when these amounts are equal.

Figure 10.2 illustrates using the previous diagram's structure. In figure 10.2

$$\sigma = \{\text{Prob}(H)/\text{Prob}(L)\}\{E[P \,|\, H] - E[P^* \,|\, H]\}.$$

The two theoretical pricing models set out here capture extreme tendencies of the current system. The balance in practice (based on U.S. cheese imports and Hong Kong textile exports) appears to be toward the first model, in which licenses have positive rent almost always. The other extreme is always possible, depending on the administrative details. The simplest interpretation of the use-it-or-lose-it requirement of import quota systems is that it offsets to some extent the protectionist bias of the option pricing. On the other hand, since this requirement is voluntarily imposed by export authorities under the VERs, its effect is to subsidize exports and

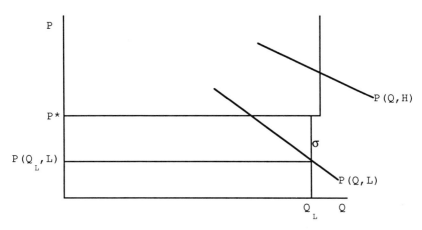

Figure 10.2

reverse the (certainty case) transfer of rent under the VER system. This may not be an intended result.

Simple characteristics of quota licensing under uncertainty are the focus of this chapter, but the results will obtain qualitatively in a more realistic option pricing model that explicitly uses the time structure of the quota system. An equation like (1) controls execution on most days of the year, save that the right-hand side is not so simple.

10.2 Optimal Restriction with Quantity Limits

Suppose that the political equilibrium produces agreement that some critical annual level of imports creates intolerable damage to producers. Below this level, consumers are to be free to purchase at given world prices.[3] Alternatively, a straightforward extension is when below the critical level there may still be need for protection, but of a form that mollifies consumer interests by restriction only on average imports (see Anderson and Young, 1982, chapter 7, for related discussion). Trade takes place in two periods within the "year." Expected surplus is the objective function.[4]

The optimal import restriction corresponding to this "noneconomic" constraint limits imports over the two periods to no more than Q in any state, and requires a uniform (non-state-contingent) markup over foreign price in states where the Q limit does not bind. For the case of no damage for imports below Q, the markup is zero. An immediate implication of the optimal structure, together with the results of section 10.1, is that the system of quota licensing and option pricing, whether by market or by internal calculation, is in general suboptimal. The optimum is, however, infeasible, due to the sequential nature of decisions. This section shows that the invisible hand theorem holds for option pricing: the option pricing system is second best provided rational expectations hold.

It follows that a number of auxiliary administrative practices must be inefficient. Two are examined in the remainder of this section. First, within-year restrictions on use are common. As the period of the licensing shrinks to the length of the period of execution (trading), unfilled quotas will imply zero markup. This must be inefficient unless the noneconomic constraint has a shrinking horizon.[5] Second, use-it-or-lose-it requirements are inefficient. They may be an attempt to offset the protection created by option valuation on below-limit sales. They can be rationalized, though unconvincingly, as optimal when the noneconomic constraint requires that second-period imports must not exceed first-period imports.

The formal analysis makes these points clear. The planner is assumed to maximize the discounted sum of domestic expected social surplus subject to the constraint that places an upper bound on imports.

The second best is defined by optimal selection of $Q_1(s)$, first-period imports contingent on state s (known in period 1), prior to knowing the state s' in the second period. For states s' when the constraint will bind, the second period surplus is

$$\int_0^{Q-Q_1(s)} \{P_2(v, s') - P_2^*(s')\}\, dv. \qquad ,$$

For states when the constraint will not bind, selection of $Q_1(s)$ does not affect surplus in the second period, and the second-period import $\tilde{Q}_2(s')$ is the unconstrained solution to $P_2(\tilde{Q}_2, s') = P_2^*(s')$. Thus the planner solves, for each s,

$$\max_{Q_1(s)} \int_0^{Q_1(s)} \{P_1(v, s) - P_1^*(s)\}\, dv$$

$$+ \delta \underset{s'}{E}\left[\int_0^{Q-Q_1(s)} \{P_2(v, s') - P_2^*(s')\}\, dv \,\Big|\, H\right] \mathrm{Prob}(H) \qquad (4)$$

$$+ \delta \underset{s'}{E}\left[\int_0^{\tilde{Q}_2(s')} \{P_2(v, s') - P_2^*(s')\}\, dv \,\Big|\, L\right] \mathrm{Prob}(L),$$

where

$|H$ denotes $Q_1(s) + Q_2(s') = Q,$

$|L$ denotes $Q_1(s) + Q_2(s') < Q$,

$$\tilde{Q}_2 = Q_2 \,|\, P_2(Q_2, s') = P_2^*(s'), \qquad s' \in L.$$

The solution to (4) is attained by, for each s,

$$P_1(Q_1(s), s) - P_1^*(s)$$

$$= \delta \underset{s'}{E} \left[\{ P_2(Q - Q_1(s), s') - P_2^*(s') \} \,|\, H \right] \mathrm{Prob}(H). \tag{5}$$

The solution (5) is essentially the two-period discounted version of (1′) for competitive equilibrium with rational expectations, the added element being the discount factor and $\mathrm{Prob}(H)$.[6] (5) shows that option pricing of licenses with an efficient market is in fact (constrained) Pareto optimal, provided expectations are rational.

The "distortion" of option pricing can be avoided by reducing the period of validity of licenses, and real world quota systems do in fact have restrictions on within-year use. Intertemporal arbitrage is frustrated, but it seems possible there might be a gain in lowering protection in the first period. It is easy to see, however, that this policy must be inferior under rational expectations.

Formally, this insight may be based on considering the choice of an optimal ex ante period-1 quota. The planner's problem of selecting an optimal period 1 limit $\hat{Q}_1$ with $\hat{Q}_2 = Q - \hat{Q}_1$ is the solution to

$$\begin{aligned} \underset{\hat{Q}_1}{\max} \; \underset{s}{E} & \left[\int_0^{\hat{Q}_1} \{ P_1(v, s) - P_1^*(s) \} \, dv \,|\, H_1 \right] \mathrm{Prob}(H_1) \\ & + \underset{s}{E} \left[\int_0^{\tilde{Q}_1(s)} \{ P_1(v, s) - P_1^*(s) \} \, dv \,|\, L_1 \right] \mathrm{Prob}(L_1) \\ & + \delta \underset{s'}{E} \left[\int_0^{Q - \hat{Q}_1} \{ P_2(v, s) - P_2^*(s) \} \, dv \,|\, H_2 \right] \mathrm{Prob}(H_2) \\ & + \delta \underset{s'}{E} \left[\int_0^{\tilde{Q}_2(s')} \{ P_2(v, s') - P_2^*(s') \} \, dv \,|\, L_2 \right] \mathrm{Prob}(L_2), \end{aligned} \tag{6}$$

where variables H_i, L_i, $\hat{Q}_i$ are defined analogously with (4). By construction, Q_1 may do as well as the optimal $Q_1(s)$ for some state s, but obviously not in general.

(4) and (6) imply that the optimal period of licensing with efficient markets in licenses is the length of the period of the noneconomic constraint. Naturally, shorter period restrictions as in (6) may evolve because

they better fit the domestic producers' loss function. The amount of inter-temporal flexibility permitted is obviously an important issue, which can only be resolved with deeper consideration of producers' costs, storage possibilities, etc. The same may be said for flexibility over states.

The final wrinkle to consider in this section is the use-it-or-lose-it requirement. The analysis of section 10.1 [see (2)] shows that it subsidizes imports, thus tending to counteract the protection given by the option pricing of quota licenses. The reason for the policy may be to mollify consumers. (5) shows that this is an inefficient solution to (4).

On the other hand, there are circumstances where the requirement could be optimal. Suppose the constraint system is $Q_1(s) \leqslant Q$ and $Q_2(s') \leqslant Q_1(s)$. This might be rationalized as reflecting high costs of adjustment to unanticipated changes in trade. In this case the planner's problem is, for each state s in period 1,

$$\max_{Q_1(s)} \int_0^{Q_1(s)} \{P_1(v, s) - P_1^*(s)\} \, dv$$

$$+ \delta \mathop{E}_{s'} \left[\int_0^{Q_1(s)} \{P_2(v, s') - P_2^*(s')\} \, dv \,|\, H \right] \mathrm{Prob}(H) \qquad (7)$$

$$+ \delta \mathop{E}_{s'} \left[\int_0^{Q_2(s')} \{P_2(v, s) - P_2^*(s')\} \, dv \,|\, L \right] \mathrm{Prob}(L)$$

subject to

$$Q_1(s) \leqslant Q \qquad [\lambda(s)],$$

where $Q_2(s') \,|\, L$ implies $Q_2(s') < Q_1(s)$.

The solution to (7) requires, when $\lambda(s) = 0$ (the original quota does not bind),

$$-\{P_1(Q_1(s), s) - P_1^*(s)\}$$
$$= \delta \mathop{E}_{s'} [\{P_2(Q_1(s), s') - P_2^*(s')\} \,|\, H] \mathrm{Prob}(H). \qquad (8)$$

(8) is the two-period discounted version of (3). With rational expectations, a competitive equilibrium will optimally price licenses to attain (8).

While this model does give a rationale for the use-it-or-lose-it require-ment, it is not a very convincing one, especially since governments typically do not destroy the excess $Q - Q_1(s)$ in period 2, but redistribute it.

10.3 Optimal Restriction and Expenditure Limits

The structure of the optimal restrictions on expenditure is exactly analogous to the quantity restrictions save that the tax equivalents are now in *ad valorem* form (see Anderson and Young, 1982, chapter 7, for the same progression). The formal structure needs development only because the option pricing of foreign exchange licenses must be considered.

Let $r(Q_1(s), s, s')$, the limit on imports in period 2, satisfy the foreign exchange constraint

$$R \geqslant P_1^*(s)Q_1(s) + P_2^*(s')Q_2(s').$$

Explicitly,

$$r = R/P_2^*(s') - P_1^*(s)Q_1(s)/P_2^*(s').$$

The problem facing the planner is to, in each state s.

$$\max_{Q_1(s)} \int_0^{Q_1(s)} \{P_1(v, s) - P_1^*(s)\} \, dv$$

$$+ \delta E_{s'} \left[\int_0^r \{P_2(v, s') - P_2^*(s')\} \, dv \,\middle|\, H \right] \mathrm{Prob}(H) \tag{9}$$

$$+ \delta E_{s'} \left[\int_0^{\tilde{Q}_2(s')} \{P_2(v, s') - P_2^*(s')\} \, dv \,\middle|\, L \right] \mathrm{Prob}(L).$$

The first-order condition is, for each s,

$$\frac{P_1 - P_1^*}{P_1^*} = \delta E \left[\frac{P_2 - P_2^*}{P_2^*} \,\middle|\, H \right] \mathrm{Prob}(H). \tag{10}$$

The first-order conditions are sufficient since the objective function is concave. Evidently the optimal policy can be decentralized with foreign exchange licensing under competitive rational expectations equilibrium in the market for licenses.

The same steps as in section 10.2 can be taken to show that attempts to subsidize below limit imports are inefficient, especially shorter interval licenses and use-it-or-lose-it requirements.

A novel element in expenditure controls is that the government can vary the exchange rate. Exchange rate variation in conjunction with binding foreign exchange constraints is in fact rather common. In (9), this amounts to the ability to tax differently in each period. The structure of (9) shows us that this added instrument gains no additional welfare. Its sole effect is on the distribution of rent, provided the instrument is optimally used. There are, of course, good reasons for varying the exchange rate that are not built into the structure of (9).

10.4 Resale Prohibition: VERs and the Large Country Case

The reason resale prohibition is interesting is that it reveals a new element in the analysis: distribution of licenses (by source). While this is a ubiquitous issue in quota systems, it is most natural to study it in the context of Voluntary Export Restraints (VERs). The multilateral VERs are supposed to be country specific. Instead, it is often alleged by importing countries, resale of licenses takes place on a fairly widespread basis. This is efficient from the point of view of the world, but may run afoul of protectionist motives that conceal restrictiveness by allocating quotas that cannot be filled. For simplicity, in the text I suppress such "hidden protection" aspects of the quota distribution: the allocation and production structures of exporters are assumed to be such that all quotas bind or none do. Appendix 10.B shows that analysis of the more general case proceeds along the same lines, and supports the same conclusion: resale prohibition has an ambiguous effect on the importer's price.

Under the assumption that all quotas bind or none do, from the importer's point of view resale of licenses among exporters should be irrelevant in a certainty model. When uncertainty and option pricing of licenses is considered, on the other hand, the distribution will always have an effect on domestic prices. Resale prohibition may either be in the domestic consumers' or producers' interest. A casual reading of the rationale for such resale prohibition supports either interpretation—prohibition of "profiteering" in licenses should help consumers, or halting redistribution to cheap suppliers should help domestic producers. Below, I show that the effect can go either way. In an important special case, linear supply, there is no effect.

The distribution-by-source problem is trivial save in the "large country" case. The minimum-sized model required has two exporters and an importer, all large enough to have interdependence of price. In the case of a large country, the foreign price P^* is a function of the quantity of imports. Welfare maximization from the point of view of the importing country will involve an optimal tariff argument of the standard trade-theoretic type as well as the "noneconomic" distortions. In practice the principal quota arrangements in the world do not appear to involve the selfish optimal tariff type of behavior. The "voluntary" export quota (VER) system exemplified in the Multifiber Arrangement deliberately transfers quota rent to the exporters in return for their acceptance of the "noneconomic" constraint imposed by importers. Welfare evaluation from the world point of view is perhaps more reasonable. That is the approach taken below. A domestic welfare analysis only involves the addition of terms familiar to trade theorists in any case.

Turning to the formal model, I assume a planner selects voluntary export restraints for two countries across two periods for alternately a single total export constraint $X + Y$, and a separate constraint, X and Y, for each country. It is straightforward that the latter yields generally lower welfare. Study of the first-order conditions shows that competitive arbitrage of licenses in a world market solves the less constrained problem. Resale prohibitions are of course optimal if the latter constraint system is imposed by political requirements. This is unlikely save in special circumstances, but such prohibitions may be instrumental in raising or lowering average price. Thus, the second model is further analyzed to reveal the effect on prices of a marginal redistribution of licenses. This turns out to be ambiguous.

The constraints are alternately

$$X_1(s) + X_2(s') + Y_1(s) + Y_2(s') \leqslant X + Y \tag{11}$$

or

$$X_1(s) + X_2(s') \leqslant X, \qquad Y_1(s) + Y_2(s') \leqslant Y. \tag{12}$$

Let P_1^* be the price of the exporter of X, and Γ_1 be the price of the exporter of Y. Period-1 decisions do not affect welfare for period-2 states in which the constraints do not bind. Then, using constraints (12) and following the analogous steps in previous models, the planner's problem is, for each state s in period 1,

$$\max_{Y_1(s), X_1(s)} \int_0^{X_1(s)+Y_1(s)} P_1(v,s)\, dv - \int_0^{X_1(s)} P_1^*(v,s)\, dv$$

$$- \int_0^{Y_1(s)} \Gamma_1(v,s)\, dv + \delta E_{s'}\left[\int_0^{X+Y-X_1(s)-Y_1(s)} P_2(v,s')\, dv \,\Big|\, H\right] \mathrm{Prob}(H)$$

$$- \delta E_{s'}\left[\int_0^{X-X_1(s)} P_1^*(v,s')\, dv \,\Big|\, H\right] \mathrm{Prob}(H)$$

$$- \delta E_{s'}\left[\int_0^{Y-Y_1(s)} \Gamma_1(v,s')\, dv \,\Big|\, H\right] \mathrm{Prob}(H).$$

In constructing the objective function above, the assumption that both constraints bind in H has been used (see appendix 10.B for analysis of the more general case). The first-order conditions (which are sufficient with downward sloping import demand at home and upward sloping supply in the exporters) are

$$P_1 - P_1^* = \delta E_{s'} [P_2 - P_2^* | H] \operatorname{Prob}(H) = \delta E[P_2 - P_2^*],$$

$$P_1 - \Gamma_1 = \delta E_{s'} [P_2 - \Gamma_2 | H] \operatorname{Prob}(H) = \delta E[P_2 - \Gamma_2]. \tag{13}$$

It is easy to see that a world market in export licenses will equalize Γ_1 and P_1^* (and $E[P_2^* | H]$ and $E[\Gamma_2 | H]$). This will effectively solve the less constrained problem where the constraint is (11). Thus it must be more efficient, provided (11) is the true political constraint.

Now consider the effect of a marginal redistribution of licenses on domestic price $[P_1$ or $E(P_2)]$. This can be studied by totally differentiating (13) with $dX = -dY$ (a redistribution of licenses satisfying the total constraint) and deriving dX_1/dX, dY_1/dX, and $d(X_1 + Y_1)/dX$. These then imply dP_1/dX and $E[dP_2/dX | H]$. With downward sloping import demand and upward sloping export supply, it is straightforward that $dX_1/dX > 0$ and $dY_1/dX < 0$. The sign of $d(X_1 + Y_1)/dX$ is the sign of [7]

$$\delta E_{s'} \left[\frac{\partial P_2^*}{\partial X} \bigg| H \right] \bigg/ \frac{\partial P_1^*}{\partial X_1} - \delta E_{s'} \left[\frac{\partial \Gamma_2}{\partial Y} \bigg| H \right] \bigg/ \frac{\partial \Gamma_1}{\partial Y_1}. \tag{14}$$

The intuition of (14) is fairly simple. A rise in X raises both X_1 and $X - X_1 = X_2$ (for the latter, see appendix 10.A). At the same time, Y_1 and $Y - Y_1 = Y_2$ are reduced. If the ratio of (expected) selling price in period 2 relative to selling price in period 1 rises in the expanding country at the same rate that it falls in the contracting country, then there is no intertemporal misallocation at an equilibrium that preserves $X_1 + Y_1$. (14) is analogous to the famous critical ratio condition of the transfer problem. An immediate implication of (14) is that for the linear supply case (which means additive uncertainty as well), there is no effect of resale prohibition on total imports, hence on period-1 or expected period-2 price in the impacting country. If (14) is positive, an increase in X (implied by resale when $P_1 - P_1^* > P_1 - \Gamma_1$) will lower P_1 (and raise $E[P_2 | H]$) and conversely for (14) negative.

An implication of the results of this section would appear to be that resale prohibitions are unattractive instruments. They are inefficient so far as a simple approach to the noneconomic constraints can take us, and it is not even clear whether the interests of domestic consumers or producers are advanced by them.

10.5 Conclusion

This chapter has shown that administrative details of quota systems can make a difference in their effect on the sequence of prices, welfare, and trade. Empirical studies can eventually be done to cost out various quota schemes along the lines suggested in this chapter. I suspect they will show substantial added burden.

To carry out this work properly, a more elaborate theoretical development of option pricing of licenses will be needed. Quota licenses are a nontrivial extension of option pricing models for two reasons. First, the use-it-or-lose-it requirement has no counterpart in financial options. Second, and more fundamentally, the quota license exercise systematically affects the price of the import good. In contrast, the basic model of financial option literature assumes the option exercise is too small relative to the total spot market volume in the underlying security to affect its price.

The extended model should examine three important areas, one empirical and two theoretical. The empirical investigation should develop the implications of the option value model for modeling import demand under quota constraint. The protective effect of quotas is more complex than previous models have permitted.

Second, the private and social efficiency of arbitrage of licenses should be explored. In section 10.2, I show that competitive rational expectations equilibrium as in (1′) is efficient. An interesting question is whether the real world structure of licensing is attaining (1′) or may even be *amplifying* fluctuations.

The second interesting theoretical issue for future research raised by option pricing of quota licenses is, What is the optimal frequency (period) of licenses? Typically, quota systems are run with annual limits. They are often supplemented by a limited amount of carry-forward from year to year, and constrained by within-year (in some cases weekly!) smoothness limits. As an example of the latter, the People's Republic of China has an informal annual textile export limit. Its exports are monitored weekly, and a deviation of more than 30% above 1/52 of its annual quota induces administrative consultations, with the threat of formal limits enforcing "good" behavior. In the limit, the latter type of policy implies weekly licenses, with some carry-forward.

In the financial options markets, competitive forces and transactions costs interact to determine the periods of options purchased. In some circumstances, at least, the range offered is (second-best) optimal. For quotas, no economic criteria have ever been used to determine the right period, and it is unlikely that current methods are efficient. For example, shortening the period of licensing, in the absence of all administrative costs, can seemingly be desirable, since it reduces the protective effect of the option value of a license on below-limit sales. On the other hand, it reduces intertemporal arbitrage. The analysis of section 10.2 shows that the latter inefficiency dominates, so that licensing should allow flexibility within the period of the "noneconomic" constraint. This further suggests the importance of an attempt to model more deeply the loss function behind the constraint, probably in a dynamic stochastic environment.

Economists have largely ignored administrative details of quota systems; this has been a mistake, since they matter and economic models give a great deal of insight into their implications. Substantive resource allocation issues are involved. Furthermore, the growing use of quotas in world trade suggests the great practical importance of better understanding the implications of quota systems. For example, it has been estimated that textile export licenses in Hong Kong account for 3–6% of national income.

Appendix 10.A: Derivation of Comparative Statics

The system of comparative static derivatives is taken from differentiating (13) and using $dX = -dY$:

$$\begin{pmatrix} \dfrac{\partial(P_1 - P_1^*)}{\partial X_1} - \delta E\left[\dfrac{\partial(P_2 - P_2^*)}{\partial X_1}\bigg| H\right]\text{Prob}(H) & \dfrac{\partial P_1}{\partial Y_1} - \delta E\left[\dfrac{\partial P_2}{\partial Y_1}\bigg| H\right]\text{Prob}(H) \\[2em] \dfrac{\partial(P_1)}{\partial X_1} - \delta E\left[\dfrac{\partial P_2}{\partial X_1}\bigg| H\right]\text{Prob}(H) & \dfrac{\partial P_1 - \Gamma_1}{\partial Y_1} - \delta E\left[\dfrac{\partial P_2 - \Gamma_2}{\partial Y_1}\bigg| H\right]\text{Prob}(H) \end{pmatrix}$$

$$\times \begin{pmatrix} dX_1 \\[1em] dY_1 \end{pmatrix} = \begin{pmatrix} -\delta E\left[\dfrac{\partial P_2^*}{\partial X}\bigg| H\right]\text{Prob}(H) \\[1em] \delta E\left[\dfrac{\partial \Gamma_2}{\partial Y}\bigg| H\right]\text{Prob}(H) \end{pmatrix} dX. \tag{A.1}$$

We solve for the comparative static derivatives by inverting and simplifying, using

$$-\delta E\left[\frac{\partial P_2^*}{\partial X_1}\bigg| H\right]\text{Prob}(H) = \delta E\left[\frac{\partial P_2^*}{\partial X}\bigg| H\right]\text{Prob}(H),$$

$$-\delta E\left[\frac{\partial \Gamma_2}{\partial Y_1}\bigg| H\right]\text{Prob}(H) = \delta E\left[\frac{\partial \Gamma_2}{\partial Y}\bigg| H\right]\text{Prob}(H),$$

and

$$\partial P_i / \partial X_1 = \partial P_i / \partial Y_1, \qquad i = 1, 2.$$

The determinant in (A.1) is positive and all its elements are negative under the stipulated conditions. Furthermore, it is immediate that $dX_1/dY > 0$ and $dY_1/dX < 0$. A bit of additional algebra implies (14). Let Δ be the determinant and note $\Delta > 0$. Then

$$\begin{pmatrix} dX_1/dX \\ dY_1/dX \end{pmatrix} = \frac{1}{\Delta} \begin{pmatrix} a + d_1 & -a \\ -a & a + d_2 \end{pmatrix} \begin{pmatrix} -c_1 \\ c_2 \end{pmatrix}, \qquad (A.2)$$

where

$$a = \frac{\partial P_1}{\partial Y_1} - \delta E \left[\frac{\partial P_2}{\partial Y_1} \bigg| H \right] \text{Prob}(H) < 0,$$

$$d_1 = -\frac{\partial \Gamma_1}{\partial Y_1} - \delta E \left[\frac{\partial \Gamma_2}{\partial Y} \bigg| H \right] \text{Prob}(H) < 0,$$

$$d_2 = -\frac{\partial P_1^*}{\partial X_1} - \delta E \left[\frac{\partial P_2^*}{\partial X} \bigg| H \right] \text{Prob}(H) < 0,$$

$$-c_1 = -\delta E \left[\frac{\partial P_2^*}{\partial X} \bigg| H \right] \text{Prob}(H) < 0,$$

$$c_2 = \delta E \left[\frac{\partial \Gamma_2}{\partial Y} \bigg| H \right] \text{Prob}(H) > 0,$$

$$\Delta = a(d_1 + d_2) + d_1 d_2.$$

Then

$$dX_1/dX = \frac{-c_1 a - c_2 a - c_1 d_1}{\Delta} > 0,$$

$$dY_1/dX = \frac{c_1 a + c_2 a + c_2 d_2}{\Delta} < 0. \qquad (A.3)$$

Adding the two equations in (A.3) we have

$$d(X_1 + Y_1)/dX = \frac{c_2 d_2 - c_1 d_1}{\Delta}$$

$$= \frac{(\partial P_1^*/\partial X_1)(\partial \Gamma_1/\partial Y_1)}{\Delta} \text{Prob}(H) \left\{ \delta E \left[\frac{\partial P_2^*}{\partial X} \bigg| H \right] \bigg/ \frac{\partial P_1^*}{\partial X_1} \right. \qquad (A.4)$$

$$\left. - \delta E \left[\frac{\partial \Gamma_2}{\partial Y} \bigg| H \right] \bigg/ \frac{\partial \Gamma_1}{\partial Y_1} \right\}.$$

The term outside curly brackets in (A.4) is positive and the term inside is (14).

It is also of interest to make the following computation:

$$\frac{d(X - X_1)}{dX} = \frac{\Delta + a(c_1 + c_2) - c_1 d_1}{\Delta}$$

$$= \frac{-a(\partial P_1^*/\partial X_1) + (\partial \Gamma_1/\partial Y_1) + d_1 d_2}{\Delta} > 0.$$

(A.5)

Appendix 10.B: Resale Prohibition in the General Case

The text analyzed the effect of the transfer of licenses assuming that both VER constraints bind or neither does. This may be justified as an analysis based on small alterations in a reasonably efficient allocation where suppliers have similar production structures. Here I consider the general case. Essentially the same factors operate.

The objective function of the text is augmented by added terms reflecting the added possibilities of the X or Y constraint alone binding. H now refers to the set of outcomes where both constraints bind. B_x refers to the X constraint alone binding and B_y refers to the Y constraint alone binding. Since such terms are obvious, I omit writing out the full maximization problem. The first-order conditions analogous to (13) are now

$$P_1 - P_1^* = \delta \underset{s'}{E} [P_2 - P_2^* | H] \text{Prob}(H) + \delta \underset{s''}{E} [P_2 - P_2^* | B_x] \text{Prob}(B_x),$$

$$P_1 - \Gamma_1 = \delta \underset{s'}{E} [P_2 - \Gamma_2 | H] \text{Prob}(H) + \delta \underset{s''}{E} [P_2 - \Gamma_2 | B_y] \text{Prob}(B_y),$$

(B.1)

or

$$P_1 - P_1^* = \delta E[P_2 - P_2^*],$$

$$P_1 - \Gamma_1 = \delta E[P_2 - \Gamma_2].$$

(B.2)

This is the same as (13). The critical condition analogous to (14) is

$$\frac{d(X_1 + Y_1)}{dX} \gtreqless 0 \text{ as}$$

$$\frac{E[\partial P_2^*/\partial X | H] \text{Prob}(H) + E[\partial P_2^*/\partial X | B_x] \text{Prob}(B_x)}{(\partial \Pi_1/\partial X_1)}$$

$$\gtreqless \frac{E[\partial \Gamma_2/\partial Y | H] \text{Prob}(H) + E[\partial \Gamma_2/\partial Y | B_y] \text{Prob}(B_y)}{(\partial \Gamma_1/\partial Y_1)}.$$

(B.3)

The main message of (B.3) is that unless the distribution is markedly skewed against an efficient producer, resale prohibition has complex and ambiguous effects on domestic price: these effects operate along the lines of (14) in the text.

Now consider the effect of skewed distribution. A high value of $\text{Prob}(B_x)$ implies an allocation systematically too low for X. We see from (B.3) that as $\text{Prob}(B_x)$ rises, a transfer increasing X will definitely raise total supply in the first period, $d(X_1 + Y_1)/dX > 0$. Moreover, for states in B_x, the increase in the X quota will increase supply in the second period, since $dX_2/dX > 0$ [see (A.5) and will not affect the level of Y_2 (since the Y constraint does not bind). Then domestic price falls in both periods (in expected value terms for the second period). As $Prob(B_x)$ grows, we thus have the uncertainty case analogue to the "hidden protectionism" of a license distribution skewed against the most efficient producer.

The simplest special case reveals a nice intuition. If supply is linear, then (B.3) implies $d(X_1 + Y_1)/dX \gtreqless 0$ as $Prob(B_x) \gtreqless Prob(B_y)$. A "neutral" distribution of licenses would equate $Prob(B_x)$ with $Prob(B_y)$; hence $d(X_1 + Y_1)/dX = 0$. As in the text, the linear case implies distribution has no effect on (expected) domestic price in either period. Naturally, neutral distributions need not be efficient.

Notes

1. After this chapter was completed, I discovered that Eldor (1982) suggested that quota licenses were options and could be valued as in the financial literature.

2. PV is formed iteratively. If the agent uses a below-limit license, he receives a new one. In the next period, with below-limit conditions, the equilibrium value of the license will be zero, by (2). With limit conditions, the value is, with rational expectations shared by all, $Prob(H)\{E[P|H] - E[P^*|H]\}$. PV is a stream of such values. Iterating, and simplifying the polynomial in $Prob(H)$, (2) becomes

$$-\{P(Q(s), s) - P^*(s)\} = \frac{Prob(H)}{1 - Prob(H)}\{E[P|H] - E[P^*|H]\}.$$

This yields (3).

With discounting, the formula replaces $Prob(H)$ with $\delta\, Prob(H)$, where δ is the discount factor.

3. In Anderson and Young (1982, chapter 7), we rationalized tariff quotas (a tariff schedule in which the rate steps upward with volume of imports) as optimal when the distribution of imports was to be restricted in its average value in two ranges. This approximated a loss function to domestic producers that stepped upward with imports, yet allowed some flexibility to mollify consumer interests.

4. There are several ways to rationalize this convenient assumption. One is to assume perfect securities markets exist. Another is to assume that the traded good forms a small enough portion of total expenditure so that variations in the marginal utility of income are neglected (see Young and Anderson, 1982, for relaxation of this restriction).

5. Are consumers' or producers' interests advanced, at least in the sense of average price being higher or lower, by within-year restrictions on use? This question is formally similar to the question of the effect of resale prohibition on average price, examined in section 10.4. The answer is similar too—it depends.

6. Assume an infinite horizon, stationarity so that $P_i(Q, s) = P_j(Q, s) = P(Q, s)$ for all i and j, and $\delta \leqslant 1$. Then (5) is going to be

$$P_1 - P_1^* = E[P \mid H] - E[P^* \mid H]\,\mathrm{Prob}(H)\{1 + \mathrm{Prob}(L)\delta + \mathrm{Prob}(L)^2\delta^2 + \cdots\}$$

$$= \{E[P \mid H] - E[P^* \mid H]\}\,(\delta\,\mathrm{Prob}(H))/(1 - \delta\,\mathrm{Prob}(L)).$$

This is the form of (1′) with discounting, and obviously converges to (1′) at $\delta = 1$.

7. See appendix 10.A.

References

Anderson, James, E. (1985), "The Relative Inefficiency of Quotas: The Cheese Case," *American Economic Review*, 75, 178–190.

Anderson, James E., and Leslie Young (1982), "The Optimality of Tariff Quotas under Uncertainty," *Journal of International Economics*, 13, 337–352.

Bhagwati, Jagdish, and T. N. Srinivasan (1983), *Lectures in International Trade*, Cambridge, MA: MIT Press.

Black, Fischer, and Myron Scholes (1973), "The Pricing of Options and Corporate Liabilities," *Journal of Political Economy*, 81, 637–659.

Eldor, Rafael (1982), "On the Valuation of Currency Options, Exchange Rate Insurance Policies, and Quota Licenses," Working Paper 40-82, Foerder Institute of Economic Research, Tel-Aviv University.

Young, Leslie, and James E. Anderson (1980), "The Optimal Policies for Restricting Trade under Uncertainty," *Review of Economic Studies*, 47, 927–932.

Young, Leslie, and James E. Anderson (1982), "Risk Aversion and Optimal Trade Restrictions," *Review of Economic Studies*, 49, 291–305.

Index